COMPUTER LITERACY

Academic Press Rapid Manuscript Reproduction

Based on the
National Computer Literacy Goals for 1985 Conference
Reston, Virginia, December 18–20, 1980

COMPUTER LITERACY
Issues and Directions for 1985

Edited by

Robert J. Seidel
Human Resources Research Organization
Alexandria, Virginia

Ronald E. Anderson
Minnesota Educational Computing Consortium
St. Paul, Minnesota

Beverly Hunter
Human Resources Research Organization
Alexandria, Virginia

1982

ACADEMIC PRESS
A Subsidiary of Harcourt Brace Jovanovich, Publishers
New York   London
Paris   San Diego   San Francisco   São Paulo   Sydney   Tokyo   Toronto

This publication is based on a conference supported by funds from the National Science Foundation under Grant No. SED 7918987 to the Minnesota Educational Computing Consortium (MECC), St. Paul, Minnesota, under a project directed by Dr. Ronald E. Anderson. The conference was organized by the Human Resources Research Organization (HumRRO), Alexandria, Virginia, under a subcontract directed by Dr. Robert J. Seidel. Additional support for transcription and technical editing was provided by a grant to HumRRO from the American Telephone and Telegraph Corporation (AT&T). Any opinions, findings, conclusions, or recommendations expressed herein are those of the authors and do not necessarily reflect the views of the National Science Foundation, MECC, HumRRO, or AT&T.

ACADEMIC PRESS, INC.
111 Fifth Avenue, New York, New York 10003

United Kingdom Edition published by
ACADEMIC PRESS, INC. (LONDON) LTD.
24/28 Oval Road, London NW1   7DX

Library of Congress Cataloging in Publication Data
Main entry under title:

Computer literacy.

"Based on a ... conference entitled, 'National goals
for computer literacy in 1985' held in Reston, Virginia,
on December 18-20, 1980 ... sponsored by the National
Science Foundation ... organized by the Human Resources
Research Organization"--Pref.
   Includes index.
   1. Education--United States--Data processing--Con-
gresses. 2. Computer-assisted instruction--United States
--Congresses. 3. Computers--Study and teaching--United
States--Congresses. I. Seidel, Robert J., Date.
II. Anderson, Ronald E. III. Hunter, Beverly.
IV. National Science Foundation (U.S.) V. Human
Resources Research Organization.
LB1028.43.C65   370'.28'54   82-1677
ISBN 0-12-634960-6   AACR2

PRINTED IN THE UNITED STATES OF AMERICA

82 83 84 85   9 8 7 6 5 4 3 2 1

This Book Is Dedicated to Future Generations
Who Will Continue to Struggle
with the Changing Perspectives
of an Information Society
R. J. S.

CONTENTS

III COGNITIVE RESEARCH AND SOLVING PROBLEMS USING THE COMPUTER

IV COMPUTER LITERACY AND CURRICULUM DEVELOPMENT

V.   ALTERNATIVE POLICIES AND IMPLEMENTATION OF GOALS FOR COMPUTER LITERACY DURING THE NEXT FIVE YEARS

PANELISTS:

CONTRIBUTORS

Numbers in parentheses indicate the pages on which the authors' contributions begin.

Ronald E. Anderson (10, 211), *Minnesota Educational Computing Consortium, St. Paul, Minnesota 55133*

Alfred Bork (91), *Department of Physics, University of California, Irvine, California 92717*

Ludwig Braun (103, 271), *Department of Technology and Society, College of Engineering and Applied Sciences, State University of New York, Stony Brook, New York 11794*

John Seely Brown (161), *Cognitive & Instructional Sciences, Xerox Palo Alto Research Center, Palo Alto, California 94304*

Kenneth E. Brumbaugh (233), *Minnesota Educational Computing Consortium, St. Paul, Minnesota 55133*

Sylvia Charp (99), *Instructional Systems, Instructional Computer Center, School District of Philadelphia, Philadelphia, Pennsylvania 19140*

John Clement (171), *Department of Physics and Astronomy, University of Massachusetts, Amherst, Massachusetts 01003*

Dorothy K. Deringer (3), *Science Education Directorate, National Science Foundation, Washington, D. C. 20550*

Richard A. Diem (227), *Division of Education, University of Texas, San Antonio, Texas 78285*

Thomas Dwyer (193), *Department of Computer Science, University of Pittsburgh, Pittsburgh, Pennsylvania 15260*

Jane D. Gawronski (223), *Planning, Research and Evaluation, Department of Education, San Diego County, San Diego, California 92111*

Beverly Hunter (34, 217), *Educational and Training Systems Division, Human Resources Research Organization, Alexandria, Virginia 22314*

J. C. R. Licklider (281), *Laboratory of Computer Science, Massachusetts Institute of Technology, Cambridge, Massachusetts 02139*

Joseph Lipson (167), *Division of Science Education, Development and Research, National Science Foundation, Washington, D. C. 20550*

Jack Lochhead (171), *Department of Physics and Astronomy, University of Massachusetts, Amherst, Massachusetts 01003*

Phyllis R. Marcuccio (229), *Directory of Elementary Education, National Science Teachers Association, Washington, D. C. 20009*

Richard E. Mayer (129), *Department of Psychology, University of California, Santa Barbara, California 93106*

Andrew Molnar (301, 3), *Science Education Directorate, National Science Foundation, Washington, D. C. 20550*

David Moursund (74), *Computer and Information Science Department, University of Oregon, Eugene, Oregon 97403*

Gary Olson (187), *Department of Psychology, University of Michigan, Ann Arbor, Michigan 48109*

Robert J. Seidel (20), *Educational and Training Systems Division, Human Resources Research Organization, Alexandria, Virginia 22314*

Elliot Soloway (171), *Department of Computer and Information Science, University of Massachusetts, Amherst, Massachusetts 01003*

John Sonquist (70), *Department of Sociology, University of California, Santa Barbara, California 93106*

Robert Taylor (86), *Center for Computer Information Management Service, Teachers College, Columbia University, New York, New York 10027*

Nellouise Watkins (267), *Computer Center, Bennett College, Greensboro, North Carolina 27420*

Daniel H. Watt (54), *LOGO Project, Massachusetts Institute of Technology, Cambridge, Massachusetts 02139*

Karl L. Zinn (275), *Center for Research on Learning and Teaching, University of Michigan, Ann Arbor, Michigan 48104*

PREFACE

This publication is based on a two-and-a-half day conference entitled National Goals for Computer Literacy in 1985 held in Reston, Virginia, on December 18–20, 1980. The conference was sponsored by the National Science Foundation under a grant awarded to the Minnesota Educational Computing Consortium (MECC). The conference was organized by the Human Resources Research Organization (HumRRO), under a subcontract directed by Dr. Robert J. Seidel. A steering committee for the conference was composed of Dr. Ronald E. Anderson, Dr. Beverly Hunter, Dr. Daniel Klassen, and Dr. Robert J. Seidel.

The purposes of the conference were as follows:

(1) to provide a forum for opposing views on computer literacy and to move toward greater consensus on needs and goals;

(2) to bring research implications and instructional expertise to bear upon computer literacy;

(3) to consider methods for infusion of computer-related objectives and activities into existing curricula for different age levels;

(4) to identify considerations, issues, and barriers to developing national goals for achieving a computer-literate society in the United States;

(5) to focus attention on computer literacy needs and the precollege education process;

(6) to plan directions and national goals for computer literacy for a five-year period.

The nature of this working conference was participatory with all attendees actively contributing to its outcome. Participants were sought who could contribute to the above purposes and goals. Experts were identified in each of the levels of precollege education, teacher training, each major area of curriculum development (e.g., science, mathematics, social studies), various educational application areas, and research in cognitive science and computer literacy. The search was conducted via telephone in order to obtain cross-sectional representation from industry, research foundations, academic institutions, and governmental and educational research agencies.

The conference was conducted in five sessions over a two-and-a-half day period. Each session addressed one of the following major computer literacy areas: perspectives; definitions and requirements; cognitive research; curriculum development; policies and implementation of goals.

The first session consisted of separate presentations by the project sponsor and conference organizers on various perspectives on computer literacy. The second and third sessions were each divided into three parts: presentations, individual discussant remarks, and general group discussions. The fourth and fifth sessions were panel discussions. In keeping with the working nature of the conference, a critical component was the assembling of working discussion groups during the conference. Each of these groups was charged with addressing a series of questions and reporting their summary and recommendations to the complete body.

The following list provides the breakdown of these topics and groups as they are presented in this book:

Section II: Definitions and Requirements
>   Working Group I: Computer Literacy for Teachers and School Administrators
>   Working Group V: Ethics and Values for Computer Literacy

Section III: Cognitive Research
>   Working Group II: Developmental Sequence of Computer Literacy for Grades K-12

Section IV: Curriculum Development
>   Working Group III: Computer Literacy Learning Materials for Grades K-8
>   Working Group IV: Computer Literacy Learning Materials for Grades 7-12
>   Working Group VII: Computer Literacy in the Mathematics Curricula
>   Working Group VIII: Computer Literacy in the Science Curricula
>   Working Group IX: Computer Literacy in the Social Studies Curricula

Section V: Policies and Implementation of Goals
>   Working Group V: National Strategies for Implementing Computer Literacy

ACKNOWLEDGMENTS

Our heartfelt appreciation begins with acknowledging the role of Dr. Dorothy Deringer, our Technical Monitor, and her colleague, Dr. Andrew Molnar of the Science Education Directorate at the National Science Foundation. Without their vision, encouragement, and continuing guidance this conference could not have taken place.

We extend our thanks to all the conference participants. Not all of them prepared papers for inclusion in this book; however, their earnest contributions and lively exchanges of ideas during the general conference sessions and individual working groups are reflected in the included discussion summaries. We gratefully acknowledge everyone's contribution. We wish to first thank those participants who took on the onerous task of moderating a disciplined session with many creative voices actively seeking the floor simultaneously: Dr. John Haugo, Dr. David C. Johnson, Dr. Kenneth C. Laudon, and Dr. Daniel Klassen, and all the other participants whose names appear at the end of this volume.

The HumRRO Conference Staff provided their invaluable aid and encouragement in the various preconference arrangements and conference activities. The success of the conference was due in large measure to the preconference arrangements and typing provided by Doris Stein. Coordination of the various conference activities was greatly facilitated by Carol Hargan, Michael Hillelsohn, Greg Kearsley, Richard Rosenblatt, Russell Schultz, Doris Stein, and Harold Wagner.

Finally, we wish to extend our appreciation to Judith Paris, our production editor, for her diligent and creative efforts at creating a coherent product from excellent, but diverse conference papers, transcripts, and dialogues. In addition, we wish to note the excellent typing support of Lisa A. Pettipas. Last, but not least, we wish to extend extreme gratitude to American Telephone and Telegraph Corporation for its support in the transcription of the conference proceedings and subsequent technical editing.

Robert J. Seidel
HumRRO
Ronald E. Anderson
MECC
Beverly Hunter
HumRRO

SECTION I

PERSPECTIVES ON COMPUTER LITERACY

Four major approaches to a perspective on computer literacy are presented: (1) impact of computer literacy on our
citizenry; (2) major national components of a computer literacy program; (3) the development of an information handling
curriculum for an evolving computer literacy concept; and (4)
a 30-year historical overview of "computer events in three
strands" -- (a) research/development/technology; (b) education; (c) social/political institutional. These papers provide the reader with a foundation for interpreting the issues
addressed in the remainder of the book.

KEY COMPONENTS FOR A NATIONAL COMPUTER LITERACY PROGRAM[1]

Dorothy K. Deringer
Andrew R. Molnar

National Science Foundation

In 1968, the National Science Foundation was directed by the President and Congress to provide a leadership role in the use of computing in science and in education in the United States. During the last decade, the Science and Engineering Education Directorate of the National Science Foundation has invested over $70 million for a wide variety of efforts on computers in science education.

All of these innovative and exemplary projects concerning computers in education have contributed to the notion that computing has become a new imperative in education and that a new and important national requirement is emerging for children and adults, students and teachers who will live, work, and consume goods and services in what is now being called the information or knowledge society. The ability to deal effectively with information technologies in business, industry, and government, and increasingly in our homes and our schools, has created a need for what has been called "computer literacy." The ability to use and understand computing is becoming as important as our ability to understand and handle the written word. A computer-literate populace is as necessary to an information society as raw materials and energy are to an industrial society.

In response to these concerns, the National Science Foundation recently supported a conference on computer literacy which attempted to identify issues, considerations, and

---

[1]*The opinions and views expressed herein are those of the authors and do no necessarily reflect the views of the National Science Foundation.*

3

barriers to developing a national goal for achieving a computer-literate society in the United States. This conference
to explore national goals for achieving computer literacy was
an attempt to study the many facets of this problem. At the
conference, jointly organized by the Minnesota Educational
Computing Consortium (MECC) and the Human Resources Research
Organization (HumRRO), ninety people gathered for three days
to discuss computer literacy in our society. This conference
included computer scientists, classroom teachers, principals,
creators of educational materials, publishers, vendors, and
governments officials.

The conference agreed that there is a national need for
"computer literacy." Though there were many different opinions expressed, there were also many common themes. There was
an agreement that we are experiencing a growing national problem and there is an urgent, national need to create an educational system that fosters computer literacy in our society.

Due to the decline in national productivity, the increase
in foreign trade competition, and national defense and safety
needs, computers have emerged as the major force for amelio-
rating these conditions. Consequently, the shortage of computer specialists and knowledge workers has raised the problem
of computer literacy to the level of a national crisis.

A computer-literate workforce is necessary to maintain
our national defense and to improve our national productivity.
At the individual level, computer literacy is needed to participate in a knowledge society. To insure equality of opportunity, all of our citizens must have access to these skills
and tools. Other nations recognizing the importance of computers to their society have already begun national programs
designed to introduce the widespread use of computing into
their educational systems. Today, no such national programs
exist in American education. It has been said that American
education is not only missing a great opportunity, it is failing to discharge a crucial responsibility (Licklider, 1979).

It is believed that this national challenge requires a
broad-based solution with the participation of all segments of
our society. Although education is a state and local function, it is believed that a national effort is needed to
transform and retool our educational establishment to fulfill
this need. While the educational establishment has the crucial role and prime responsibility, we, as a nation, can only
succeed with the active cooperation and involvement of the
many key segments of society. Therefore, we are offering a
report of our discussions.

The conference found that key components for achieving computer literacy are:

1. *The recognition that the concept of computer literacy is multi-faceted.*

The term "computer literate" has many different definitions. Many or most of these differences are a matter of perspective. Some define computer literacy as it is taught; some see computer literacy as it should be taught; and some visionaries see computer literacy as it could be taught given the sophisticated technology predicted to be soon available. The conference proceedings will provide not absolute goals and requirements, but a road map. It is a description of the territory with a variety of suggested approaches for arriving at a variety of destinations; the shortest route, the scenic route, and, the cheapest route.

For example, to some a general awareness of computers is sufficient; to others, a technical skill that can only be acquired by hands-on experience is mandatory; to still others, students must learn to write programs that do things -- solve differential equations or create poetry.

Diversity of opinion, and even fervent advocacy is a characteristic of any rapidly advancing field and should be viewed as an opportunity. It should not be used as an excuse for lack of action. Ideas should be advanced, developed, and disseminated for users to judge their worth and value.

2. *The identification and development of a significant number of knowledgeable people both to create new tools and materials and to effective use them.*

The available pool of talent for instruction and research in computing fails by far to meet our national needs. People are the most important resource. At least two kinds of special people are not critically needed -- knowledge creators and knowledge users -- to develop the nation's human resources necessary and to act as catalysts for educational change.

The shortage of computer scientists and engineers, programmers, curriculum developers, and "creators," is widely documented and discussed in the *President's Report on Science and Engineering Education -- 1980's and Beyond* (National Science Foundation, 1980). We must now devise strategies so that concerted action can be taken to produce these people. It is clear that the educational system, as it now exists, cannot meet our needs for a decade or more without a major restructuring.

Teachers, faculty, board members, parents, and administrators are all potential "users" of these new technologies, and they play the key role in preparing our students for the future. To fulfill this role adequately, they must become computer literate. Also, we must remember that the educational pipeline is a long one. If we are concerned about human resources in the year 2000, we must begin *now*.

3. *The involvement of the home, the workplace, and the community as well as the school in creating literate society.*

In an information society, educators will have to broaden their domain and assume the responsibility and leadership for fostering computer literacy in the home, the workplace and the community as well as in the school. This component recognizes that important reinforcement and learning takes place outside the school environment. Television, libraries, amusement centers, retraining and continuing education programs in business and industry all play a role in helping us become more familiar with computers, and educators must become active participants in this arena.

4. *The presence of computers for instruction in all schools for all students.*

It is believed that we are now at a point where such a recommendation is both economically and technically feasible. In order to begin, a computer should be in every classroom from kindergarten through eighth grade; in grades 8 through 12 computers should be available in a laboratory environment for every student. In higher education, at least one university is already considering *requiring* each student to have his or her own personal computer; this is clearly an achievable goal for all colleges and universities.

5. *The availability of a critical mass of high-quality curricula and courseware.*

While there are outstanding examples of high-quality courseware, educators lack sufficient materials to implement a total curriculum which can take maximum advantage of computers in education. A comprehensive curriculum and critical mass of high-quality courseware are needed in mathematics, science, and social science. A nationally organized effort involving schools, colleges, and universities is needed to address this need. Support will also be required at both local and national levels by citizens' groups, business and industry, and

local and state governments as well as the Federal Government
if we are to provide this critical necessity.

6. *Continued innovation, research, and development to iden-
    tify new opportunities for the use of computers.*

     Further study, research and development should be under-
taken on an accelerated basis to identify the individual and
societal opportunities and potential dangers of computers in
education and of the impact of computers in society. Of
special concern is fundamental research on such areas as human
cognition, person/machine interactions, and ethics and values.
Policy studies are needed to identify issues related to the
growing impact of computers on the worlds of work and education. "Think" tanks should be established to identify and
systematically develop new and compelling uses of computers to
improve productivity and identify new ways that education can
be used to turn these skills into social, economic, and academic benefits.

     Our educational system faces a new problem of unprece-
dented proportions. The computers has the potential for having an impact on every facet of education. Already the computer has revolutionized our society. It has made certain
occupations and skills obsolete. It has been instrumental in
major discoveries in science, medicine, and space exploration.
It has abetted and accelerated the information explosion. The
computer has created a need for a plethora of new skills and
new knowledge. If education is to meet the rapidly changing
needs of an information society, it will require the introduction of many new innovations and perhaps the major restructuring of our institutions. We must now begin the important
tasks of exploring these new horizons and the difficult task
of re-evaluating the basic assumptions underlying American
education.

REFERENCES

Licklider, J.C.R. (1979). "Impact of Information Technology
     on Education in Science and Technology" in *Technology
     in Science Education: The Next Ten Years,* National
     Science Foundation, Washington, D.C.

National Science Foundation (1980). *Science and Engineering
     Education for the 1980's and Beyond,* National Science
     Foundation, Washington, D.C.

NATIONAL COMPUTER LITERACY, 1980[1]

Ronald E. Anderson

Minnesota Educational Computing Consortium
Special Projects Division

On December 18, 1980, a select group of leaders in education and computing research convened in Reston, Virginia, to address the issues suggested by the title of the conference: "National Computer Literacy Goals for 1985." This meeting was "national" in its' representation but, more importantly, national in its focus. Our goals at this conference concerned learning and literacy for all, not a privileged few. In the spirit of a democratic diffusion of computer expertise, we did not limit the conference focus to any particular grade level or social group. The citizenry is the only justifiable target of any national program for literacy and, by analogy, computer literacy. However, it stands to reason that the elementary and secondary schools must shoulder the greatest burden for computer literacy instruction because the major responsibility for socialization for citizenry resides in the precollege educational institutions. This state of affairs mandates the conference on "National Computer Literacy Goals for 1985" to devote extensive, but not exclusive, attention to the precollege educational process.

Why should we single out 1985 as the milestone for progress in computer literacy? A brief history will add some perspective. About ten years ago a number of us began thinking about what the citizenry needed to know about computers. It was about this time that the American Federation of Infor-

[1]*This report is a product of the "Instructional Materials for Computer Literacy" project which is supported by the National Science Foundation under Grant Number SED-7918987. Any opinions, findings, conclusions or recommendations expressed (herein) are those of the author and do not necessarily reflect the views of the National Science Foundation.*

mation Processing Society (AFIPS) and Time, Inc. (1971) sponsored a computer-related opinion survey of the nation's
adults. Ironically, it was the only national adult survey of
computer literacy taken during the past decade. Two years
ago, under National Science Foundation sponsorship, a conference was held in Reston, Virginia, on the social issues of
computers. Computer literacy was one of the major issues
discussed (Amara, 1974).

Years ago, before the advent of the microcomputer, few
were convinced that the masses should know about computers.
Now that many homes and most schools have computers, computer
literacy is no longer the concern of a select few. But now
the challenge is much greater -- there is much more to learn
about and there are new issues of public concern.

Electronics and computing are changing so rapidly that it
is pretentious to try to plan for a ten or twenty year period.
It is necessary, however, to take a long range perspective in
planning educational change because educational institutions
are not able to respond rapidly to changing social and technological conditions.

In setting 1985 as the milestone for growth in the computer literacy of our society, we are assuming implicitly that
there is a body of knowledge and techniques that can be
learned and that this body will not be made obsolete within a
five year period. While some facts and assertions in such a
body of technical knowledge will become outdated, there appears to be enough stability to warrant goal setting and
curricular planning. The widespread excitement over the
potential of microcomputers in education makes it difficult to
delay such evaluation and planning. Thus, one major goal of
the conference was to focus attention on computer literacy
needs and to plan directions and national goals for a five
year period.

Another major goal of the conference was to provide a
forum for opposing views on computer literacy and to move
toward greater consensus on needs and goals. Not only is
there presently a lack of agreement on needs and goals but
many use the term "computer literacy" differently. The underlying issues are more significant than semantic confusion.
The different definitions arise from differences in educational philosophy. Computer literacy has two common educational meanings: one meaning relates to the variety of specialized literacies, e.g., scientific literacy, and technological literacy; and the other refers to general language

literacy which encompasses reading, writing, and understanding. There are two generally accepted dictionary definitions of language literacy. One is the state of being informed, "cultured" and well-versed, and the other is the ability to communicate, e.g., reading and writing. The descriptor, "literate," is generally used to suggest a threshold on the literacy continuum. For instance, we might speak of a literate society as one where almost everyone can read and write. Or, we might refer to a learned, knowledgeable, well read person as literate. This discrepancy arises from "literate" sometimes meaning a "minimal" literacy level and other times meaning a very high level of literacy.

It is not surprising that the term computer literacy shares the semantic ambiguity of language literacy. Since communication with computers via a computer language is directly analogous to interpersonal communication via ordinary language, the conjunction of "computer" and "literacy" has had an intuitive appeal. There is also a great deal of knowledge about computers to be acquired, so it is appropriate to use the term computer literacy to refer to varying levels of knowledge about computers. Indeed, the tradition of scientific literacy, and related ones such as technological literacy, economic literacy, and geographic literacy, to name only a few, suggests that the term literacy is a matter of being informed rather than a communication skill. Scientific literacy (Pella, O'Hearn, and Gale, 1966) and technological literacy both have generally been defined as scientific and technical knowledge pertaining to social implications. Thus, for example, scientific literacy does not so much refer to one's knowledge of biology but to one's understanding of the implications of biology, or more generally, the science-society interface. It is no wonder that in the computer literature we see the term computer literacy equated with "computers and society."

Discussions about computer literacy began appearing in the literature in the mid-1970's. A number of these discussions took a middle ground approach to defining computer literacy. The Conference Board of the Mathematical Sciences (1972) released a report recommending a junior high school course in computer literacy, which was defined as an understanding of computer capabilities, applications, and algorithms. This definition of computer literacy, however, largely ignored issues of social impact. But other writers, including Lykos (1974), Moursund (1976), and Rawitsch (1978), presumed that computer literacy even included emphasis upon social issues. Moursund (1976) conceptualized computer literacy as "a knowledge of the non-technical and low-technical aspects of the capabilities and limitations of computers, and of the social, vocational and educational implications of computers." Both his early writing and his later texts (Moursund, 1978; Billings and Moursund, 1979) propose that "low-level" knowledge is best acquired by a combination of programming and non-programming instructional materials.

Other discussions have focused on one or the other of the two meanings of literacy. Luehrmann (1980) and others tend to equate computer literacy skills with programming skills which implies that computer literacy is a minimal communication skill, analogous to reading and writing.

On the other end of the continuum are those who view literacy as a matter of being well-informed about general aspects of computers. Elementary school textbooks such as Ball and Charp (1977) exemplify this point of view by proposing to make one computer literate with less than 100 pages of instruction consisting mainly of drawings. Rawitsch (1978) suggests that students should also learn how to access computers and to have some understanding of the social issues, but he stops short of insisting that students should learn how to program in order to become computer literate. A more extreme but conservative view is taken by Carpenter, Corbitt, Kepner, Lindquist, and Reys (forthcoming) who define computer literacy as a low level understanding of what computers do or can do in society. Following the lead of the Conference Board of the Mathematical Sciences (1972) they explicitly assume that such a low-level understanding includes comprehension of algorithms but not necessarily the ability to program an algorithm.

The diversity of these various views of computer literacy is obvious but the significance of this dissensus is perhaps overrated. If one adopts the perspective that computer literacy is a matter of functioning effectively within a given role (cf. Anderson and Klassen, 1980) then it becomes more obvious why some people need low-level understanding and others, e.g., students and engineers, need higher level understanding.

It is clear that many social roles, including student roles, in 1980, to say nothing of 1985, require a high level of understanding about computers and computer programming. It is this premise that underlies the position taken by the Computer Literacy Project at the Minnesota Educational Computing Consortium (MECC). This project claims that each of the following domains are essential to computer literacy for students: hardware concepts, software and data processing concepts, programming and algorithms, application principles, social implications, and a favorable or well-informed affective orientation. This position is most explicitly laid out in Anderson and Klassen (1980) but the domains, or dimensions of computer literacy, are specified in earlier publications (Johnson, Anderson, Klassen, and Hansen, 1980; and Klassen, Anderson, Hansen, and Johnson, 1980).

The disagreements over what should be included within the definition of computer literacy have not only academic but curricular import as well. If one accepts the perspective that computer literacy is role specific, then considerable diversity in curriculum programs is justified because not all students have the same needs. A national program of computer literacy does not necessarily produce a single curriculum or requirement for every citizen. The goals of the conference on "National Computer Literacy Goals for 1985" allowed flexibility in educational philosophy and instructional requirements. The most important considerations are how to infuse any computer related activities into the curriculum and what instructional methods should be utilized in this endeavor.

Another major goal of the conference was to bring research implications and instructional expertise to bear upon computer literacy. While one session was devoted exclusively to research results, the major emphasis was upon psychological and instructional research. To effectively implement initiatives for changing the state of computer literacy, it was necessary to include social research as well. In order to ascertain what people know and feel about computers it is necessary to conduct broad-based surveys. Very little is known about the state of computer literacy at this time, but the limited data that are available are very instructive and will be summarized here.

Numerous research projects have included measures of attitudes, knowledge, and skills related to computers but rarely have these studies included samples beyond one or two classrooms. Some noteworthy exceptions are the studies conducted in Minnesota (Klassen, et al., 1980), Nebraska (Stevens, 1980), and Illinois (Dennis, 1978). The AFIPS/Time, Inc. (1971) survey of attitudes toward computers is the only nation-wide computer-related survey of adults conducted within the U.S. within the past ten years. The results show that at the beginning of the decade the populace felt generally favorable toward computers although expressing considerable ambivalence and hesitancy. Many of the questions in the survey asked about awareness of general applications of computers in society, and the results indicated that the public had a general awareness of computer capabilities but many people held misconceptions about computers. Because the survey was taken almost 10 years ago, when the role of computer technology was dramatically different, these data need not be discussed in greater depth here.

Unfortunately, I do not have a 1980 survey of computer literacy to report to you, nor is it likely that over the next five years we will have an annual assessment of national computer literacy. However, there is a wealth of data available from the National Assessment of Educational Progress (NAEP) that is relevant to our interests. The data were collected during the 1977-78 school year in the most recent mathematics assessment performed by the NAEP. This recent survey was the first time that questions pertaining to computers were included in a NAEP assessment, but future NAEP assessments of mathematics will probably include additional items pertaining to computers. The computer related questions were asked of two samples of students, 13-year olds and 17-year olds. Approximately 2500 students were tested in each age group (National Assessment of Education Progress, 1980).

The NAEP data reveals some important though disturbing findings:

1. Perceived access to computer facilities was rather low. Only 12% of the junior high (13-year olds) and 25% of the senior high (17-year olds) students indicated they had "access to a computer terminal to learn mathematics."

2. Very few claimed to be able to program a computer. Only 8% of the 13-year olds and 13% of the 17-year olds said they could write a program.

3. Only 11% of the 17-year olds reported having some coursework in computer programming.

4. Performance on flowchart reading exercises and simple BASIC programs revealed very poor understanding of algorithmic processes involving conditional branching.

5. About half of the students who had taken computer programming classes were still unable to read a simple flowchart.

   *6. A few of the students who had taken computer pro-
gramming classes seemed to have little or no understanding of
general computer capabilities, even though students in general, even those lacking computer experience, seem to have such
an understanding.*

   *7. Many students both with and without computer pro-
gramming coursework did not seem to have a sense of the value
of computers for themselves personally or for society.*

While these conclusions are based on data gathered about two
and a half years ago, there is reason to believe that the
overall opportunity for computer experiences and literacy has
not dramatically improved at the present time.

   In brief, the best data we have suggest that few students
in either senior or junior high school have opportunities for
computer experience; few have algorithmic problem-solving
skills; and many lack an awareness of the role and value of
computers. Since these findings are true for 17-year old
students, most of whom were in the 11th grade, we would speculate that many students are graduating from high school and
perhaps from college without a minimal level of computer literacy.

   What is equally disturbing is the evidence in the data
that what little literacy exists in the nations' students is
unequally distributed across social groups. Computer experience is much less common among minorities, women, and those
living in the Southeastern U.S. or in rural areas. Not only
is computer experience less common among these groups but
there is good evidence that computer knowledge and skills are
lower as well.

   These assessments of the state and national computer
literacy at the end of the 1970s give us cause for great concern. To function effectively as students, especially in
science and mathematics classes, our nation's youth needs to
know how to use and program computers. To function effectively as scientists, engineers, managers, and teachers, the professionals of today, to say nothing of 1985, need to learn how
to use computers to enhance their specialized skills. To
function effectively as citizens in 1985, we will all need to
know how the computer impinges on and enhances our everyday
lives.

   The need for improving the general state of computer
literacy is compelling without a doubt. It is time to tackle

the specifics of instructional objectives and instructional strategies. The "National Computer Literacy Goals for 1985" conference was indeed opportune and hopefully the beginning of a concerted national agenda for change.

REFERENCES

AFIPS and Time, Inc. (1971). *A National Survey of The Public's Attitudes Towards Computers.* AFIPS Press, Arlington, VA.

Amara, R. (1974). "Toward understanding the social impact of computers." Institute for the Future, Menlo Park, CA.

Anderson, R.E. and Klassen, D.L. (1980). "A conceptual framework for developing computer literacy instruction." *Minnesota Educational presented at the annual meeting of the ACM Computing Consortium,* St. Paul, MN: Paper.

Ball, M. and Charp, S. (1977). *Be a Computer Literate.* Creative Computing Press, Morristown, NJ.

Billings, K. and Moursund, D. (1979). *Are You Computer Literate?* Dilithium Press, Forest Grove, OR.

Bukoski, W.J. and Korotkin, A.L. (1976). "Computing activities in secondary education," *Educational Technology,* January, 9, 23.

Carpenter, T., Corbitt, M., Kepner, H., Lindquist, M. and Reys, R. (1980). "Results of the second NAEP mathematics assessment: secondary school," *The Mathematics Teacher,* May, 73, 5, 329-338.

Carpenter, T., Corbitt, M., Kepner, H., Lindquist, M., and Reys, R. (forthcoming). "The current status of computer literacy: NAEP results for secondary students," *The Mathematics Teacher.*

Chambers, J. and Bork, A. (1980). "Computer assisted learning in U.S. secondary/elementary schools," (Research Report No. 80-03). Center for Information Processing, California State University, Frensno, CA.

Conference Board of the Mathematical Sciences (1972). "Rec mendations regarding computers in high school educatic Conference Board of the Mathematical Sciences, Washing ton, D.C.

Johnson, D.C., Anderson, R.E., Hansen, T.P., and Klassen, D (1980). "Computer literacy: what is it?" *Mathematic Teacher*, February, 73, 91-96.

Klassen, D.L., Anderson, R.E., Hansen, T.P., and Johnson, D (1980). "A study of computer use and literacy in scie education, Final Report." MECC, St. Paul, MN.

Luehrmann, A. (1980). "Computer literacy: a national cris and a solution for it," *BYTE*, July, 5, 7, 98-102; also reprinted in Proceedings of the 1980 Personal Computin Festival, *American Federation of Information Processin Societies, Inc.*, 167-170, Anaheim, CA.

Lykos, P.G. (1974). "The computer illiteracy problem: a partial solution," *American Mathematics Monthly*, April 81, 4, 393-398.

Moursund, D. (1978). "Basic programming for computer lite- racy." McGraw-Hill, Inc., New York, NY.

Moursund, D. (1976). "What is computer literacy?" *Creative Computing*, November/December, 2, 6, 55.

National Assessment of Educational Progress (1980). Proce- dural Handbook: 1977-78 Mathematics Assessment. Edu- cation Commission of the States, Denver, CO.

Pella, M.O., O'Hearn, G.T., and Gale, C.W. (1966). "Referen to scientific literacy," *Journal of Research in Science Teaching*, 4, 199-208.

Rawitsch, D.G. (1978). "The concept of computer literacy," *The MAEDS Journal of Educational Computing*, 2, 2, 1-19.

Stevens, D.J. (1980). "How educators perceive computers in the classroom," *AEDS Journal*, Spring, 13, 3, 221-232.

ON THE DEVELOPMENT OF AN INFORMATION
HANDLING CURRICULUM:
COMPUTER LITERACY, A DYNAMIC CONCEPT

Robert J. Seidel

Human Resources Research Organization

I. CURRENT PROBLEMS

The focus of this volume and the conference that generated it is computer literacy. Yet, the diversity of view-
points expressed by conference participants and found in the
chapters of this volume indicates an ambiguous definition of
the term "computer literacy." Throughout the various chapters
and participant comments is the implicit or explicit need to
deal with broader topics of "information know-how" or "information handling" (see Licklider's comments). This chapter
attempts to provide a broader informational context for the
development of a curriculum. The curriculum is intended to
address the varied needs for computer literacy for groups and
individuals with different societal roles.

Regardless of the term's ambiguous definition, there are
a number of common threads which represent the premises of the
argument for computer literacy on a national scale:

Premises:

- Our society, collectively and individually, must
  handle increasing amounts of information;

- Individuals need to become better problem-solvers;

- Computers are a major component of the work environment to help solve problems and handle information; *therefore,*

Conclusion:

- All persons should be computer literate.

Given the above, it appears that the argument for universal computer literacy is approached with significant gaps in logic. At the very least, those premises demand a separation of research questions from those of implementation and policy decisions. For example, computers can be used to solve problems, to act as a tool for teaching people how to solve problems, and more specifically, to solve computer programming problems. One *research question* is: Does this mean that people with computer programming skills are better problem solvers in the domain of computing? (see Mayer, pp. 129).

Another research issue that should be addressed deals with whether teaching someone to solve computer programming problems or to solve algebra problems phrased in computer programming terms will make people better problem solvers in *domains other* than those of computer programming and/or algebra. Soloway's research (see pp. 171) suggests "yes" to the question of helping people solve algebra problems by using rephrased computer programming statements as the focus. But, the other issue -- the value of computer programming for teaching better problem solving in various domains versus teaching problem solving equally well without computer programming -- is still open for research (Milner and Seidel, 1979).

II.   VARIETIES OF NEED

The arguments that not all individuals or groups need to learn about computers to the same degree or in the same way draws upon an analogy for me with "transportation" or "telephone literacy." Clearly, these technologies changed our communication modes and our conception of cultural awareness. Those of us who have traveled as passengers in an automobile have developed an appreciation for the value of the automobile as a transportation device. There are others who have driver's licenses and control the machine. The use of the telephone is a similar case in point. However, in none of these technologies have we needed to learn the elements of the technology (e.g., the elements of a carburetor, the mechanical problems and solutions to those problems) in order to incorporate their features into our understanding of how society could benefit from their usage. I believe the same holds true in the use of computers in society today. In many of the

current groups within society, adults can benefit clearly from
knowledge of the advantages, impact, and requirements that the
use of computers place upon our communication systems and of
interactions with societal institutions. Yet, much of this
can be done without making everyone a computer programmer.

As noted in Figure 1, there are many kinds of people who
have to deal with information. Let's take one example within

School   *Home*

        Policymakers   Spouse
        Administrator   Parent
        Teacher   Child
        Student   Sibling
        PTA Member

Job   *Society*

        Executive   Friends
        Manager   Service Personnel
        First Line Supervisor
        Worker

                        Governments

                        Federal
                        State
                        Local

        Figure 1. A Variety of Information Handlers

the school environment in which there is a variety of different actors (e.g., school board member, principal, teacher,
student, etc.). On the surface, it appears that the amount of
involvement or training using computers required by each actor
differs based upon *who* they are in the school environment. It
is also the case that the *same* individual may be located in
different environments (e.g., school or home), depending upon
the role the individual is seen as depicting as illustrated in
Figure 2. We know that the activity of learning is readily
placed within the activities of the home, work environment,

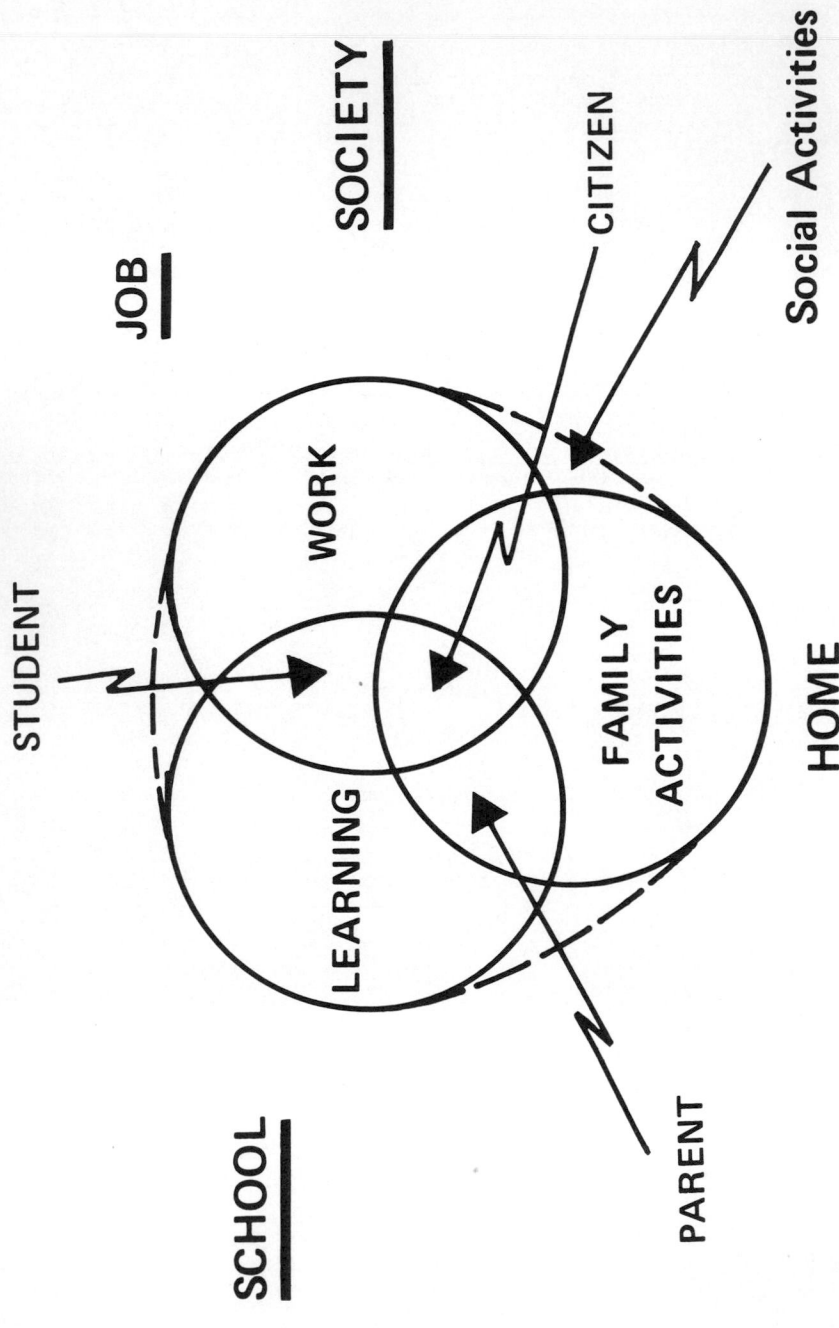

Figure 2. Varieties of environment for handling information.

school environment and society at large. At the intersection
of all these activities, we find the *citizen* (see Watt, pp.
53).   That citizen may be a student or a parent as well as
friend; or all three at the same time! So, there are multiple
roles for people, multiple activities, and therefore, multiple
needs within our society.

All of these roles will require the individual to cope
with the increasing amounts of information being produced and
disseminated throughout our society. There is increasing
involvement of technology in our working environment and day-
to-day existence. Our simple assertion is that an individual's societal roles and tasks place different contingent
demands on the computer and the individual involvement with
the computer.

In order to deal with these issues, it is necessary to
consider the variety of individuals who need to handle information, the context in which they handle information, and the
distinction between present and future needs. From this kind
of analysis, I feel that a flexible curriculum for teaching
people how to handle information based upon their needs should
evolve.

Before describing the proposed outline for an information-handling curriculum, there remains for us to consider
both a *present* and *future* orientation to the needs of these
multiple groups in our society. For example, we discussed at
the conference the needs for computer literacy over the next
five years. The question we must consider is, do we ignore
today's adults? To do so would be a mistake. Those not directly employed or connected with the existing school system
today have needs of their own for processing increasing
amounts of information. Moreover, these individuals are potentially significant educational change agents for school
systems and society. For example, these adults will have
offspring who will be, or currently are, students, and these
adults can influence school boards, local government resource
allocations, as well as providing information lobbying resources for important individual and policy groups on a national scale. Therefore, to hasten the achievement of the
educational goals for computer literacy, we should include in
our focus of interest the development of adult education
courses or curricula on information-processing, handling, management, and other related activities.

As discussed earlier (see Figure 1), an administrator in
a school, or a policymaker, must be able to appreciate how
computers can be used to, for example, augment the existing

disciplines or how they might aid in managing student schedules. However, it is debatable whether such individuals need
to become computer programmers in order to attain this appreciation. My guess is that for now the latter is not the case.
Similarly, an executive responsible for a large corporation
may need a broad appreciation of information technology and
its benefits. S/he may even need to know how computers (e.g.,
information technology) will play a role in such areas as in-
ventory and production. However, the needs of this executive
would be different from those of a first-line supervisor, or a
worker who might be required to use computer-aided design
techniques for performing productive work.

    Equally important in considering the needs of today's
adult population is the distinction between training and education. The work force (e.g., managers, secretaries, various
newspaper employees) have needs to handle increasing amounts
of information, and technology can help. But these groups
require computer literacy in a *specific job context*. Literacy
for the secretary means helping her/him understand the benefits of text manipulation, and the organization of files, as
implemented through the use of word processing machines. Once
this is learned, other aspects of information technology can
be pursued as desired in a modular curriculum. Such an approach for adult information handling courses has at least two
immediate advantages: (1) it solves an immediate, relevant
need; and (2) by designing a training/literacy course as a
first step, a concrete basis for understanding the value of
(information technology) computers is established and will
likely lead to greater awareness and acceptance of other
societal applications as well.

    Public awareness of the need to educate the entire popu-
lation to manage information was given a boost at the April
1980 House Hearings of the Subcommittee on Science Research
and Technology and the Subcommittee on Select Education. During the hearings, it was emphasized several times that television and the computer have helped to realize the importance of
this need to process information (Melmed, pp. 27; Hollenbeck,
pp. 29-30). One answer at those hearings to the question of
how much computers should be a part of the lives of individuals in our evolving information society was to give all people, at least, a minimal amount of computer knowledge that
would enable them to become "computer comfortable." The
meaning of "computer comfortable" is to allow people to be
able to "interact easily with the computer" (Rockoff, pp. 120-
121).

Other individuals at that very important set of hearings emphasized the increasing value of a computer delivery system in the field of education, and the need for appreciation of how much computers could do for delivering individualized instruction cost-effectively. From my point of view, the unifying themes for the terms "computer literacy," "computer comfort," "computer appreciation," or "information processing" is the term "information handling." What is required is a flexible curriculum for information handling which deals with the various facets of awareness, knowledge, and skills that have been stressed both in those April 1980 public hearings, in the conference discussions, the presentations, and the related papers in this volume.

III.   MARKET VS. NATIONAL NEED

Just as recognizing the distinction between the needs for training and education, and today's adult versus future generations as important to a national strategy for attaining computer literacy, it is also essential to distinguish a market from a need. An employer who believes business productivity will increase as a result of his/her employees, and his/her becoming knowledgeable and/or skillful in using computers, will pay for an information handling course. Developers of computer literacy and information-handling curricula can, therefore, gauge both a need and a market for cost recovery and profits; publishers or vendors will produce accordingly to satisfy that market.

A need also exists in education. But, who will pay for the curriculum development? For example, is there a market for computer literacy within teacher training? The need exists but with the current paucity and dim near-term prospects of funding for public education -- or even its very existence -- the creation of a market seems doubtful. It became quite clear at the conference that teacher training institutions are a natural focus for creating a tremendous multiplier effect in order to attain national computer literacy. However, until a market can be seen as clearly as the need and the societal value, a curriculum tailored to meet this need on a national scale is not likely to be developed. This commentary is by no means novel. Numerous times before suggestions have been made for a unique, national partnership, or consortium, among industry, government, and education to achieve critical mass of academic computing usages in the U.S. (Levien, 1972; Seidel and Rubin, 1975; and recently Gillespie,

1981). The sad fact is: the suggestions are still valid and nothing has been done. (See Section V in this volume)

Another view of national markets is seen in the continuing growth of personal computer sales to the private consumer, business and hobbyist (350,000 units annually by 1979, with a value estimated at $500 million) (Nilles, 1981). A computer literacy course that is sold or provided as part of a package when the computer is purchased, at a retail store, would seem very appealing.

For education to benefit, however, local or state school districts will probably have to support development and/or acquisition of computer literacy curricula along with computer purchases. So far, Minnesota and MECC provide a reasonable State model to follow. HumRRO, with National Science Foundation support, is attempting to infuse computer literacy in K-8 at the county level. But federal support will be diminishing shortly. This model requires sustaining monetary investment and commitment at the *local* level. It is not clear at this time whether other school districts on their own will be able to take advantage of this approach (see Hunter, Section IV in this volume) without outside funding support for development and implementation. If some viable arrangement can be made between public education and industry, patterned after some combination of the elements described above, then computer literacy levels can be raised dramatically for pre-college students within the next five years. The much rumored voucher system might be the catalyst to create the market to serve the needs in public education. If not, then it is likely that business, home consumers, and private schools will be the near term, five-year market for information handling curricula.

IV. PROPOSED CURRICULUM

The curriculum which I stress has a domain as indicated in Figure 3. The sequence of topics and emphasis would vary contingent on need and interest. In this curriculum, need is relevant to the primary role being served (e.g., worker, home consumer, or pre-college student). The continuum of an information handling curriculum contains three basic areas: (1) awareness of information impact; (2) generic knowledge of information handling; and (3) the specific knowledges and skills related to the use of computers. The latter, in turn, encompasses three basic components. The first component is the specific knowledge related to application programs and databases. These may be uniquely relevant to different disci-

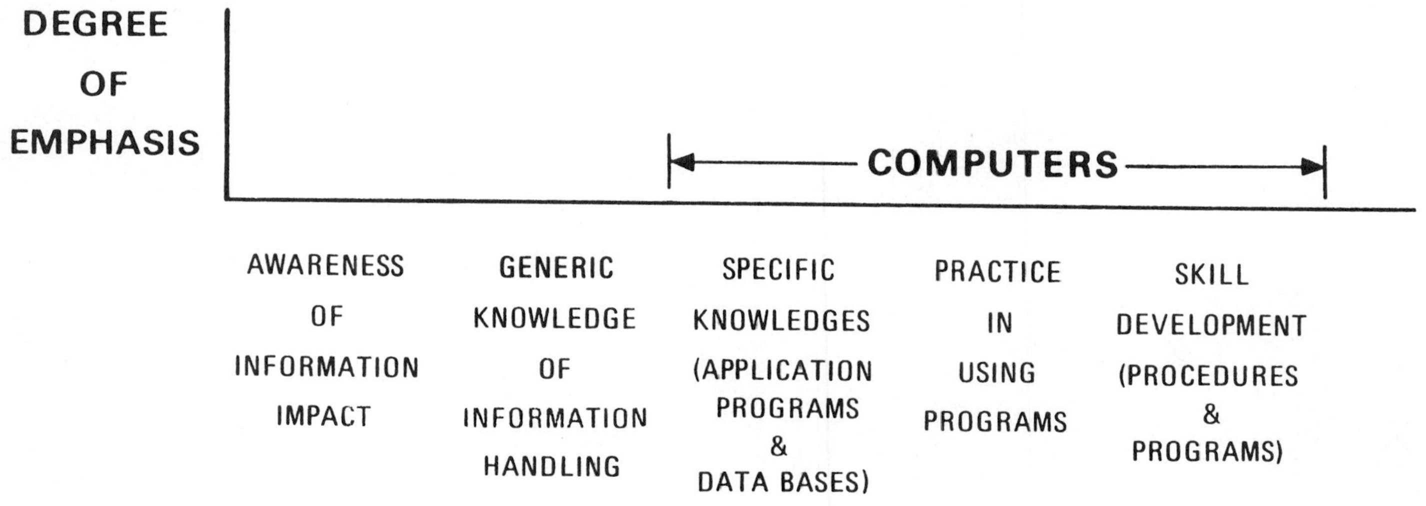

Figure 3. Continuum of an information handling curriculum.

plines. Secondly, this portion of the curriculum involves practice in using computer programs without necessarily having a computer programming skill. Lastly, there is the component involving the development of skill in producing and modifying computer programs, as well as the more general process of creating and executing procedures.

In Figure 3, on the Y-axis is the term "degree of emphasis" which indicates that the particular implementation of a course in information processing or handling will differ based upon the needs of the target population (see Figure 1). This point demands emphasis in respect to the developmental stages of readiness of the pre-college student. The focus of our conference was on pre-college education. We should carefully note that there is still a good deal of disagreement concerning whether the computer programming should be introduced as a separate course to learn or as an integral part of study in various subject matter areas to young children (e.g., K-4). As part of a course of study, the computer can serve as a performance aid on a simple level (e.g., drill and practice spelling) and on a more complex level (e.g., simplified simulation and game applications).

What I propose is consistent with MECC and HumRRO categorization (Anderson and Klassen, 1980; Hunter, 1980) of types of knowledge and skills. But for the adult in business or industry I propose a tailored curriculum. This curriculum can be conceived of as an inverted pyramid with the starting point as job-relevant knowledges and skills. Modules for broader understanding, awareness of impact on society at large, and additional applications would be added as later options.

The *awareness of information impact* should take into account whether it's an impact on the school, the job, the home, or society in general. By and large, a type of impact awareness using the various media, such as television programs, radio spots, as well as lecture offerings in adult continuing education centers would be appropriate for the citizen. There have been excellent examples on television of such a possibility. One such effort was two TV episodes of the *Lou Grant Show*. The viewer was exposed to how word processing and financial functions could be accomplished with computers, and how potential social problems such as job displacement, strikes, and businesses collapsing could result without adequate awareness of institutional impact.

Secondly, the *generic knowledge of information handling* should deal with old and new conceptual ways of storing, retrieving, transmitting, transforming, and otherwise processing

information. This module would include a section on creating
and following explicit procedures to accomplish these functions. This part of the curriculum would deal with such problems as the value of information, ethics of ownership, and
privacy. The *specific knowledge of databases and applications
programs* would be relevant, again, to the different target
groups as noted in Figure 1 -- school, job, home and society.
Similarly, this would be the case for *practice in using existing programs*. The *development of skills* and recognizing, modifying, and writing various computer programs and procedures
could be included in any curriculum relevant to the subject-
matter involved. It would also be consistent with a developmental approach having separate courses in computer programming or computer science, starting at the 7th or 8th grade
level.

The entire information handling curriculum should involve
experiential learning at some level and to some minimal degree. The format envisioned is description of function, dem-
onstration of how available tools can accomplish these functions, and practice by the students in using the available
tools. However, *now*, administrators, teachers, and other
adults may need to feel more "computer comfortable" -- not
necessarily become programmers. As noted earlier, adult curricula would be tailored to job (role) relevance. The inverted pyramid approach would readily permit expansion of understanding and competence using technology based on interest and
need, and build upon the familiar (e.g., my job and how it
will change).

Where would each course be offered? They could be given
on-site for business and other consumers of personal computers. They could be offered courses at computer stores or as
part of the software package to take home for self-study.
Also, there could be adult education center programs located
at local public schools, and universities, and offered after
hours. In future generations, course offerings should probably be in the educational mainstream. All students in a few
years from now should have some experience as computer programmers, albeit in a minor discipline-oriented mode. (See Fig. 4.)

Perhaps, what I am proposing could be characterized as a
transition curriculum which a few years from now will require
extensive revision. We are just breaking new ground in the
videodisc field. It is likely that processing information
through visual analogues will, in less than ten years, open up
other vast fields for an information handling curriculum.
Holographic developments may add a technology that will totally alter our view of knowledge and information processing.

AWARENESS OF
IMPACT OF
INFORMATION

SPECIFIC KNOWLEDGE
OF DATA BASES
& APPLICATIONS PROGRAMS

PRACTICE IN
USING PROGRAMS

ON MY:

FOR MY:

IN MY:

(a) School
(b) Job
(c) Home
(d) Society

(a) School
(b) Job
(c) Home
(d) Society

(a) School
(b) Job
(c) Home
(d) Society

GENERIC KNOWLEDGE OF INFORMATION
HANDLING . . . (COMPUTERS, ESPECIALLY)

DEVELOPING
SKILLS IN

Old and New Conceptual Ways of Storing, Retrieving,
Transmitting and otherwise processing Information

Value of Information

Ethics of Ownership

Ethics of Privacy, etc.

Recognizing, modifying and writing
Procedure & Computer Programs

Figure 4. Information handling needs.

V.   EVOLVING CULTURE

As asserted throughout this paper, bounding the domain of
an information technology or handling curriculum must take
into account that the cultural setting within which the curriculum is being offered is time-bound (i.e., computer literacy as a concept is evolving). This, too, was a point of
universal agreement at the conference (see Moursund, pp. 73).
A significant evolutionary factor to consider concerning how
information is to be managed at any point in time is the
nature of any existing data base of knowledge. For example,
our knowledge of astronomy prior to Galileo was considerably
limited as compared with our knowledge after his discoveries.
Our knowledge of flight changed in a similar manner subsequent
to the invention of heavier-than-air aircraft. These and
other significant advances have continually changed the nature
of the information we are required to process in order to
understand our world.

As another example, for generations we have learned the
multiplication tables and the four arithmetic functions (addition, subtraction, multiplication, and division) during the
first few grammar school grades. This practice has recently
been called into question because of the availability of the
hand-held calculator. If the *elements* of our mathematical
knowledge called "arithmetic" previously had been the four
functions, one could now raise the question of whether a
consolidation and quantum jump in the data base has occurred.
Thus, "arithmetic" takes on a lower order position as an *element itself* in a *new* knowledge base. A similar change in the
nature of information handling requirements seems likely over
the next generation with the widespread use of microcomputers
in homes, schools and the work environment. The term "computer programming" may have the same fate as "arithmetic."

Let me emphasize that as we learn more about and with
computer technology, our culture will change. And, with this
change our means of communicating with each other will add yet
another dimension. With videodisc and holographic technologies, the processing of information will reach a new electronic level. The question that will be relevant to consider *then*
is: What knowledge and/or skills does an individual need in
order to take advantage of the future level? Five years
hence, what will the definition or concept of computer literacy be, and how will we deal with it at that time? Prior to
1900, "flight" was either restricted to meaning airborne
travel by birds or earth-based avoidance by others. Technol-

ogy has added to that meaning considerably. Hopefully, computer literacy will similarly become part of an organic and
open-ended evolving curriculum for developing *information
know-how* by the individuals and groups of our society.

REFERENCES

Anderson, R.E. and Klassen, D.L. (1980). "A Conceptual Frame-
     work for Developing Computer Literacy Instruction," *Pre-
     sentation at the Association of Computing Machinery* in
     Tennessee, October 28, 1980.

Dwyer, T.A. (1981). "Multi-Micro Learning Environments: A
     Preliminary Report on the Solo/NET/works Project," *Byte,*
     January, pp. 104-114.

Gillespie, R.G. and Dicaro, D.A. (1981). *Computing in Higher
     Education: An Accidental Revolution,* 42 page pamphlet,
     University of Washington. (ERIC Document Reproduction
     Service No. HE 014-069).

Hunter, B. (1980). "An Approach to Integrating Computer
     Literacy Into the K-8 Curriculum," Professional Paper 2-
     80, Human Resources Research Organization, October, pp.
     2-80.

Levien, R.E. (1972). *The Emerging Technology: Instructional
     Uses of the Computer in Higher Education.* A Carnegie
     Commission on Higher Education and Rand Corporation
     Study, McGraw-Hill, New York.

Nilles, J.M. (1981). *A Technology Assessment of Personal
     Computers,* (Report), National Science Foundation.

Rockoff (1980). Expert witness on *Information Technology in
     Education,* Joint Hearings before the Subcommittee on
     Science, Research and Technology of the Committee on
     Science and Technology and the Subcommittee on Select
     Education of the Committee on Education and Labor House
     of Representatives, April, No. 134, pp. 114-125.

Seidel, R.J. and Rubin, M.L. (1975). "Alternative National
     Models: Strategies for Change," in *Learning Alternatives
     in U.S. Education: Where Student and Computer Meet,* by
     B. Hunter, C.S. Kastner, M.L. Rubin, R.J. Seidel, Educa-
     tional Technology Publications, Englewood Cliffs, NJ.

COMPUTER LITERACY: 1949-1979

Beverly Hunter

Human Resources Research Organization

Our mission at the conference was to recommend goals for computer literacy, and ways of achieving those goals. If our work is to be useful, we must build upon lessons we have learned from the past as well as upon visions we have for the future.

Each of us has seen the experienced benefits that come for skilled, informed, ethical, and wise uses of computers and information systems. Each of us has seen and experienced negative consequences that result when people use computers in unskilled, uninformed, unethical, or unwise ways. Each of us has tried to improve the level of computer literacy in ourselves, our colleagues, and our students.

Thus, the history of computer literacy is contained in a distributed data base. It is distributed among all our individual memories. During this next half hour, please search through your own data banks for events and lessons you have learned that may contribute to our collective wisdom. Build for yourself a special working file of these events and ideas to draw upon during our work over these next three days.

To help you extract these events from your own memories, I will mention some 100 or so events that I think have some relevance. You will use the characteristics of those events, as keys for searching your own memories. When you find these pertinent events and ideas, you will tag them in some way to make them readily accessible for use during the conference.

These events will be presented in three strands, corresponding to the three screens in front of you. The strand on the left-hand screen depicts events that relate to research, development, and technology. The middle screen depicts edu-

cational events. The right-hand screen depicts events that
are social, political and instructional.

The events I suggest are not claimed to be the most important. The most important events are those with which you
have had personal experience and have learned from. The
events are not claimed to be causal, either. I do think these
events can teach us something about needs for computer literacy, about resources for achieving computer literacy, and
about ways of accomplishing goals.

(The items on the following pages correspond roughly to
the events and ideas that are depicted on the three screens.)

RESEARCH/DEVELOPMENT/TECHNOLOGY	EDUCATION	SOCIAL/POLITICAL/INSTITUTIONAL
1949	*1949*	*1949*
ENIAC -- 5000 Additions/second	*Giant Brains* by E.C. Berkeley -- "This book is intended for everyone."	"Machines that Think and How Society May Control Them"
	1950	*1950*
	ACM and Rutgers College of Engineering: Computing Conference. "To help engineers and executives understand the numerous things that a computer of moderate cost can do."	Alan Turing, "Computing Machinery and Intelligence"
	1953	
	Math Department brochure encourages student interest in computing: "The growing use of modern electronic machines (often referred to as *Giant Brains*) provides an exciting new field for mathematicians.	

RESEARCH/DEVELOPMENT/TECHNOLOGY	EDUCATION	SOCIAL/POLITICAL/INSTITUTIONAL
1956		*1956*
IBM 704 computers -- gifts to MIT & UCLA		NSF Institutional Computing Services grants to colleges and universities.
	1958	
	All freshmen required to learn computer programming -- Colorado School of Mines	
1959		
University of Illinois PLATO Project -- R&D on computers in instruction for undergraduates		
	1961	*1961*
	George Washington High School in Denver begins computer science program	NSF sponsors summer conference on computer programming for college teachers.
		Conference on CAI sponsored by SDC and Office of Naval Research

36

RESEARCH/DEVELOPMENT/TECHNOLOGY	EDUCATION	SOCIAL/POLITICAL/INSTITUTIONAL
	1962	*1962*
	Authorities at Dartmouth agree that a digital computer should be as easily accessible to everyone as the library	Association for Educational Data Systems (AEDS) formed
1963	*1963*	*1963*
Institute for Mathematical Studies in the Social Sciences at Stanford University begins R&D in CAI with funding from NSF and Carnegie Corp.	Dartmouth builds timesharing BASIC	Commission of College Geography formed. New Yorker Magazine, "The Analytical Engine" by Jeremy Bernstein
1964	*1964*	
Research at HumRRO on teaching problem-solving via assembly language programming	College of Engineering Faculty vote to require all freshmen to take a one-credit course in "Basic Computer Programming" (several universities)	
Florida State University CAI Center founded		
IBM Field Engineering CAI national network		

RESEARCH/DEVELOPMENT/TECHNOLOGY	EDUCATION	SOCIAL/POLITICAL/INSTITUTIONAL
1965	*1965*	*1965-1971*
ENTELEK CAI-CMI Literature and Program Abstract	University of Texas CAI Laboratory	USOE funds more than 500 projects using computers in education
	Computer Curriculum Corporation in Palo Alto markets computer-based drills in math and reading to elementary schools.	
	Public school systems adopt CAI: Philadelphia, McComb County, MS; New York City; Waterford District, MI	
1966	*1966*	*1966*
HumRRO research on teaching computer programming via CAI	Oregon's Computer Instruction Network. 25 terminals in schools	Coleman Report on Role of CAI in education of ethnic minorities: "CAI is nearly perfect instrument..."
NCECS/TUCC network. "PALS" model for sharing instructional programs	Fairfield University -- Teacher Training in Computing	Association for Development of Instructional Systems formed
IBM 1500 system provides R&D vehicle for CAI.		

RESEARCH/DEVELOPMENT/TECHNOLOGY	EDUCATION	SOCIAL/POLITICAL/INSTITUTIONAL
	1967	*1967*
	Estimated 6% of college students use computers.	Carnegie Commission on Higher education established to study future role of technology.
	Dartmouth Secondary School project to explore the use of computing in secondary schools: "The average student can learn to program in the seventh grade."	President's Science Advisory Committee: Need for computing opportunity for almost all undergraduates
	Dorn article in *Datamation* on computer role in high school: Computer science course is of less value than integration of computer into math and science curricula	U.S. Forest Service study shows foresters, engineers, statisticians, need computer-related skills for modelling, data management, statistical analysis
1968	*1968*	*1968*
Communications network established for sharing computer resources among 19 public California State Universities and Colleges	Philadelphia School District provides CAI in elementary math; computer programming courses in high schools	NSF begins support of regional academic computing networks
	Boy Scouts of America has computer merit badge	

RESEARCH/DEVELOPMENT/TECHNOLOGY	EDUCATION	SOCIAL/POLITICAL/INSTITUTIONAL
1968 (con't)	*1968 (con't)*	*1968 (con't)*
First Index to CAI, Helen Lekan (ed.), includes 456 programs	Knox College; Wilber Pillsbury develops CompuGuide accounting	George Leonard in Education and Ecstasy describes Learning Dome; "The high interactive, regenera-time technological society now emerging will require something akin to mass genios, mass crea-tivity, and lifelong learning."
CAMP (Computer Assisted Mathematics Program) is developed	Beloit College: Social Sciences Instructional Programming Project: "I have found that undergraduate students are the only reliable, low-cost, high-output resource in educational computing." (M. Hall)	Educational Technology Act passed by Congress
Languages used for educational computing: (Zinn Summary)	Highline School District, Seattle, Washington: Long-range plan for computer education established by District administration. Plan includes computer literacy for all students; problem-solving use of computers; pre-vocational training	
CRICISAM: Calculus, a Computer-Oriented Presentation, developed by authors from several institutions		
HUNTINGTON Project initiated -- outgrowth of Engineering Concepts Curriculum Project		
ELIZA		

RESEARCH/DEVELOPMENT/TECHNOLOGY	EDUCATION	SOCIAL/POLITICAL/INSTITUTIONAL
1969	*1969*	*1969*
ARPANET established	Physics Computer Development Project -- University of California, Irvine, Alfred Bork, Director	USOE has spent $35.6 million on educational computing
60% of colleges and universities have computers -- SR&B Survey		Anthony Oettinger: *Run Computer Run*
		ACM SigCue formed
1970	*1970*	*1970*
Lekan Index shows 910 CAI programs	University of Iowa; First conference on computers in the undergraduate curricula	Silberman (*Crisis in the Classroom*) fears instructional use of computers will amplify failures in education
Bernard Luskin projections of breakeven points in adoption of CAI: 1984	Computer instruction network in Oregon: To provide students with a basic understanding of computers and how to use them as a problem-solving tool	*Computers and Crisis* -- ACM
Dartmouth Secondary School project summary of teacher needs: 2-4 weeks training; release time; summer institute; 1 computer/60 students	13% of secondary schools use computers for instruction (Darby, Korotkin, Romashko)	Commission on Instructional Technology -- Sterling MacMurrin: "A society hurtling into the satellite can no longer be held back by an educational system which is limping along at the blackboard and textbook stage of communication."

RESEARCH/DEVELOPMENT/TECHNOLOGY	EDUCATION	SOCIAL/POLITICAL/INSTITUTIONAL
1970 (con't)	*1970 (con't)*	*1970 (con't)*
	Project SOLO, Pittsburg, PA, Tom Dwyer, Director	ACM SigCSE conference on C.S. education: "Computer Education for Secondary School Mathematics Teachers"
	Some universities offer introductory computing courses designed for social science, humanities majors.	IFIP World Conference on Computer Education.
1971	*1971*	*1971*
PLATO and TICCIT projects	Administration of some colleges declare goal of universal computer literacy for students.	NSF grants for PLATO and TICCIT
"Twenty Things to Do With a Computer," Papert & Solomon: What you really want to teach the child to program is not the computer but himself."	Project REACT develops teacher training materials in computing	CONDUIT established. Computers at Oregon State University NCECS, Dartmouth, and the Universities of Iowa and Texas.
Buckminster Fuller: "We must make *all* the information immediately available over the two-way TV's ready for the different individual human chromosomal ticker tapes to call for it."		EDUCOM -- "Computing in Higher Education: Successes and Prospects"

42

1972

Carnegie Commission finds inadequate supply of quality instructional materials (*The Fourth Revolution*)

Moursund -- "Computer Science for Elementary School Teachers" SigCSE

Luehrmann at the Spring Joint Computer Conference -- "Should the Computer Teach the Student, or Vice Versa?"

Interactive classroom graphics -- Kelley, OR

Anastasio and Morgan -- "Study of Factors Inhibiting Widespread Use of Computers in Education": Lack of materials and evidence of effectiveness

Computers and Society, by Mossman

1972

Computer graphics in physics -- (Bork and Peckham)

Denison University Administration adopts goal of computer literacy for all students

Peoples Computer Company formed

Montgomery County Public Schools, MD, reports on progress with CAI (Kay Morgan, Director)

1972

Conference Board of Mathematical Sciences: Recommendations regarding computers in high school:

- junior high course to understand roles computers play in our society
- teacher training, all disciplines
- clearinghouse for materials

TimeShare and Houghton Mifflin join to provide computing services and instructional materials to high schools

MECC -- Minnesota Education Computing Consortium is an organization formed by Community College system, Department of Administration, Department of Education, State College System and University of Minnesota

RESEARCH/DEVELOPMENT/TECHNOLOGY	EDUCATION	SOCIAL/POLITICAL/INSTITUTIONAL
1972 (con't)		
What is a Computer?, by Marion Ball		
1973	1973	1973
A Guided Tour of Programming in BASIC, (Dwyer and Critchfield)	Students at George Washington High School develop carpooling program. Disseminated nationally by Department of Transportation.	Advisory Committee on Issues in Educational Technology. National Academy of Engineering: *Issues and Public Policies in Educational Technology*
	Students at Sehome High School, Washington, laying cable to computer center at nearby college	
	Teaneck High School, New Jersey, instructional computing department established to teach computer literacy, obtain programs for teachers in all disciplines	
	Lawrence Hall of Science Computer Literacy Program	

RESEARCH/DEVELOPMENT/TECHNOLOGY	EDUCATION	SOCIAL/POLITICAL/INSTITUTIONAL
1974	*1974*	
Creative Computing Magazine	Bennett College, southern black women's college, initiates major project using computers to remediate deficiencies in language arts and math, and provide computer literacy.	
HumRRO study of computer-based learning materials finds 5,560 items documented nationally		
Computer Lib, by Ted Nelson		
Learning Alternatives in U.S. Education: Where Student and Computer Meet, by Hunter, Kastner, Rubin and Seidel		
1975	*1975*	*1975*
Altair announces personal computer	26.7% of high schools report instructional use of computers -- Bukoski and Korotkin	Educational Computing in Minority Institutions -- ECMI Funded by NSF
		Conference sponsored by NSF: "Ten-Year Forecast for Computers and Communications: Implications for Education, 1985"

RESEARCH/DEVELOPMENT/TECHNOLOGY	EDUCATION	SOCIAL/POLITICAL/INSTITUTIONAL
1976	*1976*	*1976*
The Compleat Computer, by Van Tassel	Los Nietos School District, CA. Role of CAI in Education of Ethnic Minorities	Study for Environmental Protection Agency finds 4,000 EPA engineers, scientists, managers, clerks, need computer-related skills to define data requirements, manage projects, use lab automation, write programs.
My Friend the Computer, by Jean Rice		
Sophie, by J.S. Brown		
Artist and Computer		
Evaluating Instructional Computing, by Mossman		
1977	*1977*	*1977*
Personal Computing Magazine	Sehome School District submits to voters a special levy for purchase of terminals and lease of computer time for student use. 80% favorable vote.	Congressional Hearings: "Computers and the Learning Society"
MECC Computer Literacy Objectives	68% of colleges have computers (SREB Survey)	

46

RESEARCH/DEVELOPMENT/TECHNOLOGY	EDUCATION	SOCIAL/POLITICAL/INSTITUTIONAL
1978	*1978*	*1978*
Braun: Some bases for choosing a computer system suggestions for educators	Rosemount School District in Minnesota institutes computer literacy for grades 3-8	President Carter's reorganization project finds lack of computer literacy on part of management
Computer Awareness Book — computer coloring book for children		*The Next Great Crisis in American Education: Computer Literacy*
Evaluating a Computer Literacy Curriculum, by Kurshan and Sherman		ACM sponsors Elementary and Secondary School Subcommittee (Dave Moursund, Chairman)
The Source information utility		
1979	*1979*	*1979*
Explosion in commercially available computer products for education and personal computing	Schools buy thousands of PETs, Apples, TRS-80's	HR 4326, a bill "to establish a national commission to study the scientific and technological implications of information technology in education"
	Computertown, USA	
Northwest Regional Education Lab establishes MicroSift to be a clearinghouse for educational programs that run on microcomputers	*K-12 Course Goals in Computer Education*, Multnomah County, Oregon	AFIPS convenes panel to study scientific and technical implications of information technology in education

AUDIENCE COMMENTARY

•   Spurred on by the difficulties experienced in reliably
operating and synchronizing the three screens for Ms. Hunter's
presentation, one observation was made about the lack of use
of multiple screen slides or other technologies in the classroom. There is a sizeable set of research studies indicating
that split screen displays are very effective. In fact, the
mind can take in more information from those split screens.
On the other hand, how many classrooms do you observe using
split screen displays? Teachers do not really seem to be
aware of that bit of technology. Going even a step further,
some of the research has indicated that if you have some sort
of disruption of something failing in the system, you find the
impact on learning is considerable. In fact, quite often the
learner goes away with learning and remembering something
about the disruption rather than the information. One of the
reasons teachers are not using the multiple or split screen
displays is because these displays break down, and rather than
suffer with that they say they won't use the technology until
it gets better. What does this mean in terms of microcomputers? When a child is using it with our grandiose expectations, think of the implications for teachers regarding
reliability of equipment, maintenance skills, and so forth.

SECTION II

DEFINITIONS AND REQUIREMENTS FOR
COMPUTER LITERACY

The definitions and requirements of computer literacy as
they impact society students, and teachers are discussed in
three separate presentations. Individual discussants were
selected per presentation to share their perspectives and
concerns as well as differences and similarities. This section concludes with summaries of the working groups addressing: computer literacy needs for teachers and administrators
(Working Group I); computer literacy materials for students in
grades 7-12 (Working Group II); and ethics and values for
computer literacy (Working Group V).

EDUCATION FOR CITIZENSHIP IN A
COMPUTER-BASED SOCIETY

Daniel H. Watt

Research Associate, MIT LOGO Group
LOGO Project Coordinator, Brookline Public Schools
Director, Computer Resource Center,
Technical Education Research Centers

With this paper I hope to focus discussion on some issues and problems connected with providing the education needed by citizens of a computer-based society. Rather than offer a laundry list of requirements for computer literacy, I have chosen to focus more broadly on the kinds of skills and understandings that might be needed by the majority of the population during the next decade or so, and to focus more narrowly on our role as educators in developing programs to meet those needs. As someone whose professional career for the last fifteen years has been concerned with pre-college education as a teacher, teacher trainer, curriculum developer and educational researcher (most recently with the LOGO Group at MIT), one of my major concerns is whether public schools in this country will be able to play a significant role in facing the education challenges of the 1980s.

In the body of this paper I will suggest some of the ways that the widespread proliferation of computers may have an impact on the lives of ordinary citizens, and offer my understanding of what should be meant by the term "computer literacy." I will also discuss the role of public education in developing a computer literate populace, raise some issues for consideration in planning for computer literacy education, and suggest one particular activity as a step in meeting some of the goals of computer literacy education.

I. THE IMPACT OF COMPUTERS ON PEOPLE'S LIVES

A. *Computers and Work*

   In the past, only a small percentage of the population
was directly concerned with computers in their work. Those
who had direct contact with computers were professional technicians, programmers or computer scientists, who required
specialized technical training. People who made use of information processed by a computer only had to be comfortable
reading printouts. Automation was a major economic and labor
relations issue, as society tried to balance the increased
productivity expected from automation against the dislocation
and hardship experienced by workers whose skills were made
obsolete in the process.

   In the future, we can expect the overwhelming majority of
our working population to have significant interactions with
computers as part of their daily work. As our economy becomes
more dependent on information processing, those whose work
involves such information will need to have a great deal of
direct involvement with computers. Word processors connected
with computer-based filing, copying and communication systems
will transform the nature and conditions of office work. In
addition to economic and social issues concerning the pros and
cons of replacing human workers by machines, automation will
raise real issues of control of the work environment. Information systems will not only improve an organization's ability
to produce and distribute their product -- they will also
provide managers with an unprecedented degree of control over
the moment-by-moment functioning of employees whose work
requires interaction with the system. "Big Brother in the
workplace" may become as significant a labor relations issue
as replacement of workers by automation has been in the past.

B. *Computers and Personal Life*

   In the past, most people's contact with computers was
limited to receiving bills from the telephone company. A
small, somewhat isolated minority had access to computers for
professional and occasionally recreational pursuits.

   In the future we can expect to see dramatic increases in
the contacts between individuals and computer systems in their
daily lives. Personal computers and special purpose computer
devices will find their way into the homes of many people for
family, business, household management, intellectual and
educational development, recreational activities, and creative

expression. Personal computers are so new that it is difficult to predict their consequences, but I personally believe
that they will eventually have as much impact as the automobile or television. I expect that we will see mind-expanding effects for many people who learn to program their home
computers and use them as creative personal tools for writing,
composing and playing music, graphic arts, animation, communication and information retrieval. For others, there may be
mind-deadening effects if they become dependent on limited
forms of computerized instruction or addicted to fast-paced
and exotic, but fundamentally, meaningless arcade games.

Contact with large computer systems is also becoming a
part of the personal lives of most people. When such a system
is functioning smoothly and effectively, it is hardly noticed.
It is undeniable that such systems may produce many gains for
the public welfare. On the other hand, when a public system
malfunctions the irritations are more obvious than the benefits of smooth operation. When a terminal is down or when an
employee of a bank, travel agency, or supermarket can't seem
to find the correct magic word to make the system listen to
him, or when the computer is seen as the *cause* of someone
being denied a credit purchase, check cashing privileges, or a
seat on an airplane, people tend to exaggerate the negative
consequences of living in a computer-based society, as opposed
to the positive ones. Alienation seems to be one of the
characteristics of life in the late twentieth century, and
regular public contact with computer systems whose functioning
is too complex to understand may well increase rather than
reduce such alienation.

C.   Computers and a Citizen's Responsibilities

A society ceases to be functionally democratic when deci-
sion-making must be left in the hands of an influential minority with technical expertise and economic power, or when it is
exercised by the population-at-large if that population cannot
make informed judgments about crucial technical matters. For
the past twenty years, we have had to face a series of public
issues requiring understanding of technology and its impact on
society. As we have progressed from concern about the testing
of nuclear weapons, through a series of environmental and
energy crises, to a renewed concern about the effects of nuclear power, we have had to make many decisions involving complex technological considerations.

Our society has a poor track record for preparing its
citizens for making judgments about such issues. Concerns
about the impact of computers are not substantially different

from other issues concerning technology and society. Some
computer-related issues have become fairly clear to the public
in recent years -- for example, issues of privacy and individual rights that arise due to the existance of large data
bases containing personal information. Many other issues have
not yet had serious public consideration. The rapid rise of
electronic banking, changes in the fabric of social organization brought about by large-scale computer systems, the
increasing influence of computer modeling on a host of public
policy decisions, and the question of how society is going to
regulate the functioning of massive computer-based communications systems, are among the issues that require public attention, but do not yet seem to have reached public conscious-
ness.

     It seems to be characteristic of such concerns that they
don't become public issues until potentially harmful systems
are deeply entrenched in the functioning of our society. When
mass production of private automobiles began early in this
century, no one could foresee the problems to be caused by air
pollution, or the energy crisis. Many as yet unknown issues
about the impact of computers on individuals and on society as
a whole may be lurking ahead of us. The fact that we cannot
clearly perceive them argues strongly for the development of a
citizenry able to deal effectively with technological issues.
In particular, it points to the need for universal computer
literacy.

II. WHAT SHOULD THE TERM "COMPUTER LITERACY" MEAN?

     My view of computer literacy follows from my sense of
what the impact of computers will be, and from my understanding of what is commonly meant by the term literacy. When I
consider a person literate, I usually mean that s/he can read
and write well, and can use reading and writing fluently in a
variety of contexts. Further, a literate person in our society will have had a range of experiences with the literature
of our common cultural heritage. S/he will be able to read,
understand, interpret, and make judgments about a news article
or a literary work, and will be able to compare the works of
different writers.

     A more complex aspect of literacy is its effect on a
person's intellectual functioning. Without going into detail
here, I will simply assert that a literate person can make use
of a wider range of intellectual strategies than someone who
is non-literate.

Children grow into literate adults by growing up in a culture pervaded by literacy and pro-literacy values. Older playmates and siblings, parents and teachers, are all carriers of the culture. For the earliest years, at home and in school, children *use* literacy skills in a wide variety of every day tasks of importance to them.

My concept of "computer literacy" goes beyond its common definition as a body of information primarily *about* computers, how they work, how they are used, and their impact on society (Ball and Charp, 1977; Billings and Moursund, 1979; Johnson, et al., 1980). I believe that such a body of subject matter should more appropriately be termed "computer awareness" (Luehrmann, August 1980). Rather, I think of computer literacy as a cultural phenomenon which includes the full range of skills, knowledge, understandings, values and relationships necessary to function effectively and comfortably as a citizen of a computer-based society. The computer literacy needs of any individual will vary according to that person's particular involvement with computers, but computer literacy requirements for the average person should expand dramatically during the next decade (Molnar, 1978).

To make this notion of computer literacy more specific, I have divided it into four distinct but interrelated categories (Watt, 1980):

1. The Ability to Control and Program a Computer to Achieve a Variety of Personal, Academic, and Professional Goals. This includes the ability to write programs in one or more computer language, read, understand, and modify more complex computer programs, to use a computer as a problem-solving tool, and to analyze information generated by a computer program (for example, predictions about economic trends), in terms of how the program itself operates and the particular data chosen at program input (Luehrmann, July 1980).

2. The Ability to Use a Variety of Pre-Programmed Computer Applications in Personal, Academic, and Professional Contexts. This includes the ability to make informal judgments about the suitability of a particular software tool for a particular purpose, and to understand the assumption, values, and limitations inherent in a particular piece of software.

Both computer programming and the use of computer applications will require a greater familiarity with representing and processing visual information than has been required in the past. Similarly, the understanding of hierarchically

organized data structures has become significantly more important as people have access to previously inconceivable quantities of information stored in computerized data bases.
(Molnar, 1978).

   *3. The Ability to Make Use of Ideas from the Cultures
Surrounding Computer Programming and Computer Applications as
Part of an Individual's Collection of Strategies for Information Retrieval, Communication, and Problem Solving.* This
aspect of computer literacy corresponds to the effect on intellectual functioning of learning to read and write, and is
probably the most difficult to incorporate specifically into
educational programs since the effects themselves are not yet
well understood (Papert, 1980; Turkle, 1980; Papert, et al.,
1979). The fact that these concepts are difficult to integrate into school programs at present does not make them any
less important to the functioning of a computer literate citizen.

   *4. The Ability to Understand the Growing Economic,
Social, and Psychological Impact of Computers on Individuals
and Groups Within Our Society and on Society as a Whole.* This
includes the recognition that computer applications embody
particular social values and can have different kinds of impacts on different individuals and different segments of society. It includes the understandings necessary to play a serious role in the political process by which large and small
scale decisions about computer use are made, and to transcend
the dependent roles of consumer or victim (Turkle, 1980; Kling
and Lundegaard, 1980; Weizenbaum, 1976; Wessel, 1974).

III. PUBLIC EDUCATION AND COMPUTER LITERACY

   Education for computer literacy, as I have defined it,
should be thought of as more like the life-long process of
acquiring a culture, than like the mastery of a well defined
body of subject matter. Education for computer literacy requires many years of experience with computers and a long term
fostering of concerns and values related to the use of computers and their impact on society. Above all, education for
computer literacy implies the need for a computer literate
culture of parents, teachers and older students for a child to
grow into. The growth of computer literacy among teachers and
the gradual incorporation of computers and ideas relating to
computers into all subject areas should be of the highest
priority to a school system trying to educate a computer
literate public.

Education for computer literacy is occuring in many places outside of formal education institutions. Companies that use and manufacture computers provide training for their employees and their customers' employees. Computer stores, popular computer magazines, and local and national interest groups are all aiding the growth of knowledge about personal computers and their use. Adult education courses in computer programming are now being offered in many areas. Public access to computers in libraries, museums, and community centers is also likely to contribute significantly to the growth of computer literacy.

Nevertheless, I believe that there is a clear need for an all-out-effort by public school educators. Only public schools can help ensure that all citizens have equal access to the opportunity of computer literacy education, and only the public schools in our society have responsibility for the education of citizens who can make effective decisions about the impact of technology on society.

How can we ensure that less affluent segments of our society will have equal educational opportunities? Affluent students already have more access to computers in their homes or parents' places of business than students from less privileged backgrounds. It is also generally the case that schools in more affluent areas are finding it easier to incorporate computers in their educational budgets. Given the ways in which present social, economic, demographic, and political trends impact on public schooling, providing equal educational opportunity will be a difficult challenge for public school systems.

A more subtle concern relates to precisely *how* computers are being introduced into different types of school settings. It is my personal observation that when computers are introduced into suburban schools, it is often in the context of computer programming and computer awareness courses. In less affluent rural or inner city schools, it is more likely to be in the context of computer-assisted instruction. Affluent students are thus learning to tell the computer what to do, while less affluent students are learning to do what the computer tells them! I am not aware of any statistics confirming this observation, but I believe it bears careful examination. I am concerned that both the *amount* of computer access in schools and *the ways in which computers are used* in different communities may serve to reinforce existing socio-economic inequities rather than to foster educational equality.

I do not care to debate here the relative merits of
computer assisted instruction and instruction in computer programming, but I would like to point out the relevance of the
issue for computer literacy education. For the next few years
at least, computers in the schools will remain a relatively
scarce resource. I believe that schools should make a clear
commitment to using those few computers they have to develop
the computer literacy of their teachers and students. Given
existing social and economic inequities, this should be especially the case for schools serving less affluent popula-
tions.

IV.   SOME ISSUES IN PLANNING FOR COMPUTER LITERACY EDUCATION

A.   *Computer Literacy and Job Training*

Many school officials seem to be unclear about their
responsibility in educating and training students for computer
related jobs and professions. Are computer related skills and
technical understandings issues that should be left to vocational schools and to business and industry? Or are they
basic survival skills that should be taught to all students in
school? Opinion among educators is beginning to shift to the
latter view, but this shift raises other issues of schools'
resources and competence to provide the necessary background
education, as well as specific technical training needed for
computer-related employment.

Consideration of a particular example may help to clarify
some of the difficulties that schools face in dealing with
this issue. In many high schools, computer related skills are
taught within vocational and business education departments.
Data entry by means of keypunch is often a required course in
these departments. This has persisted despite the widespread
shift to more interactive forms of data entry in the business
world. The equipment is in place, the curriculum already
exists, and the teachers are familiar with them. Substantial
investments have been made in equipment and training. Shifts
in what is taught will require new material investments as
well as retraining and recruitment of teachers at a time when
schools are facing a serious economic crunch. Nevertheless,
many schools, vocational and business departments are ahead of
their colleagues in introducing and upgrading computer-related
courses.

The problem of recruiting and retraining teachers for
such courses is made considerably more difficult by economic

pressure from computer related industries. At the same time that high technology companies are decrying the shortage of qualified personnel, they are recruiting heavily from among high school and post-secondary teachers with technical and mathematical training, offering them substantially higher salaries than they can earn as teachers. This type of economic pressure is cutting deeply into schools' ability to provide students with adequate computer related skills.

Recent conversations with two friends who are professionally involved in recruiting and training entry-level programmers and computer technicians helped me put the problem of job training into a broader perspective. Having researched industrial needs by talking directly with lower level managers and shop foremen, they found that their contacts were not primarily concerned with their recruits' technical skills with a particular programming language or piece of equipment. Rather, they were worried about their new employees' lack of familiarity with computer systems and electronic equipment in general, and especially about their ability to engage in thoughtful problem solving and clear logical thinking -- especially in debugging or troubleshooting situations -- as well as their ability to work independently and responsibility on job-related tasks. These concerns go beyond the usual role of the vocational or business education department and raise again the question of the role of a student's entire educational experience in preparing for technically related jobs.

B.   *The Psychological Impact of Computers*

The psychological impact of computers on individuals is not yet well understood. While it seems possible that some individuals may become overly dependent on, even adicted to, interaction with computers (Weizenbaum, 1976; Zimbardo, 1980), a kind of computer phobia seems to be more common among a wide section of the population. While programs for computer literacy education are generally directed at reducing computer phobia, developers of such programs do not usually take into account the wide variation in individual reactions to involvement with computers. Since it will be increasingly important for individuals to understand their own reactions to computers if they are to function comfortably with them and avoid pathological effects, understanding the psychology of human/computer interactions should be part of the computer literacy education of teachers, as well as explicitly built into computer literacy programs for students.

Turkle (1980) has been carrying out a series of studies relating to the development of computer cultures and the

infiltration of our general culture by concepts and values
that have originated in computer cultures. Her work has included interviews with pre-college teachers and students who
have been exposed to computers, young children interacting
with computer toys, and students at university computer centers, as well as a number of computer professionals and hobby-
ists. She has begun to shed some light on an area in which
much more research needs to be done. In her work (1980) she
has raised a number of issues explicitly for consideration by
computer literacy educators. Other issues related to the
psychological impact of computers on individuals have been
raised by a team of researchers at Bolt, Beranek, and Newman,
a Cambridge, Massachusetts, consulting firm (Bolt, Beranek &
Newman, internal document, 1980), and by a study group of
Boston-area educators (Computer Education and Human Values
Study Group, 1980). Drawing on these sources I would like to
raise a few specific concerns for consideration by educators.

    *1. Computer Use May Lead to Isolation and Separatism
Among Students, Or to Cooperation and Appropriate Social
Interactions, Depending Largely on Pedogogical and Classroom
Management Decisions Made About Their Use*. If a group of
student "computer freaks" is seen as forming a powerful but
isolated clique within a school, this could adversely effect
the attitudes of the majority of students toward computers.
In particular, such polarization could reinforce male/female
role stereotypes with regard to computers if computer cliques
are predominantly male.

    *2. Educational Programs that Focus on Only One Approach
(Structured Programming for Example) May Result in Only Some
People Coming to Feel Comfortable with Computers*. There are
many different styles of·relating to computers. My own
experiences teaching LOGO to children (Watt, 1979; Papert, et
al., 1979) reinforce this concern. There were several different approaches to using the computer among a diverse group
of sixth-grade students. Because we explicitly recognized
these differences and allowed for them in our planning, all
the students attained some degree of comfort with the computer.

    *3. If We Acknowledge That Computer Literacy Education
Involves Training in Habits of Thought, How Do Different
Styles of Relating to Computers Transfer to Non-Computer Situations?* Computer programming is often used explicitly to
teach problem solving, yet current research has only begun to
scratch the surface in exploring whether what students learn
about problem solving by programming computers has any carry
over into non-computer situations. Suppose it does have some

carry over, even if we can't detect it yet -- can we help
students understand which kinds of problems are most amenable
to computer-related problem solving techniques? As computer
literacy education becomes more widespread, such issues will
become more interesting and important.

4. *Anthropomorphic Imagery Pervades the Computer Culture, Both in the Way that Computer Users Tend to Project
Human Qualities onto Computers, and in the Use of Anthropomorphic Metaphors in Problem Solving* (Solomon, 1976). Even
more pervasive is the attribution of human characteristics to
the computer by those who write educational programs for young
children. While the consequences of these almost universal
phenomena are not well understood, it is clear that they could
have major impact on human/computer relationships, especially
for young children. This concern requires immediate attention
from educators and researchers before our culture is flooded
with computer programs aimed at young children.

5. *The Presence of Computer Programs Which Simulate
Intelligent Behavior, As Well As Actual Effort to Create
Artificial Intelligence (Weizenbaum, 1976), Raise Disturbing
Questions in Politics, Religion, Psychology, and Education.*
Computer literacy educators should be prepared to deal openly
with such questions and with the anxiety created by them for
some people.

C. *The Impact of Computers On Society*

Existing computer literacy curriculum materials and
objectives usually include some information about the impact
of computers on society (Johnson, et al., 1980). While the
primary emphasis is usually on positive impacts of computers,
some treatments of potentially harmful aspects of computers
are also usually included. The privacy issue is probably the
most common example. What are not commonly considered seriously in such materials are the changes in social, political,
military and economic decision making owing to the use of
computer-based models, or changes in the nature of social
organizations and the overall organization of society brought
about by widespread computer use (Weizenbaum, 1976; Anderson
and Sim, 1978).

Also lacking in most such materials is a concern for the
particular social values embedded in a given social application of computers. An application may support the values and
goals of one particular social group and be harmful to others,
but this type of subtlety is rarely considered in material
intended for school use. The work of Kling and Lundegaard

(1980) dealing with values conflicts involved in the implementation of Electronic Funds Transfer systems provides a
useful model for considering such issues.

The issues involved in considering the social impact of
computers (or other complex technology) are complex and con-
troversial, and transcend the boundaries of traditional academic disciplines. For these reasons, and because computer
literacy advocates are usually computer enthusiasts whose
broad aim is to *reduce* public fear and anxiety about computers, computer literacy materials often tend to ignore or
oversimplify such issues, to the detriment, I believe, of the
more sophisticated understandings needed by citizens of our
society.

V.   INVESTIGATING THE SCHOOL AS A MICROCOSM OF SOCIETY

I think that there are ways that schools can begin to
educate students for roles as citizens of a complex technological society. I would like to suggest one approach here as a
technique for enhancing the computer literacy of both teachers
and students in ways that may effect their functioning as
citizens. I suggest treating the school itself as a microcosm
of society for the purpose of investigating some of the types
of issues I have raised. By investigating the psychological
effects of increased student interaction with computers, as
well as changes occuring with in the social organization of
the school, students may gain insights that will serve them
well as citizens. Students who are exposed to a range of
experiences including being a full control of a computer as
well as having their actions fully or partially computer-con-
trolled will learn to distinguish modes of computer use along
such a spectrum. By investigating any number of situations
within their own schools, students can learn an approach to
social inquiry, relating the personal to the general, that
will help them cope with a range of social issues. While
particular issues to explore will vary with students' age and
sophistication, I would like to suggest a few examples to
serve as models of what I have in mind.

*1. Are computers resources within a school available
equally to all students? How are decisions about computer
access made? By whom?*

*2. Do certain groups of students spend more time using
computers than others? Are certain teachers more comfortable
with computers than others? What are some of the character-*

istics of computer users and non-users? Is one of the groups more heavily male and the other female? Some of the causes of this can be explored. Can or should anything be done about it?

3. Given limited computer terminals and computer power, who decides how the computers are to be used? Are students encouraged to write their own programs? To play computer games? To use the computer as a personal tool? Are there certain programs which all students must use? What are the rationales for such decisions? Are there competing rationales?

4. How do teachers feel when students know more about the computer than they?

5. Are students concerned about data bases containing student records? Can these records be abused? What safeguards exist? What rights of access and privacy do students have? Who decides these questions, and what rationales are used to justify the decisions?

6. What are the concerns of other members of the school community -- janitors, secretaries or administrators -- with regard to non-instructional computer use? Have computers simplified or complicated their jobs, as they see it? Do they perceive their work as more or less "human" when computers are involved?

7. What kinds of changes have occurred in school organization as a whole as a result of administrative use of computers for scheduling, reporting, attendance, etc.? Are schedules more flexible or more rigid? Are grades reported more promptly and accurately, or are there more delays and errors? When an error or inefficiency in a computer program is found, who has responsibility for correcting it? How long does that typically take to accomplish?

This type of exploration could be extended to the use of computers in particular academic departments, or to polling the attitudes of school committee members and the community at large, or to comparing the extent and kind of computer use in the schools of neighboring communities with different socio-economic levels, etc.

The learning attained by students engaged in such activities will depend heavily on teachers' skills in leading discussions and on their knowledge of well developed techniques such as role playing, values clarification, moral dilemmas and

other approaches to personal growth and social inquiry (Shaftel
and Shaftel, 1967; Simon, et al., 1972; Kohlbert, 1978; Hawley,
1975). One useful result of such activities might be a collection of data for researchers investigating the impact of
computers on education. Another consequence might be that
teachers oriented toward humanistic education and teachers who
specialize in the social sciences might collaborate directly
with those who usually dominate computer literacy education --
the mathematicians and scientists. This would be advantageous
for the computer literacy education of the faculty as a whole,
and it could also serve as a model for the collaboration of
humanists, social scientists, and computer scientists in
investigating some of these issues in the wider world.

     With a broad definition of computer literacy, and the
development of some creative collaboration among teachers and
students, it is still possible for schools to play a critical
role in developing the computer literacy needed by all citizens for the 1980s and beyond.

REFERENCES

Anderson, R.E. and Sim, F. (1978). "Sociology of Computing:
     Conceptual Framework and Curriculum Development," in
     Bailey (Ed.) *Computer Science in Social and Behavioral
     Science Education,* Educational Technology Press, Engle-
     wood Cliffs, NJ.

Ball, M. and Charp, S. (1977). *Be A Computer Literate,* Crea-
     tive Computing Press, Morristown, NJ.

Billings, K. and Moursund, D. (1979). *Are You Computer Lite-
     rate?* Dilithium Press, Forest Grove, OR.

Bolt, Beranek and Newman (1980). *Study of Issues Related to
     the Implementation of Computer Technology in Schools,*
     (Internal Document, Proposal #P80-1SD-97), Cambridge, MA.

Computer Education and Human Values Study Group (1980). *A
     Position Paper,* c/o D. Watt, Technical Education Research
     Centers, 8 Eliot Street, Cambridge, MA 02138.

Hawley, R.C. (1973). *Human Values in the Classroom,* Education
     Research Associates, Amherst, MA.

Johnson, D.C., Anderson, R.E., Hansen, T.P., and Klassen, D. (1980). "Computer Literacy: What is it?", *The Mathematics Teacher,* February, 73, 91-96.

Kling, R. and Lundegaard, K. (1980). "Passing the Digital Buck," *Society,* Vol. 17, No. 2.

Kohlberg, L. (1975). "The Cognitive Development Approach to Moral Education," *Phi Delta Kappa.*

Luehrmann, A. (1980). "Computer Illiteracy: A National Crisis and A Solution," *Byte,* July, 5, 7, 98-102.

_____(1980). "Computer Literacy: What Should It Be?", August.

Molnar, A. (1978). "The Next Great Crisis in American Education: Computer Literacy," *THE Journal, Technological Horizons in Education,* July/August.

Papert, S. (1980). *Mindstorms: Children, Computers, and Powerful Ideas,* Basic Books, New York, NY.

Papert, S., diSessa, A. Watt, D. and Weir, S. (1979). *Final Report of the Brookline LOGO Project,* (LOGO Memos 53,54), MIT LOGO Group, Cambridge, MA.

Shaftel, F.R. and Shaftel, G. (1967). *Role Playing for Social Values: Decision Making in the Social Studies,* Prentice-Hall, Englewood Cliffs, NJ.

Simon, S., Howe, L. and Kirschenbaum, H. (1972). *Values Clarification, A Handbook of Practical Strategies,* Hart Publishing Company, New York, NY.

Solomon, C. (1976). *Problem Solving in an Anthropomorphic Computer Culture,* (Unpublished masters thesis), Boston University.

Turkle, S. (1980). "Computer as Rorschach," *Society,* Vol. 17, No. 2.

Watt, D.H. (1979). "A Comparison of the Problem Solving Styles of Two Students Learning LOGO," *Proceedings, National Educational Computing Conference,* June. Reprinted, *Creative Computing,* December 1979.

_____(1980). "Computer Literacy: What Schools Should Be
    Doing About It," *Classroom Computer News,* November/Decem-
    ber.

Weizenbaum, J. (1976). *Computer Power and Human Reason,* W.H.
    Freeman, San Francisco, CA.

Wessel, M. (1974). *Freedom's Edge: The Computer Threat to
    Society,* Addison Wesley, Reading, MA.

Zimbardo, P. (Ed.) (1980). "The Hacker Papers," *Psychology
    Today.*

DISCUSSANT REMARKS

John Sonquist

University of California at Santa Barbara

SUMMARY

● Watt does not directly address the differential abilities of organizations to use
computers, their use of computer technology
and the subsequent impact on individual,
organizational, and national power relationships.

● Increasing individual alienation is increasing because of the design of large and impersonal bureaucracies, as well as by designers of non-friendly computer systems.

● The fear of technocracy is based on a dangerous myth that ignores or prevents the
necessity for a careful look at existing
power structures in society that use computing.

● We must remember that computer technology is
created and used by people -- not an external
force.

● We should create institutions that will
forecast and examine existing trends to help
us "take a look" into the future.

John Sonquist

NARRATIVE

   Dr. Watt's paper sets the issues very well; however, I
come to similar conclusions but from a different perspective.
I agree that computers in work is one of the most important
ways in which most people will be seriously impacted by computing in their citizen lives. This topic has come up repeatedly and I think it deserves emphasizing. If one analyzes
specific types of computer users and their types of work, one
will likely find different literacy requirements. Literacy
requirements for production workers is the use of the computer
as a production tool rather than management information tool.
The blue collar worker is subjected to an automated production
situation and will have a certain kind of literacy requirement. The white collar worker, usually involved with computers as a management tool, may have a different kind of literacy requirements.

   Again, with respect to computers in the worklife, Dr.
Watt's fear of big brother watching the worker, is with foundation, but my reading of the literature indicates that management control over the workers is a far less complete and a
far more complicated phenomenon than his remarks indicate. An
important topic is omitted: the idea of the differential
abilities of organizations to utilize computer technology and
the way in which that computer technology is used has an
impact on power relationships between people within an organization, between organizations, and between countries.

   In Dr. Watt's section on computers and personal life, he
emphasizes the possibility that children will be either
exposed to mind-deadening or mind-expanding computer technology. I would expand his statement that the personal lives
will be affected by large bureaucratic organizations having
large computers systems over which the individual has very

little power. These large systems are usually designed by
engineers with little systems design training, and are designed to suit the needs of high level management. These are
not friendly systems for the citizen who must deal with them.
This is the second area in which computer literacy for citizenship is needed. I don't think computers are likely to be
major factors responsible for the increasing alienation. I
think that the chief factor is essentially having to deal with
large and impersonal bureaucracies. It is true that many
computer systems designers through their creations have
fostered large bureaucratic systems, but I don't think this is
necessary. I think, in fact, that computers can help to make
large bureaucratic systems more, rather than less, person-
oriented, but that will require different kinds of systems
designers than those currently graduated by our universities
today.

Let's turn to computers and the citizen's responsibilities. Dr. Watt makes the point that democracy vanishes when
decision making is in the hands of an influential minority
with technical expertise and economic power. This is a
modern version of the old theory of domination by the tech-
nocrats, and I think it is a mistake to use this imagery. The
critical factor is the economic power. Most decisions are not
made by computer people or even technically sophisticated
managers. Decisions are made higher up the corporate ladder
or, in a government agency. The fear of technocracy is a
dangerous myth because it prevents a careful examination of
the structures of power that, in fact, exist in modern society
and use computing.

Now, having used the word *impact* repeatedly let me now
say that I think we ought to get rid of this word. The words
you use for dealing with the problem *structure* your approach
to it. I would prefer to stop using imagery that conjure up
visions of some external force controlling us. Computer
technology is created by people in industry and used by
people who make decisions that are based on their own personal
value systems, company goals, and bureaucratic goals. These
are intrinsic to people and are not some external force
impacting us.

I would add another point to Dr. Watt's list of literacy
requirements for a responsible citizen; citizens ought to know
something about the technical, administrative, and legal
control mechanisms that a society has available to it to deal
with issues that need public attention. Some of the future-
ologists have been concerned with such things, for example,

Bettina Hubert's work includes concepts of forecasting but does not examine existing trends. Some of the ideas that have come up, especially prior to my discussion, include "you can't anticipate what's downstream." In a sense, part of computer literacy is knowing just that. Thus, we should try to set up institutions to perform the functions of "looking downstream" as far as we can. People need literacy with respect to the relationship between value and technology. All of these things need to be a part of this facet of coping with computer technology. The total society level is not the only level in which one needs coping mechanisms. Individuals and organizations also need coping mechanisms to help them deal with technological change.

Let me conclude my tirade against the use of the word *literacy*. Let's focus on the particular situation that people find themselves in their work life, personal life, and as a citizen. Individuals currently utilize their existing skills to deal with their workplace and personal problems. We ought to try to isolate exactly what kinds of skills people need in different circumstances.

PERSONAL COMPUTING FOR ELEMENTARY
AND SECONDARY SCHOOL STUDENTS[1]

David Moursund

Department of Computer and Information Science
University of Oregon

I. PERSONAL COMPUTING (noun)

Convenient and readily available access to an electronic
digital computer for personal use. An idea which gained prom-
inence in the late 1970's with the advent and rapid proliferation of microcomputers.

ENIAC, the first general purpose electronic digital computer, became operational in December 1945. It was neither
convenient to use nor readily available. The situation
changed slowly, as computers became commercially available in
1951, and as both hardware and software became more reliable
during the late 1950s and early 1960s. Thus, by the mid-
1960s, quite good quality computers were in widespread use,
and computer usage was well established in higher education.
A number of undergraduate and graduate degree programs in computer science had been established. However, the idea of personal computers was probably still not even a dream in most
people's minds.

Timeshared computing and minicomputers became available
during the 1960s, and microcomputers became available during
the latter half of the 1970s. A battery-powered computer, the
size of a hand-held calculator and programmable in BASIC, be
came commercially available at a retail price of about $250 in
1980. These advances have opened up the possibility of
personal computing for the general population. The industrial

[1]*The editors wish to express their appreciation for Karen*
Billings' presentation of this paper at the conference.

might of this country could produce a microcomputer for every
home, office, and student desk at school, and these individual
units could be tied into each other and to larger computers
through our telephone system. Not only is this possible, but
it is likely to occur -- if such a computer system can be
shown to be sufficiently useful.

The idea of "computer literacy" for the general population is relatively new, probably first emerging in the late
1960s. Leaders in the field of computer and information science began to suggest that all people needed to know something
about computers. The goal of universal computer literacy has
gained in popularity as computers have become more and more
widely used and readily available, and as their overall usefulness has become more evident to the general population.
The Conference Board of the Mathematical Sciences recommended
universal computer literacy in its 1972 report (Conference
Board of the Mathematical Sciences Committee on Computer Education, 1972). It suggested that this could be achieved via a
junior high school computer literacy course. Although its re-
quest to the National Science Foundation for funding to develop such a course was denied, many individual teachers began to
offer computer literacy units or entire courses, and authors
began to develop materials useful at the elementary and secondary school levels.

The meaning of "computer literacy" has never been particularly clear and it seems to have changed over time. Initially, computer literacy tended to mean a level of understanding
at which the student could talk about computers but could not
actually work with the computer. (This is now called computer
awareness.) Students were exposed to movies and talks about
computers, allowed to handle a punched card, discussed ways
that computers are used in business, government and science,
and perhaps toured a computing center. There was little or
nothing personally relevant about this for most students, and
being aware of computers had little impact upon them.

But even in the early 1970s computers were having a
personal impact upon a few students. Computer assisted instruction had already reached into some elementary and secondary schools. Some secondary schools were offering instruction about computers, and some computer clubs existed for students. The federal government recognized and encouraged this
interest via support of a large number of teacher training
institutes in the computer field, and by support of some major
research projects in the area of computer assisted instruction.

This situation prompted Art Luehrmann, and others, in the early 1970s, to raise an important issue: what are appropriate uses of computers in education (Luehrmann, 1972)? Should the computer teach the student -- or vice versa? Or, as Tom Dwyer put it, should the student be the passenger or the pilot (Dwyer, 1981)? The basic issue is what, and how much, students should learn about computers. When a computer acts upon a student in a computer-assisted learning mode, the student need not learn much about computers. But when a student acts upon a computer, developing programs and solving a variety of problems, the student must learn a lot about computers. Also, in this situation, the students' teacher(s) are apt to need to know quite a bit about computers; at least, if their knowledge about computers is small they are apt to feel quite uneasy about the situation.

These questions have not been resolved, perhaps because not enough people have considered them to be important. Even now the school that can provide one microcomputer or time-shared terminal per 25 students is rare. Rarer still is the school that has even one teacher with a knowledge of computers in education equivalent to a strong bachelor's degree in this field.

But both of these situations are changing; they could change quite rapidly if society, working through its school system, decided that it was important to have it happen. Currently, computer literacy is not accepted as an important goal, either by the majority of teachers or by the majority of students. Computer literacy needs to become a relevant goal, both for educators and for students. The remainder of this paper discusses some aspects of personal computing and how they help to define some goals for computer literacy.

II. PERSONAL COMPUTING: A FORMAT FOR EXPLORATION

Students at all grade levels can learn to use a computer in a manner and at a level that is meaningful to them and makes a difference in their lives. Personal computing for students can be divided into several categories. The following uses of computers are neither disjoint nor all inclusive, but will serve to guide our exploration of the concept of computer literacy. Computers can be personally useful to students:

1. *As a general aid to learning.*
2. *As an aid to problem solving.*

3. *As an object of learning in itself: the*
    discipline of computer and information science.
4. *As entertainment.*

We will discuss each of these, and indicate how each
contributes to a definition of computer literacy. The discussion will be from the student point of view. Thus, the goals
for computer literacy that emerge will tend to be student
oriented and acceptable to students. Moreover, they will be
flexible, easily adapting with changes in computer capability
and availability, and with changes in the curriculum.

III. COMPUTER ASSISTED INSTRUCTION

Computer assisted learning (CAL), the use of computers as
an aid to learning, is a well established and extensively researched field. In essence, CAL is a computer simulation of
certain aspects of the teaching/learning process. Initially
much CAL material was quite poor, and even today this remains
a major problem. But, like any computer simulation, CAL quality can be improved by continued work on the underlying
theory, the software, the hardware, and the other supporting
materials. Thus, we now have some quite good CAL materials,
with strong evidence that many students learn more, better,
and faster using these materials. Moreover, CAL is an excellent educational research tool, contributing significantly to
an understanding of what students learn and what helps them to
learn. Good CAL embodies what is known about learning theory,
and makes explicit the model(s) of instruction being used.

Another idea that can be made explicit in education is
learning to learn. The jobs of a student are learning, and
learning to learn. The computer provides a good motivation
and/or vehicle for specific instruction on learning and on
learning to learn. Since computers can help students to learn
more, better, and faster, all students can benefit from learning the capabilities of CAL and having access to CAL. Any
student can learn to use CAL, and all can learn how (for them
personally) CAL compares with other aids to learning.

Ideally, a computer literate student has experienced CAL
in a variety of disciplines and has developed insight as to
its value relative to other modes of instruction/learning.
The student has been taught what it means to learn, and has
specifically studied various modes of instruction/learning.
The student understands what best fits his/her needs in a wide
variety of situations.

Notice that this aspect of computer literacy is sensitive to changes in computer technology, and to changes in CAL quality and availability. We need to acquaint students with the best that is currently available, and help them to understand that this "best" is rapidly changing. We should also stress that CAL can occur in many settings outside the classroom, and can thus play a useful role in lifelong, continuing education.

This approach to computer literacy can begin at the elementary school level and can continue throughout a student's education. It has the potential to help revolutionize education. The responsibility for learning can be placed more explicitly upon the student, rather than upon the teacher or school system as it is now. Instruction and learning do not have to be teacher directed, nor do they require that a teacher be present. It is likely that eventually CAL will be a standard, or even dominant, mode of instruction/learning. Because of this and the other benefits of CAL discussed in this section, we should begin to make more extensive use of CAL, even in situations where it is not yet 100% cost effective relative to conventional modes of instruction.

IV.   AN AID TO PROBLEM SOLVING

Problem solving is a central and unifying theme in education. Any discipline can be framed as a hierarchical set of problems to be solved. Instruction in a discipline leads to understanding the nature of the discipline's problems: the problems that have been solved, how to solve some of the problems that have been solved, what problems have not been solved, and how to formulate and attack new problems.

A key aspect of problem solving is building upon the work of others. This work is stored in a variety of ways. For example, each discipline has its own special vocabulary. The vocabulary of a discipline has been carefully developed to aid in the precise communication of key ideas of the field. Books, journals, and other writings are "coded" in these vocabularies, and constitute a standard way of storing the accumulated knowledge of the field. Still and motion pictures, video recordings, and audio recordings are other modes of storage. Much knowledge is stored in the form of machines that people learn to use: the telescope, microscope, telephone, television, radio, automobile, and so on. A person can learn to use these machines to solve various problems without mastering all of the details of how to construct the machines or how/why they work in the manner they do.

Computers, although they are also "merely" machines, provide a uniquely new way to store knowledge. We can (roughly) divide the computer storage of knowledge into two categories -- passive and active. Passive storage by means of computers is analogous to books, films, etc. -- more efficient, to be sure, but not qualitively different. Written materials can be stored on a magnetic disk or tape, and can be retrieved with the aid of a computerized information retrieval system. Similarly, pictures or sound can be digitized for computer storage, and later reassembled for play back. This may be faster and more convenient than "by hand" methods, but it adds no unique dimension.

Contrast this with the computerized storage of how to do something, in a form such that the computer can carry out the actual doing. We see this in a typical computer program to solve some problems. The program contains detailed information about how to solve a problem and the computer can carry out the steps of the program. This sort of active storage of knowledge is akin to the storage of knowledge in other machines, such as the telephone, microscope, or radio.

Progress in hardware, software, artificial intelligence, and in computer assisted problem solving in all disciplines, is continuously expanding the totality of problems that computers can solve or help solve. For any particular problem area that a student might study it is likely that computers are already a very important aid to problem solving, and that the importance of computers is growing. This leads us to a second major aspect of computer literacy.

The computer literate student understands and uses computers as an aid to problem solving. This means that the student has studied problem solving and a variety of aids to problem solving. The student has used computers as an aid to problem solving in a wide variety of disciplines, and understands their capabilities and limitations. Given a problem the truly competent student can decide if a computer is a useful aid when compared with other aids/approaches to solving the problem.

A key aspect of this part of computer literacy is substantial instruction and practice in using a computer as an aid to problem solving. There are many problems in which a library program is conveniently available. Some of these library programs are easy to use and easy to learn how to use. Others require substantial instruction and practice. Indeed, learning to use certain packaged programs is roughly equivalent to difficulty to learning a programming language.

But there are many situations in which an appropriate library program is not available. An existing program may need to be modified, several pieces of existing programs may need to be combined, or a new program may need to be written. Thus, instruction in computer programming is an important part of computer literacy. We will discuss this in more detail in the next section.

If the use of computers as an aid to problem solving is taught and integrated into the curriculum, it will substantially change some parts of the curriculum. Our curriculum contains a number of areas in which a computer can solve problems or can be of substantial assistance in solving them. We will need to decide what we want students to learn to do by "conventional" methods and to what extent "knowing" an area includes knowing how to make use of a computer to solve problems in the area.

The ideas of computer literacy raised in this section are dependent upon the capabilities of computer hardware and software, and will change over time. As with CAL, students should become familiar with the best of modern hardware and software, since continued rapid progress is to be expected in both. This type of computer literacy is multi-disciplinary. Its proper achievement requires that most teachers be computer literate with respect to their own disciplines. (Computer literacy requirements for teachers are discussed in the position paper prepared by Alfred Bork, see pp. 91). The Association for Computing Machinery's recommendations on teacher education are given in Taylor, Poirot and Powell (1980).

V.   LEARNING COMPUTER AND INFORMATION SCIENCE

Computer and information science is a new and important discipline. It is now well established in most major colleges and universities, and it is rapidly growing in stature. In the United States alone there are nearly 400 bachelor degree programs and nearly 100 doctorate programs in this field. There are hundreds of journals that devote all or part of their content to computer and information science topics, and the research journals of almost every other discipline occasionally carry computer-oriented articles.

Computer programming is part of computer and information science. Learning how to program and developing a reasonable level of programming skills are essential to understanding the field of computer and information science. We are not talking about a professional level of programming skill, but we are talking about a useful level. A student should be able to program well enough to be able to attack the types of problems being studied in the school curriculum, and to make effective use of the tools being taught. When the topic being studied is part of computer and information science then it is even more important that students write programs. Computer and information science should be taught in a hands-on environment, with considerable emphasis upon solving real world problems.

Thus, we are led to including computer programming as part of computer literacy both through our analysis of problem solving and also through the importance of computer and information science. But neither of these gives a precise statement of the level of programming skill that is appropriate to computer literacy.

College level computer literacy courses have existed for many years. The author of this paper first taught such a course in 1969. Experience in teaching Computer Literacy or Concepts of Computing courses suggests that only a modest level of programming skill need be acquired by students to support their gaining an awareness level of computer literacy. This is supported by the typical textbook for this area, which generally includes much less programming then is found in a term-long computer programming course.

Computer programming for problem solving would tend to suggest a higher level of programming skill, and a skill level that grows as one learns to attack more difficult problems. For example, as the student progresses upwards in mathematics, s/he acquires mathematical tools that can be used to attack more and more difficult problems both in mathematics and in other disciplines. The student's computer programming skills should be compatible and consistent with his/her problem solving skills.

The Association for Computing Machinery (ACM), working through its Elementary and Secondary Schools Subcommittee, has developed a year-long computer science course for the high school (Rogers and Austins, 1980). The course is intended to be roughly comparable to high school biology in its difficulty, and the hope is that eventually it will have a similarly wide audience. The course has a relatively low mathematics prerequisite. Its content is balanced between computer programming, problem solving, and a variety of topics from computer and information science.

The ACM-recommended course is at the ninth or tenth grade level. But many people recommend beginning serious instruction about computers in the seventh or eighth grade, or even earlier. Although modest experiments have been carried out at all of these levels, there is a severe shortage of appropriate instructional materials or strong research results. Moreover, there is an even greater shortage of appropriate trained teachers to present the necessary instruction.

It is perhaps too early to say that a high school level computer and information science course is an essential part of computer literacy. But already we can see a movement on the part of some colleges and universities in that direction. That is, it seems likely that ten years from now many colleges and universities will place entering freshmen into a remedial computer literacy course if they have not acquired this level of knowledge in their previous education.

It is also difficult to know what employers will expect of students entering the job market then years hence. The rapid proliferation of computers suggests that a quite high level of computer literacy will be expected. The ACM course might become part of a definition of the expected level of computer literacy.

The aspects of computer literacy discussed in this section tend to come from higher level authority (for example, the ACM) rather than being apparent to the student. Not all students will easily accept the idea that an ACM recommended body of knowledge and specific skills will be useful on the job or in college. Moreover, we cannot say with certainty that this course is indeed appropriate. For many years to come people will be able to acquire needed levels of computer-oriented skills on the job or in their higher education programs. But students who have acquired this level of computer literacy will have a distinct advantage in seeking jobs and/or in continuing with their education.

VI.   COMPUTERIZED ENTERTAINMENT

Computers are a rapidly growing form of entertainment. They compete successfully with television, hi-fi, books, and other similar forms of entertainment. Thus, they are quite important in the lives of many students, and can have either a positive or negative effect. We should remember that the typical 18-year old in the United States has watched more hours of TV than s/he has attended school!

Some computerized games can be learned and perhaps even mastered in a matter of minutes. But there are a growing collection of computerized games that require dozens or even hundreds of hours of effort to master. These may require extensive learning and/or the development of a high level of hand/eye coordination.

There now exist quite good computer programs that aid in musical composition, and computerized aids to artistic creation are also available. It is not difficult to include these in the realm of entertainment, but they also have clear educational value. A computer program to play chess, checkers, backgammon, or Othello can be an exciting opponent and an excellent aid to learning one of these games. Many other problem solving situations can be formulated as interesting games, with both entertainment and learning occurring.

There is no clear dividing line between entertainment and education. Indeed, if learning is fun, more and better learning tends to occur. Thus, students should be given the opportunity to make use of CAL materials that are both educational and fun. They should learn to be critical of learning aids that are unnecessarily dull.

There appears to be little need to give students instruction in how to use a computer as a form of entertainment. Students quickly learn this on their own and/or from their peers. But the study of entertainment, or more appropriately the study of leisure time, is now considered to be important in modern education.

A computer literate student has experienced the use of computers as a form of entertainment in a variety of situations. The student has studied various forms of leisure time activity and how computers fit into this field. The student has made a conscious and reasoned decision about the role computerized entertainment will play in his/her life at the current time.

VII. FINAL REMARKS

One common way to talk about computer literacy is to discuss knowledge, attitudes, and skills. Various instruments are developed to test these aspects of computer literacy, and scores on tests serve to define levels of computer literacy.

Another approach is to specify course goals and to develop specific program goals and objectives to implement these goals (Neill, 1976; and Rickets, 1979).

We have not attempted to use these approaches here, nor have we discussed their merits. Rather, we have used a different approach, based upon the idea that a computer can have a personal impact upon the student, and the student will be self-motivated to acquire a certain level of computer literacy because of the personal value of computers. This assumes, of course, that appropriate learning opportunities are made available to students.

The conclusion reached through this approach is that computer literacy is a working knowledge of computers. This knowledge should be at a level compatible with the other knowledge and skills a student is acquiring in school. It is a knowledge based upon understanding how computers can help one learn, how computers can help one solve problems, how computer knowledge is essential to a modern understanding of some topics, what is included in the field of computer and information science, and computers as a form of entertainment. This approach to computer literacy easily changes as computers become more readily available and easy to use, as we learn more about computers and integrate this knowledge into the curriculum, and as the use of computers becomes commonplace throughout the home, business, government, and schools.

REFERENCES

Conference Board of the Mathematical Sciences Committee on Computer Education (1972). "Recommendations Regarding Computers in High School Education."

Dwyer, T. (1981). "Multi-Micro Learning Environments: A Preliminary Report on the Solo/NET/works Project," *Byte,* January, pp. 104-114.

Luehrmann, A. (1972). "Should the Computer Teach the Student or Vice-Versa," *Proceedings of the Spring Joint Computer Conference.* Reprinted in *Creative Computing,* 1976, November/December.

Neill, M. (1976). "An Empirical Method of Identifying Instructional Objectives for a High School Computer Literacy Curriculum," (Ph.D. Thesis), University of Oregon, June.

Rickets, D. (1979). "Course Goals in Computer Education,
     K-12," disseminated by the Northwest Regional Educational
     Laboratory.

Rogers, J. and Austins, R. (1980). "Recommendations for a
     One Year Secondary School Computer Science Course,"
     Association for Computing Machinery Elementary and Sec-
     ondary School Subcommittee Report.

Taylor, Poirot, and Powell (1980). "Computing Competencies
     for School Teachers," Association for Computing Machinery
     Elementary and Secondary School Subcommittee Report,
     November.

DISCUSSANT REMARKS

Robert Taylor

Columbia University

SUMMARY

- *We need to remember that the computer is limited and mimics only part of what we do.*

- *The computer offers a key (e.g., CAI) and can provide a new way to deal with the possibility of incorporating more attention to process in the whole educational activity.*

- *We need to learn from lessons past and ensure that computing is understood as a process -- not simply end results found in a textbook.*

- *Learning and computing are communal activities as well as processes that we need to understand, nurture and build into our educational curricula.*

Robert Taylor

NARRATIVE

        I feel pretty much the way that Arthur (Luehrmann)
does -- I don't have any severe quarrel with Dave Moursand's
paper. I feel it might be more useful to deal with some of
the issues that are left out, rather than quarrel with the
typologies.

        Pat Suppes made an interesting point a few weeks ago in
New York at a meeting on computing. He said it's important to
sometimes take a global view and I always find it a little
distressing when people talk about computer access and various
things in a very closed framework. If you take some very
rough figures, and total all the computers and all the people
in the world, you have an overload of people trying to use
computers. It is going to be some time, even if we make computers as fast as we can, before that situation changes. I
think that is a useful fact to keep in mind. It's also useful
to keep in mind some of the concepts of what a computer is and
what it is not, what computer structures are logically, and
what they're not.

        A couple of years ago at Columbia we had a debate on
whether or not we can build a right brain computer. We all
knew rationally that we couldn't build a right brain computer
because we don't know what the right brain does nor how it
does it. I think it is important when thinking about the computer to realize that the computer is not going to save us
from anything. The best computer logic structures, the most
wisely designed, elegant, esthetically correct computer programs are not going to save us from anything. As far as I can
see there is only one way that the computer could possibly
save us, and that is if it could somehow absorb all the money
that we are going to waste in the MX missile system and other
weapon systems that we cannot possibly use, and won't know if

they work until we try them, and then it will be too late.   I
think that I am an educator, and that my responsibility is to
try to train people to think both rationally and irrationally.
Western thought has tended to go more and more towards what we
call scientific thinking, of which the computer is a logical
extension and epitome.   I think this is an important realization.   In the same sense that the computer won't save us,
neither will it be responsible for all the education tasks we
have to perform, nor will it necessarily help us with all of
those tasks.   Despite how exciting it is, how addictive it is
in some respects, it is important to keep that kind of global
view -- not only in terms of our current ignorance about the
human brain and how it works, and how we build devices which,
in some ways, mimic what we do.   A computer mimics only part
of what we do and it looks like we are still a long distance
from building one that will mimic a larger picture.

There are two other issues I want to comment on.   One, I
think even if we take these limitations into account, we need
to ask the larger question about the origins and nature of the
term computer literacy raised by Ron Anderson and Bev Hunter.
At this point, the concept has to be viewed with a bit of
detachment -- the idea of computer literacy itself is a reac-
tion to a situation.   You have to watch that you don't get all
wrapped up in that terminology.   Rather, what do we want to
teach human beings about computers, why do we want computers
to be an important part of what human beings are doing?   Is it
just because vendors are going to manufacture them and people
have to be defensively trained or is it because they contribute positively to some intellectual growth of human beings?
Despite the idea that computers do not deal with all of the
human intellectual capability, I think that computers do offer
a key, something that isn't stressed as often as it should be.
Certainly CAI and some of those types of uses of computers do
not really stress this even at their best.

The point is that education itself is a process.   Learning to problem solve, to write, to do anything is a process.
Most of our educational activities of the last few centuries,
particularly since 1900 in this country, have been oriented
towards measurement based on testing and therefore have tended
to shortchange process, and its' possible role in human education in favor of the end-products.   I think the computer gives
us a new way to deal with the possibility of incorporating
more attention to process in the whole educational activity.
For example, we have a project at Teacher's College where we
use the computer to teach writing, to explore how you learn to
write better, and so on.   All of you, I am sure, have used a
computer to help teach problem solving in various ways.   I

think it is very important for students to learn that great
ideas seldom come in a blinding fashion, like the cartoon
lightbulb. They take a long time, a lot of refinement, and
therefore, if there is one thing that I would say that students ought to be learning, it's that education is a process.
Computers can help to communicate this to people, through using them, sometimes in a programmatic mode when the student is
actually doing the programming, sometimes using some type of
package like word processing or linguistic analysis.

I think that the danger of failing to teach process is a
serious one. I point to the NSF report mentioned earlier by
Andy Molnar. It is very sad if you worked on PSCS, physics or
BSCS biology, or MACOS, or any of those other projects that
are discussed here, to think what has happened in most cases
today to that material. The goal of all these projects was to
teach inquiry, discovery and process. Almost everybody connected with those projects was caught up with that approach to
reality, and that these curriculum projects would convey these
ideas to students. Yet, this report now concludes from a
number of different points of view that those projects pretty
much failed to really do any such thing. What they could have
done is now gone. Instead, what happened was that some of the
surface facts that were introduced into those new curricula
have been incorporated by commercial writers or publishers
into the usual type of textbooks, and that's all that remains
of them -- not the process, not the inquiry, not any of the
better stuff, but only the end result. I think one danger
that we need to be aware of is that computing can end up the
same way. Computing can end up as a textbook that people
master parts of and they get a nice feeling that they have
covered a certain amount of the material because they covered
the first 10 chapters last term. They may have a very weak, a
very limited view of the process of computing, whether applied
to computing itself or to some other subject, and in the end
the idea, if you want to call it computer literacy, or the
idea of computing the curriculum, will be mastery of some
piece of textbook material.

I will close with what I think may be some ways to get
around this. Dave's paper is a little bit weak on how we go
about implementation. I think the very idea of computing as a
process and processes being a heart of learning, is also tied,
if it is going to be successfully built in to the curriculum,
to the whole communal idea of what are school and learning.
If we continue to think of school as a place where people are
bottled up for a certain amount of time, in a situation where
they go through a certain number of books per year and master
in some measurable way, we really are not going to get at that

process any better than we have in the past. If, on the other
hand, we see learning as a communal activity just as computing
tends to be a communal activity, then perhaps process can be
part of education. If we use older students to teach younger
ones as some people have tried to do, and as we use parents in
the community to come in and learn about computing and work
with their children, I think there is a much greater chance
that we will get a different view of computing. Perhaps this
will help us open up some of the other avenues in education
that have generally been closed. If we simply try to rely on
materials that will be very much like books and will eventually be incorporated in books, then computing will suffer the
same fate as many of the other curriculum projects. So, I
stress trying to find ways to incorporate what I think is the
essence of computing as an educational activity, namely, the
development of a true sense of learning as a process into
whatever we're about. I don't think we can do it simply by
setting objectives, although this may be an important part of
what we have to do.

COMPUTER LITERACY FOR TEACHERS

Alfred Bork

Educational Technology Center
University of California at Irvine

The term "computer literacy" has been much bandied around in recent years. It derives from a wide use of the term "literacy," as in "reading literacy," "math literacy," and "science literacy." Unfortunately literacy, in general, is one of the words that almost everybody "defines" differently. Often the implicit definitions used, reflected by what kind of courses the individuals teach under such titles, are very limited. Furthermore, a great number of variables may affect what type of literacy one is talking about (e.g., who the individuals are, the level of literacy required, the objectives of the program).

Computer literacy as a composite term is derived from the general term "literacy," as applied, among other areas, to being able to read and write in a competent fashion, to do essential arithmetic, and to understand science in a general sense. The implication is that these tools are needed for a reasonable level of survival and participation in modern society. If we extend the term to cover computer literacy, we should have a similar set of requirements. In all cases, literacy implies the ability to *do* something -- vocabulary is not enough.

My concern in this paper is with computer literacy as applicable to one group -- teachers in elementary and secondary schools in the United States. We are concerned with teachers *as* teachers aiding students in the learning process. Thus, we can focus on their use of the computer in their own classes. Nevertheless, we cannot neglect the wider issues of computer literacy with such a group. The subject of computer literacy for K through 12 teachers has received special attention through one of the subcommittees of the Association

for Computing Machinery particularly concerned with computers
in elementary and secondary education. The subcommittee's report, by Taylor, Poirot, and Powell, deserves special attention, more than is possible with a brief paper such as this.
The reader is referred to this report.

I. THE CENTRAL PROBLEM

One of the most startling developments in education the
past few years is that schools are purchasing small computers
at a very rapid rate. The number in any one school is often
small, but a recent study of fifty states indicated that over
90% of the school districts responding to the survey (over
60%) claimed to have some computer capability at the present
time. However, few use it for instruction.

Because computers are rapidly becoming widely available
is not to say that the computers are well used in the schools.
Often a school which purchases several personal computers
(with considerable fanfare) discovers that when they arrive
there is little direct use of the machines. The computer
frequently becomes the personal possession of a relatively
small clique of students and faculty. With such groups game-
playing often becomes one of the major activities, or a few
students learn simple programming techniques, often developing
a set of bad programming habits.

We can confidently expect the rate of purchase of computers to accelerate in schools. As more personal computers
are purchased for home use, there is more parent and student
pressure to have equivalent capabilities in schools. The
major problem is: what are the teachers to *do* with these
newly acquired computers?

Few teachers currently in the public school system have
any deep acquaintance with computers. While a few excellent
in-service and pre-service programs in certain parts of the
country provide teachers with introductions to computers,
these programs are few and far between. Teachers typically
find that they get little or poor advice from local universities, because the university faculty are often more backward
than the schools in the use of the computer within the educational process. In most cases the vendors are also of little
help; vendor pressure to sell their own particular equipment
is the dominating force.

The problem we face is that of training a large number of
teachers to make effective instructional use of the equipment
they will confront in the classroom, the modern computer
equipment of today and the immediate future. It is a national
problem and one that should be met as soon as possible if we
are to aid our teachers. For the teachers who will teach
computing directly, the problem is less severe since they have
several resources available.

Typically, the way of solving problems involving teacher
training is with in-service and summer programs. Many of the
new curriculum developments in the 60's led to workshops for
teachers. But the prognosis for this approach, given past
experience, is very poor. Not all teachers are close to
institutions offering such training. Furthermore, the amount
of training available is often inadequate. For example, the
programs available to elementary teachers in the "new mathematics" was quite insufficient to overcome their previous
approaches and biases in the area. Hence, major curriculum
developments failed because teacher training activities were
completely inadequate. Bold new approaches to aiding our
teachers are needed to solve the problem of computer literacy
for teachers.

II. THE COMPUTER AS A VEHICLE FOR COMPUTER LITERACY FOR
     TEACHERS

The key is the *computer* itself. The computer is an
excellent learning device and can be used to aid teachers in
learning as well as students in learning. Interactive computer programs, plus problem solving access to the computer, can
provide a range of possibilities not attainable in any other
way. The individual can be treated as an individual, with all
of the features which distinguish that person from another one
taken into account. Each person can proceed at his or her own
pace. Furthermore, the learning experience can be an active
one, with the learner a participant rather than a spectator.

Small personal computers of today can easily be made
available in any school as well as in various public and
learning institutions. Thus, a school district interested in
acquiring computers could offer materials directly to their
own teachers. Credit arrangements would be possible if desired. Thus, a new mode of teacher training is possible and
feasible. In addition, the computer material could be used
within in-service courses.

III.   LITERACY DETAILS

To expand these comments and move to the details of what
computer literacy for teachers involves, I will discuss a
number of specific areas that might be included in any program
of this kind.

It should not be assumed that all teachers will need all
aspects of this work. For example, while the material on
designing computer-based learning materials would certainly be
helpful pedagogically to teachers, whether they would or would
not actually be involved in developing such materials, it is
not reasonable to expect that all teachers would develop these
competencies. Nevertheless, the material to aid teachers
should be available as part of any full program in computer
literacy because some teachers will want to pursue this direction. The needs of the individual teacher must be taken into
account; a monolithic approach which assumes that all teachers
will be given the same material will prove to be unsatisfac-
tory.

A.   *Learning Theory Background*

Since we are addressing computer literacy for teachers,
we should place the discussion in a context of *learning*.
Hence, initial discussion of learning theories seems critical.
One might like to believe that all teachers have this background, but many relevant approaches to learning, such as
developmental psychology and cognitive psychology, are not by
any means well known by teachers today. Therefore, some
modules of this kind are important.

We would not expect to make teachers experts in this
area, but rather to make them aware. A mixed presentation,
looking at various approaches to learning, in which research
relevant to computer use in education should be introduced, is
desirable.

B.   *Types of Computer Uses in Education*

The emphasis should be on the broad spectrum of ways the
computer can be used in education, not ruling out any possibilities. We should stress the different pedagogical roles
which these computer uses provide in learning. The teachers
must see (that is, interact with) many examples of each type
of use, rather than simply view these uses in an abstract
fashion. Some of this material should be area-dependent;

thus, a mathematics teacher needs to focus on how the computer can be used in math courses. The work of Taylor, Poirot, and Powell mentioned earlier discusses specific areas.

We should include both the problem-solving uses of the computer, where the computer is used as a tool to amplify intellect, and also tutorial and dialog uses of the computer, with many different variants of each. Representative material from major projects should be represented in this panoramic perspective of types of computer use. Another reasonable role is a comparison of computer use in education with other media. This discussion might well be extended to more general societal issues oriented to the computer. In addition, projections for the future are essential.

C. Developing Computer-Based Learning Material

Although not all teachers will be developers of computer-based learning material, they will find it desirable to understand the process. Many teachers in the years ahead will participate in such development. Thus, this should be an important component of a program of teachers who should be brought to an understanding of the advantages and disadvantages of learning of the computer medium.

There is no single developmental strategy at present, so a discussion of this kind should show a variety of strategies. This section of the teacher training material should emphasize strategies that look to the future toward a time where considerable material can be produced.

As an optional activity, it may be possible to get people to produce some small amount of computer-based learning material. However, this may be difficult to do.

D. Structured Thinking and Programming

The recent work on both problem solving (with and without computers) and effective programming has indicated a variety of desirable strategies. These important strategies should be clearly understood by the teachers who are to use computers in the problem solving form with students. Also, they are important in the preparation of learning materials to aid students to become better problem solvers.

E. Algorithms

The notion of an algorithm is still one that needs to be stressed and presented to the teacher, perhaps initially in

non-computer form. The notion of a rule doing something and
the ability to carry out that rule is an important intellectual concern.

F. *Introduction to Programming*

We do not need to make expert programmers out of teachers
in a computer literacy program. But, we should give them
enough programming experience so that they can understand the
process of programming and be able to read programs in an
effective and powerful language. My bias would be Pascal as a
beginning language, although in the near future Ada may be an
important competitor. There is something to be said for
exploring the possibility of presenting several languages
together; LOGO on personal computers is a good alternative.

The choice of languages to use with teachers is an interesting one. There is no question that the most commonly used
language at present is BASIC. But BASIC has many flaws as a
beginning language. Recent speculation indicates that first
language has a considerable effect on later programming.
There are a number of features that one should look for in
language design, even for beginners. These features are
generally grouped under the name "structured programming."

Pascal is a desirable language as a beginning language.
In this regard, it is comforting to note that Pascal is now
available or soon to become available in almost all the small,
inexpensive, personal computers. Hence, it's practicality for
situations below the university level is rapidly increasing.

In aiding the teacher we must always be thinking ahead;
the student will not be out of school for many years. Education is often guilty of teaching outmoded technologies, but in
this situation we can easily avoid this problem.

It should be emphasized that one does not want the teacher to see all aspects of a language. One of the benefits of a
good computer language is that there are capabilities one can
"grow" into. Thus, in a language such as Pascal, concepts
such as pointers and records would probably not be necessary
in its' introduction to teachers.

The most desirable method of learning the language should
be through examples. These examples should start at the beginning with the notion of structure, so that procedures would
be one of the first concepts taught to the learner. An environment such as Turtle geometry might be a good beginning

point. Experience in a number of different levels at Irvine
has indicated that the "whole program" approach is very effective. That is, one does not start by expounding grammar, but
by developing full programs, thus showing the grammar in
connection with these developments. Structured programming
ideas should be emphasized in such a development.

Teaching programming as an interactive environment as
suggested in this paper, where there may be no human teachers
around, will be a challenge.

The areas indicated as necessary for teacher computer
literacy are not complete but they form a core program of this
type. Other areas might well be added to the list. It will
be noted that there is no emphasis on computer technology.

IV. CONCLUSIONS

In developing any new technology, it is important to
bring the users of that technology to the realization of its'
best uses, not just its' possible uses. Any technology can
often have harmful uses, unthought through activities that are
carried out simply because they can be done. For example, the
widespread advent of computer editors and word processing has
led to much use of right justification in typewriter-like
documents, without any thought as to whether this is a good or
a bad thing. Readability research, and the views of very
competent graphic designers, would, in this case, both agree
that it is a poor choice.

It is a thesis of this paper that older modes of teacher
training, based on in-service strategies, are inadequate for
the problem at hand. There are simply too many teachers, and
not remotely enough possibilities for training these teachers
by conventional means. This is not to say that in specialized
locations in-service training could not be important, just as
it has been in the past. These materials could also be important in that environment, but they address the wider problem
too. Very few schools in education in the U.S. and also
relatively few computer departments are willing or able to
provide the in-service activities needed.

If the computer is to be widely used in education, we
must help teachers to attain a reasonable approach to educational computer use. The penalty we pay, if the teachers do

not develop such an approach, could be deterioration of our
educational system. We cannot allow poor use of this powerful
aid to learning.

ACKNOWLEDGMENTS

    The author has discussed these issues with a number of
other people, particularly Robert Taylor, Richard Dennis, and
James Poirot. Although I have benefitted from these discussions, I do not want to attribute any of the flaws of this
paper to my helpful colleagues.

DISCUSSANT REMARKS

Sylvia Charp

School District of Philadelphia

SUMMARY

- We need to ask questions about the failure/ success of projects concerning computers in education.

- Universities are actively acquainting teachers with computers.

- Existing teacher training programs are not completely ineffectual nor are older modes of teacher training.

- School systems are purchasing and utilizing computers but not rapidly or in large quantities.

- We shouldn't stress learning theory in teacher training.

- We need state and local involvement as well as a strong university-school system link in the helping teachers to manage a classroom with computers for a classroom of students.

Sylvia Charp

NARRATIVE

As one of the old timers, I have some privileges to say things that probably the younger people can't say. First of all, I was very interested in Beverly Hunter's slide show earlier, and to be made aware of the very many projects concerning computers in education.

What I'm wondering is: What has happened to all the programs that have been initiated? How many of them are still in existence? If they fail, why did they fail? If they are still in operation, how successful have they been? Is this measurable? I think that we really can learn from answers to such questions, and yet no one has approached any of these -- we just don't seem to be learning from each other anymore. We are all starting to do things all over again. It would be interesting for me, as it may be for you, to find out what happened in this field.

There has been some concern expressed that the private sector is not involved in this conference. For years, the private sector has been telling us that educators can't make up their minds as to what they really want. Now here we have a group of educators that are meeting in a working conference to come up with some policies. I am not too sure how appropriate it is at this time for the conference leaders to be criticized for not inviting the public sector.

I would like to make some comments on the papers presented by my colleagues. In Dr. Bork's paper there were many generalizations and unfair statements. Some of the things said -- which I really don't think are true -- is that few teachers have any deep acquaintance with computers.

Since I really don't know what "deep acquaintance" means, and I don't know what "few teachers" means, I am a little concerned about these statements. Also, Dr. Bork said

that teachers typically find that they get little or no good
advice from local universities because the university faculty
are even more backward than the school concerning use of
computers directly in the educational process. I take excep-
tion to that point since I feel that there are many universities which have really tried and are helping us.

Dr. Bork also said that for the teachers who do teach
about computing, the problem is less severe since they have
several sources available. Well, if they use a variety of
sources in their teaching, are many of us aware of this
material? What are these sources? They should be shared.

Dr. Bork says -- and I disagree with these generalizations -- that the curriculum developments fail because the
teacher training activities were completely inadequate. I
don't think that was the main reason; there were many others,
but I don't believe that the existing teacher training programs are completely ineffectual.

Bork also mentions that the older modes of teacher
training are inadequate. Well, I personally have been doing
teacher training for many, many years, and I don't know how
and why the teacher training in which I've been involved is
not adequate.

It is stated that school systems are purchasing computers
at a very rapid rate. I don't think that's true. I think
that they are purchasing them, and that there is a greater
utilization, but I would never say that this is happening at a
rapid rate. Dave Johnson claims that a great deal of equipment is in the schools. I wish this were so. Though micros
are being purchased, the number is still small. For example,
one, two, or three microcomputers in a school is really inadequate.

As far as what should be in the curriculum and what
should be covered, I agree with Arthur Luehrmann when he
states we should go easy on what material we use initially to
train the teachers, because we haven't decided what is really
essential for them to know. I don't believe that we should
stress learning theory, but not initially.

What is more important, it seems to me, even after the
teachers are trained, is what happens next? What do we do
with the equipment once we acquire it and how do the teachers
use the micros? How do the students use them? How do we
manage a classroom with a few micros for a classroom of
students? As I visit the schools, I find the teachers don't

know how to manage. It is these areas of training that are
most important initially in teacher training. What is really
of concern is how to address the problem. Bork's paper may
provide part of the answer, i.e., using computer assisted
instruction to train teachers. To develop many modules may
be a national answer to CAI for all teachers. This could be
an approach, but I feel that there is a lot more to do, and
as far as I am concerned, it has to be done on a state and
local level. We really have to get the universities and the
school systems closely tied together much more than they have
been. My colleagues from universities are the ones who can
really help. We have to work together, to do a better job of
teacher training than we have done.

DISCUSSANT REMARKS

Ludwig Braun

State University of New York at Stony Brook

SUMMARY

- *There is a phenomenally rapid rate of change of computers in the schools that will increase due to the decreasing cost of technology.*

- *It is important that teachers learn about how the computer can be used as a learning environment for their students.*

- *We need to address the problems of how to get the millions of teachers trained.*

- *We need computers in order to teach computer literacy.*

- *Cost is an important factor in choosing a programming language and that in itself justifies using BASIC over others.*

Ludwig Braun

NARRATIVE

With great temerity I would like to take issue with one
thing said by Sylvia Charp. I think there is a rapid rate of
change of computers in the schools. I don't think there are
lots of computers in schools yet, but that's the number of
computers, not the rate of change of the number. The rate of
change of the number, I think, is phenomonal. I look around
Long Island, for example, and there are now 6 micros in every
elementary school. The rate is important because it tells us
that things are happening. Within a couple of years the
number will be phenomonal if the current rate continues. I
think the rate will leap up because micros are cheap and
getting cheaper. There is now a Sinclair computer available
for purchase at $200 (with added costs for a monitor or cas-
sette recorder).

Before I talk about Al Bork's paper, it is important for
us to realize that what we are talking about here is only one
segment of the question of computers in education. Computers
have an awful lot to offer in an educational environment.
Computer literacy is only one relatively narrow facet. There
is biology, language, math, physics, etc., all of which can
benefit enormously from using the computer in other ways. For
example, there were Tom Dwyer's Project SOLO, and the Hunting-
ton Project of a few years ago, both efforts NSF stopped
supporting. These projects could have contributed a great
deal more than they did had the funding continued. These two
educational computing projects are examples of mating discovery and learning, an important component of the learning environments. While not directly germane here, I want to mention
them to emphasize that what we are talking about is only a
segment of this whole problem.

It seems to me that programming, which Bork focused on
primarily in his paper as what teachers need to learn, is only

one component of what teachers need to learn about computers.
They also need to learn about how the computer is used as a
learning environment for their students. They need to be
literate in the uses, all of the uses, of computers in education. We have such a program at Stony Brook for teachers.
This is an aspect I think Al left out of his paper.

There is an element that Al lightly mentions but I think
is important to underscore. There are several million teachers -- 3 million, 5 million, I don't know exactly how many.
I'm worried about how to get that many teachers trained. I
think the computer is an important element of that training
and perhaps Al's intelligent videodisc is another element.
I'd like to suggest that the French have an interesting idea.
They have a program called "10,000 micros in the School."
They have an ongoing program for training 2 kinds of teachers.
The French train master teachers who are resource people once
they are trained for other teachers who are out there learning
by whatever means there is.

It's not sufficient in my mind to have a group of people
somewhere developing computer-based learning materials that
are sent in envelopes to the 3 million or so teachers around
the U.S. These teachers are going to need answers to questions and they need live contact with somebody. In the New
York area, for example, people have that. The teachers in our
area are pretty lucky; they can go to Karen Billings, come to
see me, or they can come to a number of other people. I don't
know how dense is that kind of help. I have a feeling that it
isn't very dense because I wind up getting two or three invitations a week to come to talk to people. I am sure there are
alot of you in this audience who have the same number of
invitations. What we need to do, I think, is have what might
be called master teachers or local consultants to help the
teachers who are learning by the impersonal means.

There is a component of the MECC proposal that concerns
me, and that is the concept of teaching computer literacy
without computers. I realize that there are schools without
computers and that may not have computers for a while. But if
they are going to teach people computer literacy you just
cannot do it without a computer.

Al mentions languages and states that his preference is
LOGO. I just came from a seminar yesterday at the New York
Academy of Sciences and found myself defending BASIC against
LOGO. I don't feel that I should be defending BASIC except

for one reason and that is cost. It's important when you
compare languages that the costs to implement are considered.
I can buy a computer that operates in BASIC for $600 and in a
matter of a couple of months I will be able to buy one for
$400 that "talks" in BASIC and gives numerous kids good
programming experiences. If I could get a $400 LOGO machine
I could give them better learning experience, but my fundamental concern is that there are people who are saying we
would rather see BASIC go down the tubes and not give the kids
BASIC at all. What they are doing is condemning another
generation of kids not to learn anything at all about computing. What really bothers me about the discussions of
language preference is a certain intolerance in the minds of
some people. It is entirely possible to let kids do terrible
programming in BASIC. It is also entirely possible to teach
them some intelligent programming in BASIC. It depends upon
what the teacher knows about programming. I personally would
much rather see twice as many kids learn programming in BASIC
as opposed to half as many kids learn programming in LOGO or
PASCAL. If you look at the cost of the equipment to provide
these other languages you are talking about factors of 2 or 3.

I am not prepared to accept sending a bunch of students
down the tube. My students never learned computing in our
high school until 2 years ago and we had less students per
computer terminal than most high schools in the United States.
We have only 16 terminals for 2500 students. That is a terrible ratio, but it's a much higher ratio than most of the
schools noted earlier. The latter generally has one terminal
for 3000 students, and my students learned no programming and
did not develop those kinds of thinking skills. I'm not ready
to accept that for the next generations students. I want
every student who is now in school to learn computing and it's
possible for schools to afford computing now if they are
willing to accept BASIC.

AUTHOR REBUTTAL

(Bork)

The rate of increase of computing in schools is great and
have some recent national survey data to support this.   The
data also indicates plans by the school districts for expanded
usage.   There are going to be a lot of machines in schools,
and certainly the rate is already great.   Possibly some of the
disagreements with Sylvia Charp are disagreements in degree.

1.   Few teachers have any competence with computers.
There is very little real acquaintance with what a teacher can
do with computers.   It is a hardware craze, at the moment, to
buy the equipment and then somehow magically find out what to
do with it.

2.   Some universities *are* certainly helping, but nationally, most students are not going to be helped by universities.   In fact, many students around the country will be short-
changed if one continues to assume that all the in-service/
pre-service summer institutes, etc., will occur through the
universities.

3.   Every educator puts very high emphasis on the problems with retraining an entire group of K-6 teachers to changing their ways of thinking and understanding new mathematical
ideas.   Most of them emphasize that the existing teacher
training modes were simply not adequate.

4.   One needs to look at a great variety of ways to use
the computer in educational processes.   So Lud and myself are
in agreement.   It is little puzzling that *he* finds me in
disagreement.

5.   My bias would be PASCAL, although in the near future
Ada may be an important competitor.   There is something to be
said for providing the possibility of presenting several
languages together.   Better languages are now beginning to
appear widely on small machines. APPLE, ATARI, TI, are about
to announce the availability of PASCAL, for example, and the

machines do cost a little more. Reasonable programming in
BASIC can be taught, but it is often not done. One of the
lessons out of modern structured programming is if programmers
are to program better generally, and this is not just teachers, but much more widely, the language should encourage the
reasonable practices that are seen in good programming.
Languages have to be chosen for the kind of students, teachers, and areas that one works with.

AUDIENCE COMMENTARY

● Work with teachers at the university level suggests 5 factors, all of which must simultaneously be achieved successfully if an adoption of this kind of technology is to be successful.

-- The teacher must be aware through information transfer of the technology.

-- The teacher must perceive the technology as being relevant to high priority items that s/he wishes to achieve in the classroom.

-- The teacher has to have some level of understanding of computer technology and at least some understanding about programming to get started.

-- Sufficient technical support must be given to bridge the gap between the teacher's own abilities to do things and what is needed in order to make programs effective (e.g., master teacher).

-- A social system (e.g., approval, money, time off) from peers, colleagues, administrators, school boards -- is a worthwhile thing to create. With university people there is relatively little social support for this sort of thing. The reward comes from publishing papers, not from improving classroom instruction.

● Perhaps because of an oversight in the way that this session was titled, the need for education on the part of school administrators has not really been directly addressed in this session, and, of course, we need to do so during the conference. In fact, perhaps we need to stress this as even more important than teacher training.

Simply emphasizing programming as a skill will turn out to be as empty as a piece of technology as is a computer without programming. In teaching the teachers and teaching

the children, the question is, to what use do we put this?
Without the context, without the science, without the social
studies, without the math, there's nothing there -- it's just
a box.

We have a moral and social responsibility to children to
teach them about appropriate uses of technology, about the
ethics of information handling, and some of these other related subjects. It is very dangerous to focus on the widgets
and omit these larger issues.

● From the context of a person who is still teaching in the
classroom in a high school, there is a culture lag between the
teachers in the schools now, and the teachers that we may produce in the future. We must have in-service training with a
course entitled, "Introduction to Microcomputer Technology,"
so that the differences between main frame computing and
microcomputing are clarified. Universities are very good with
mainframe computing now -- teaching BASIC, PASCAL and FORTRAN.
The students who learn this type of computing on time sharing
cannot handle the current math labs that are being introduced
into the high school where we deal with disc drives, formats
and interfacing. Because they never get the same computer
twice, we have all sorts of problems which the universities
are not addressing.

● Take all the people in the U.S. that you would trust to
teach people what you think they ought to know, assume that
they can teach those people, and in turn, those people can
teach other people. Assume a constant stream of teachers in
and out of teaching, and do the arithmetic of that and figure
how long it would take to have how much of an impact on some
fraction of the teachers in the country. Unless you accept Al
Bork's argument of using the media in some way to have another
source of information and knowledge for teachers other than
the classroom and direct transmission, a teacher training program to attain nationwide computer literacy will not.

● Teachers are lacking the management skills to conduct a
classroom. They depend on the textbook and are unable to meet
individual needs in all subject areas. Moreover, there is a
lack of flexibility that would allow a student know more about
something than the teacher. The teacher somehow feels that if
s/he loses control of these 30 students then chaos will occur.
The fact is also reflected in many teachers cannot and do not
use discovery measures in the classroom. This inability is
going to be multiplied when a terminal is put in the classroom. The universities are to blame. They use the same

method for teaching teachers that teachers then use in the
classroom. They use the textbook, they use the lecture, and
they do not meet individual needs. In the university, if you
don't keep up (it's like physics and math teachers have always
said) the student is either dumb or slow or won't apply him-
self or herself.

● The problem is that there is inadequate incentive for
departments of computer science or colleges of education to go
into computer training for teachers. Incentives in the way of
NSF support could be provided. If we look at the percentage
over the past two years of the pre-service or in-service
training, and support in computing, it is a very small percentage. In the area of research in computer science, there is a
lot of money, both from industry and from government. There
is very little industry support right now for providing teacher training. Computer science departments at universities
have too many students already so they need some sort of
incentive for getting into some programs that will aid teachers. One need is for the installation of microcomputers in
universities, because they aren't being trained on the little
computer yet. Micros are going to be used in the secondary
schools and elementary schools, and the universities ought to
get in-service training to get this started for teachers.

● How do you manage this huge task of producing the required number of computer literate teachers? Or helping
teachers become computer literate?

Turn around the arithmetic a little bit; also draw on
experience in schools where teachers are using computers with
students. That is, look at the arithmetic of the amount of
time teachers spend with computers compared to the amount of
time students spend with computers. Often some teachers are
willing to allow those students to be the teachers and to
carry on. Consider very seriously the notion of using students as a resource in educating other students and for educating teachers.

● It's important to draw a distinction between one kind of
number problem and another that's very different from it. If
the goal is to create computer modules which are to be used
across the curriculum in many different fields, you have a
vast retraining problem. There are problems, both logistical
and psychological, in managing that goal within the lifetime
of many of us here. On the other hand, if that goal is to
establish a beach/head course for 8th, or 9th, or 7th grade
course, where students learn to do something with computing,

the arithmetic is quite interesting. It takes one teacher to
teach all the students in a school. It takes one lab with 8-
15 computers to teach all students in school a one-semester,
40 hour hands-on course in computing. One can go from there
to other plateaus. But getting to that one takes one teacher
in each school -- about 20-25 thousand people. That's still a
big number, but that's not millions of teachers. It's tens of
thousands of teachers. If the 300 or so schools of education
were equipped with 300 teachers of teachers, 300 is still a
big number but it's not 10,000 teachers. If the schools of
education had the teachers of teachers and started teaching
them, then within a few years, it would be possible to retrain
people to teach this course. It is not an enormous obstacle.

●   There is another technology that just came down the road
in the last 5 years and that is the calculator. I'm sorry, I
think you blew it; teachers have not been taught how to use
that technology at all. It happened in the marketplace and
came in through the consumer market. The technology is coming
in recreation first, education second, and into the home.

●   One of the important teacher incentives may be, in fact,
that teachers will find ways of leaving teaching. They may
see that as an upward and outward movement. This may have
some possible evil aspects. When NSF ran all the institutes
in the 60's for science teachers, one of the things that happened was many of those teachers ceased being high school
teachers. Many of them became good enough to get other kinds
of jobs so there was a kind of migration. At the present
time, it is to our advantage that we offer something the
teacher will view as valuable.

●   Teaching the teachers with self-instructional material
will not work. Teachers aren't willing, and are not apt to
learn by themselves. What has worked better than anything is
to give the teacher all the activities and lesson plans, such
as MECC is doing with the student activity sheets with the
objectives -- a cookbook approach.

●   Many schools are getting computers that never had access
to them; we are learning lots of things. As Dave Moursund has
said, the computer will probably cause more problems than it
is going to solve. We are learning how little we know about
the technology, and the changes that are going to happen as a
result; how little we know about how children learn. So,
trying to tell people how or what the best strategies are in
using this technology is extremely difficult.

What about teachers or students who want to learn about computing but still don't have access to them? They can read about computers and the many different things computers can do. In workshops conducted for elementary teachers, particularly, the last part of the period is spent devising activities to do without a computer, and then with a computer. The teachers actually come up with more activities to do without a computer than with a computer. A lot of this has to do with the fact that they are just learning and haven't had the access yet; probably one year later this would reverse itself.

In observing classes and talking to students and teachers afterwards about their use, probably some of the most delightful answers are from the young students themselves. Asked what do you learn from a computer that you don't learn from a teacher, or vice versa, the answer repeated over and over is *thinking*.

● This comment was echoed and generalized by other participants. There is a spectrum of definitions of computer literacy and it depends upon the audience. Talking about computing as computer literacy is not appropriate as the total stress for a computer literacy course for everyone. Kindergarten children need a different kind of computer literacy. It's different for engineering students and it's different for the students in the German Department and for students who are going to become poets. It's different for teachers and different for beauticians, and so on.

WORKING GROUP I*

COMPUTER LITERACY FOR TEACHERS
AND SCHOOL ADMINISTRATORS

QUESTIONS

1. *What assumptions can we make about the current level of computer awareness and understanding among elementary and secondary school teachers and administrators? Are teachers prepared to teach with or about computers? Are teachers interested in becoming computer literate? Are administrators?*

2. *How much time is it desirable and realistic to expect average elementary school teachers to spend on computer-related in-service training? Junior high school teachers? High school teachers? Should all teachers be involved?*

3. *How should teacher training concerning use of, or teaching about, computers be organized and conducted? Take into account:*

    -- In-service training
    -- Pre-service training
    -- Incentives
    -- Practicality

4. *Should curriculum development projects conduct curriculum specific workshops in order to help prepare teachers to use their instructional materials? Are there examples of*

*Participants: Doris Lidtke, Richard Arnold, Alfred Bork, Richard Lavine, David Moursund, Charles Philipp, James Poirot, Beverly Sangston, and Martin Schneiderman.

115   Copyright ©1982 by Academic Press, Inc.
All rights of reproduction in any form reserved.
ISBN 0-12-634960-6

curriculum development efforts in the past that have been especially successful in this regard? What type of on-going support should be provided to teachers using new curriculum materials?

5. *Who is responsible for teacher training and retraining programs? What role should the federal government play? What about state government? The local school district?*

6. *How can colleges and universities be encouraged to play a more active role in educating teachers about computers? When and how will schools of education integrate computer literacy into pre-service training of teachers and school administrators?*

HIGHLIGHTS

- ● *Computer awareness and understanding are limited amongst teachers and school administrators.*

- ● *In-service and pre-service training materials and programs should be tailored to both self-initiating as well as disinterested teachers.*

- ● *The federal government should act as the prime initiator of teacher-administrator computer literacy education.*

- ● *Teachers teaching teachers is the most effective teacher training program.*

- ● *Technical and people support systems should be established.*

WORKING GROUP I

COMPUTER LITERACY FOR
TEACHERS AND SCHOOL ADMINISTRATORS

Our group discussed computer literacy for teachers and
school administrators. Also, we were challenged to discuss
the ethics and values questions.

The question of value and ethics is not specific to computer literacy alone. Interesting questions came up in the
area of ethics and values. Is it most appropriately dealt
with in computer literacy? Or, is this something we have to
tap on a larger scale? Are teachers encouraging practices
that are ethically questionable? What kind of examples are
teachers setting by duplicating and printing materials, making
diskettes, and distributing them -- borrowing from other
schools? One reason why teachers find themselves doing this
is because they don't have the budget to do otherwise. Is
this practice any different than the parent who steals food
for his child if the child is starving? Ethics and values in
public education is an explosive issue and typically parents
argue that ethics should be taught at home.

We concluded that the current level of computer awareness
and understanding by teachers and administrators is limited.
Among administrators computer awareness and understanding are
limited to the areas of data processing, and much of the
information and awareness they have is vendor and hardware
specific and comes from the industry. Math and science teachers are generally more comfortable with the issues. We can
conclude that teacher participation and interest in computers
is encouraged by opportunity and access to computers. This
kind of interest can be contagious. Activity in this area
seems to be regional; it appears that certain urban areas see
this phenomena more than others.

School districts should be encouraged to have in-service
projects during school time, demonstrating to their faculty

that they really are committed; teachers shouldn't have to
spend their weekends and after school time becoming computer
literate. There should be two approaches to teacher-administrator literacy: interest and receptivity. Certain teachers are already self-starters, are interested and are actively
seeking out information to try to find out about computers.
There is also the teacher who is not already receptive.

Our group felt most strongly that an appropriate course
of action we foresee in the future and a recommendation to NSF
deals with programs for teachers in pre-service and in-service
training. Materials and packages need to be developed for
those interested people to obtain.

A question raised at the beginning of the group's session
was: Can, or will, the public schools participate in the
computer literacy movement? What role do teachers and educators play? Schools are faced with practical limits of class
size and budgets, and these issues have limitations on the
design of programs.

The group agreed that the federal government should take
the initiative in teacher and administrator education. There
was question whether or not industry would move into this area
since the numbers are such that it might not be a lucrative
market for developing specific kinds of training materials.
This would be an appropriate area for the federal government.

There was some discussion about the notion of sharing
teachers with industry. Since teachers work about 10 months a
year in school they could work two months in industry, and for
industry. That would be an exciting experience for teachers
-- to get out of the classroom and understand the problems of
industry better, and broaden their horizons, to take back into
the classroom.

The single most important factor in predicting success of
new programs in schools is the building principal, according
to a Rand study. For that reason administrator literacy is
absolutely essential. Teachers training teachers is the most
effective way to go about teacher training; they understand
teachers' problems and communicate them.

A method for providing this training could be computer-
assisted learning with microcomputers as a means of developing
literacy among administrators and teachers. This would help
resolve the problems of the teacher colleges, the lack of
knowledge, and in a standalone mode this might be an appropriate way to proceed. Where administrators and educators

were talked at in a lecture mode over a day or two, we found
there was very little carryover in terms of what was happening
in the schools.

We took the charge of looking at what kinds of models we
see as working and those that are not, and tried to learn
something. We discussed some programs that have been dealing
with videodiscs, and the way teachers and administrators are
exposed to this technology.

Based on our own experiences, we came to the following
conclusions about the ways in which we might proceed:

1. *In areas where exemplary existing courseware was demon-*
    strated to school administrators there seemed to be
    something that sparked a fire, and something happened
    as a result. However, we found that this needed to be
    followed up with some support, some mechanism, that when
    somebody got "charged up" about a micro or exciting
    courseware, a support system to provide the necessary
    next step should be available.

2. *It makes a big difference when decision makers see pro-*
    grams that work. Also, it has been useful when students
    view a demonstration (e.g., a videotape) of what is hap-
    pening in the school or another school.

3. *Computer literacy programs provide growth for administra-*
    tors who, in many cases, were perceived as doing a lot
    of routine things. In such cases, an administrator would
    have a lot of impetus to try to proceed and make these
    programs become a more integral part of the schools' pro-
    gram. However, principals need encouragement and support
    from their colleagues and other kinds of support struc-
    tures so they will not be alone in advocating programs
    involving computers.

4. *There is a need for intermediate units, that is, organ-*
    izations between the school district, state and federal
    governments, to provide the kinds of support we are talk-
    ing about. Once programs are started, this support should
    last two or three years.

    What kinds of support are we talking about? Technical
    support is one kind of support. An 800 telephone number
    whereby the administrator/teacher or microcomputer user
    who has a problem can refer to someone who is knowledge-

*able quickly -- like a local computer store. We have to
be careful not to terminate training and people support
too soon.*

5. *Who is responsible for training teachers? On one hand,
we recognize that technically it is the state that is
responsible. In practice, it is the school district
that is responsible for the training. We feel there
should be a variety of approaches about how to proceed.
One way is to encourage the federal government to be
responsible for funding teacher training programs such
as summer institutes that might be composed of teacher-
administrator teams.*

6. *A number of people in this group felt uncomfortable with
one of the ten commandments presented by working group
III -- the privacy issue (See pp. 239). We feel that
private ownership in the competitive personal process is
working to the detriment of education. We feel it is
important that students share and see sharing as an important act rather than encourage students to feel protective
about everything they are doing. The most productive
kinds of activities that happen in education happen when
people are doing them in a cooperative fashion. We don't
want those tools to be used to segregate and segment
learning.*

WORKING GROUP V*

ETHICS AND VALUES FOR COMPUTER LITERACY

QUESTIONS

1. Should any standards or guidelines be proposed for mini-
    mal computer literacy for high school graduates? Who
    should propose such standards?

2. What are the most important subject areas for high school
    computer literacy?

3. What curricular materials are needed for high school
    computer literacy?

4. Should high school computer literacy be universal?
    Elective?

5. Should computer literacy be a separate course in high
    school? Integrated into math? Science? Social studies?

6. How can the discipline of computer science assist in
    promoting universal computer literacy? What curricular
    materials can be adapted for computer literacy?

HIGHLIGHTS

● Students and teachers should have thorough
   and comprehensive knowledge and understanding
   of communication laws and their implications.

*Participants: Bob Aiken, Richard Pollak, Irwin Hoffman,
   Bruce Taylor, Bill Underhill, and Ingrid Zadrozny.

- *All subject courses should discuss computer ethics and values as soon as students are involved with computers.*

- *Student teams should be composed of bright creative minds to positively motivate them and prevent future harmful actions.*

WORKING GROUP V

ETHICS AND VALUES FOR COMPUTER LITERACY

When should students learn ethics and values? Students
should learn about computing ethics as soon as they get on the
equipment, if it is a "doing" situation. If it is not a doing
situation but an "awareness" situation, students should learn
ethics after they learn what a computer can and cannot do. We
feel that this should apply to other situations in social
science, sociology -- all should include a unit on the importance of computers and related ethics/values considerations.

*What courses should include discussion with respect to
ethics and values?* All courses could include this topic. For
instance, even gym classes could talk about how computers were
used to measure certain components of exercise. Business
education and any other area can include these discussions.

What are a special set of ethical questions for micros?
It may seem like a dead issue since timesharing is not involved, but with micros becoming rapidly networked, the situation is changing.

*Students and teachers must be aware of state and federal
communications laws and their implications.* As Irwin Hoffman
pointed out, it is against the law to swear across the state
lines. Students must be aware that the content of their
files, programs and printouts might be seen by others. Doing
things in the public domain implies social responsibility and
possible legal jurisdiction.

What about copying of diskettes? Copying guidelines must
be explained to all and students must be aware of the consequences. Copying disks for backup use should be legal,
whereas laws regarding copying should be enforceable. It
would make more sense to license a group of systems in a
district rather than separately. To avoid copying, the site
should be given enough material to copy their needs. For

example, if you do have a district licensed for 25 systems
then you should have 25 manuals. We ran into several instan-
ces where people told us they got licenses for 10 systems and
got one manual. That encourages illegal copying. Also,
limiting a computer to one language invites disks to be
copied.

*Do not use copied material without the originator's per-
mission*. Keep the copy within the immediate environment and
do not share it with other schools. Unauthorized access --
intentional access is clearly theft; accidents are not theft.
Unintentional access is not theft, unless any use of the
access occurs. Use of access or blackmail are criminal offen-
ses. If you tap into someone's line accidentially, unless you
use that material in some way, it would not be considered
theft.

A list of rules or laws should be stated in general terms
so that illegal acts versus legal acts are known by all. The
teacher should share with the student as much knowledge about
the laws as the teacher can obtain.

*To challenge creative minds give bright students inte-
resting material to motivate them in a positive direction*.
Students who can break codes, etc., should be placed on an
"established team" to help prevent future harmful actions.
Also, teachers must enforce computing ethics. Finally, in
encouraging ethics, tell the student what is legal and illegal. Rationally explain why they should get legal programs
and most students will comply. Those who don't must be dealt
with in whatever way is necessary, maybe bringing them onto
the team if possible.

Teachers can demonstrate good computing ethics by being a
good example. It is necessary that the teacher provide the
proper atmosphere. Computer specialists and parents as well
as teachers should not laugh about and otherwise reward computer crime and other clever, though unethical, acts.

To summarize our conclusions, we offer a "Golden Rule of
Computer Ethics" and a "Ten Commandments for Computing."

The *Golden Rule of Computer Ethics* should be "do to
others' files and programs as you would have others do to
yours."

We also offer a *Ten Commandments for Computing:*

1.   Throw away old printouts. This prevents others from copying your work.

2.   Give constructive help, but do not give the answers away to others. (The Socratic method is the best way of giving help.)

3.   Share time on the system. Be punctual and give your time up when it is up; be fair.

4.   Do not use other students' disks, passwords, etc. Work only with what is assigned to you.

5.   Take proper care of equipment. No food, drinks, drugs around the machines. Do not take the system apart. Follow directions; use common sense.

6.   Do not disturb other learning situations.

7.   When you do not know what you are doing or have questions, ask a knowledgeable person for help. Do not guess when you do not know at all. (The last three are primarily for teachers.)

8.   Allow students to work on the computer outside class time. Be fair about time.

9.   Do not forget the computer is not just for your subject. Share it with others. Let the math teacher share with the physics teacher, and the physics teacher with the biology teacher, and so forth.

10. Share hardware, software, ideas and enthusiasm for computing.

SECTION III

COGNITIVE RESEARCH AND SOLVING PROBLEMS
USING THE COMPUTER

Cognitive research and its contribution to the design of computer literacy materials and the role of the computer in problem solving were presented by educational researchers. These papers highlight research implications and instructional expertise for computer literacy. Discussants with expertise in computer applications to instruction and cognitive psychology respectively shared their thoughts about the research, its' conduct, and findings. This section concludes with the summaries of Working Group II which focused on the developmental sequence of computer literacy for grades K-12.

CONTRIBUTIONS OF COGNITIVE SCIENCE AND RELATED
RESEARCH IN LEARNING TO THE DESIGN OF
COMPUTER LITERACY CURRICULA[1]

Richard E. Mayer

University of California at Santa Barbara

The goal of this paper is to examine techniques for
increasing the novice's understanding of computers and computer programming. In particular, this paper examines the
potential usefulness of five recommendations concerning the
design of computer literacy curricula, as listed below.

*1. Provide the learner with a concrete model of the
computer.*

*2. Encourage the learner to actively restate the new
technical information in his or her own words.*

*3. Assess the learner's existing intuitions about
computer operation and try to build on them, or modify them,
as needed.*

*4. Provide the learner with methods for chunking state-
ments into a larger, single, meaningful unit.*

*5. Provide the learner with methods for analyzing
statements into smaller, meaningful parts.*

For each recommendation, this paper will provide a clear
statement of the issue, an example, relevant background, and
a brief review of relevant research literature.

[1]*A more detailed version of this paper is available as a technical report from the author. Much of the work cited in this
paper was supported by grant SED77-19875 from the National
Science Foundation and grant NIE-G80-0118 from the National
Institute of Education.*

As can be seen, each recommendation is concerned with
increasing the meaningfulness of learning new computer information by novices. For purposes of the present paper, meaningful learning is viewed as a process in which the learner
connects new material with knowledge that already exists in
memory (Bransford, 1979). Figure 1 provides a general framework for discussing the conditions of meaningful learning
(Mayer, 1975, 1979a). This figure shows that information
enters the human cognitive system from the outside (e.g.,
through text or lectures, etc.), and must go through the following steps: (1) *Reception*. First, the learner must pay
attention to the incoming information so that it reaches working memory, as indicated by arrow "a." (2) *Availability*.
Second, the learner must possess appropriate prerequisite concepts in long-term memory to use in assimilating the new information, as indicated by point "b." (3) *Activation*. Finally, the learner must actively use this prerequisite knowledge
during learning so that the new material may be connected with
it, as indicated by arrow "c" from long-term memory to working
memory. Thus, in the course of meaningful learning, the
learner must come into contact with the new material (by
bringing it into working memory), then must search long-term
memory for what Ausubel (1968) called "appropriate anchoring
ideas," and then must transfer those ideas to working memory
so they can be combined with the new information in working
memory. Each recommendation is aimed at insuring one or more
of these conditions is met.

The traditional way of evaluating meaningful learning is
to test whether learners can transfer what they have learned
to new situations. For example, Wetheimer (1959) taught students how to find the area of a parallelogram using a rote
method (i.e., memorizing a formula) or a meaningful method
(i.e., involving the structure of the figure). Although both
groups performed equally well on problems like those given
during instruction, Wertheimer clained that the meaningful
learner were able to solve unusual problems requiring creative
transfer. Thus, this paper will focus on transfer as a
measure of meaningful learning of computer programming.

I.   USE CONCRETE MODELS

A.   *Statement of the Problem*

Novices tend to lack domain-specific knowledge (Greeno,
1980; Simon, 1980; Spilich, Vesonder, Chiesl and Voss, 1979).
Thus, one technique for improving the novice's understanding

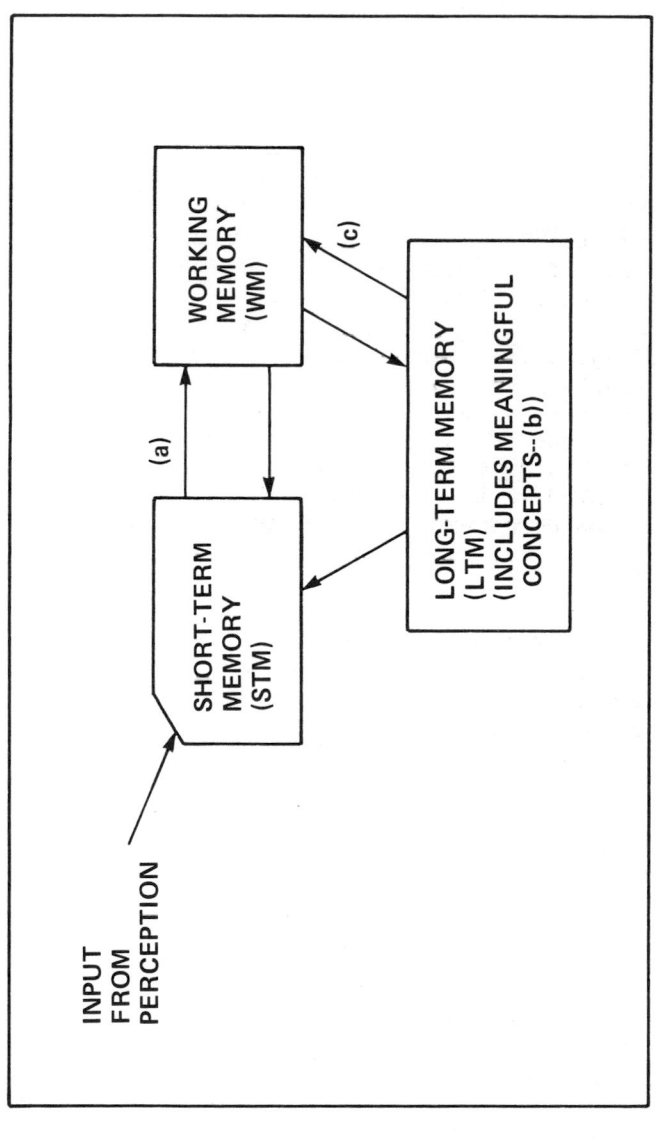

Figure 1: Some information processing components of meaningful learning. Condition (a) is transfer of new knowledge to WM. Condition (b) is availability of assimilative context in LTM. Condition (c) is activation and transfer of old knowledge to WM.

of new technical information is to provide them with a domain-
specific framework that can be used for assimilating new
information -- i.e., by allowing for "availability" as indicated by point "b" in Figure 1. The present section focuses
on the effects of concrete models on people's understanding of
computers and computer programming.

B. Example

     For example, in our own work on teaching a simple BASIC-
like language to novices, we presented a model of the computer
such as shown in Figure 2. This model provides concrete
analogies for four functional units of the computer: (1)
input is represented as a ticket window in which data is lined
up waiting to be processed and is placed in the finished pile
after being processed; (2) output is represented as a message
note pad with one message written per line; (3) memory is
represented as an erasable scoreboard in which there is natural destructive read-in but non-destructive read-out; and (4)
executive control is represented as a recipe or shopping list
with a pointer arrow to indicate the line being processed.
This model may be presented to the learner either as a diagram, or as an actual board containing these useable parts.

C. Background

     There is ample evidence that concrete models are widely
used in mathematics instruction. For example, early work by
Brownell and Moser (1949) indicated that children who learned
subtraction algorithms with the aid of "bundles of sticks"
were better able to transfer to new problems than children who
were given the rules for subtraction in abstract form with
plenty of "hands-on" experience in executing the procedures.
More recently, the important role of "manipulatives" such as
coins, sticks, blocks, etc., has been documented by Weaver and
Suydam (1972) and by Resnick and Ford (1980).

     There is also some evidence that concrete models may
enhance comprehension of text. For example, students' recall
of an ambiguous passage was enhanced when a title or diagram
or introductory sentence was given prior to reading but not
when given after reading (Bransford and Johnson, 1972; Dooling
and Lachman, 1971; Dooling and Mullet, 1973). Similarly,
Ausubel (1963, 1960, 1968) has provided some evidence that
expository learning may be enhanced by using an "advance
organizer" -- a short, expository introduction, presented
prior to the text, containing no specific content from the
text and providing a general framework for subsuming the
information in the text. More recent reviews of the advance

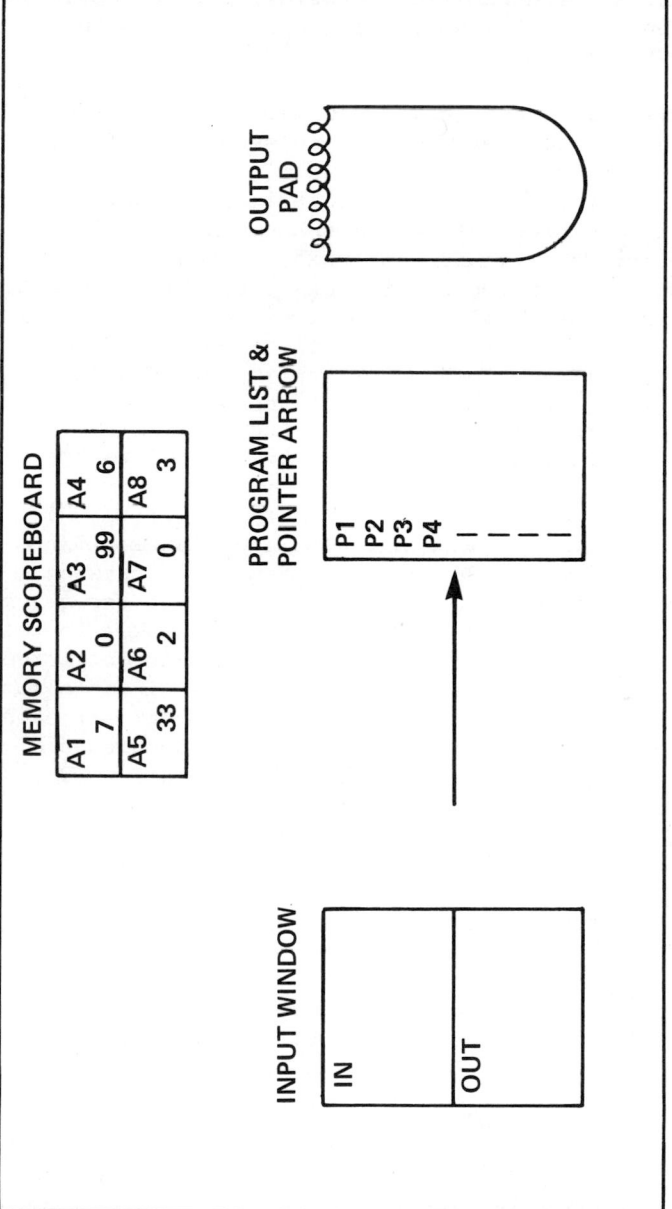

Figure 2: A concrete model of the computer for a BASIC-like language.

organizer literature reveal that advance organizers tend to
have their strongest effects in situations where learners are
unlikely to already possess useful prerequisite concepts --
namely, for technical or unfamiliar material, for low ability
subjects, and when the test involves transfer to new situations (Mayer, 1979a, 1979b).

Royer and his colleagues (Royer and Cable, 1975, 1976)
have demonstrated that concrete models may serve as effective
advance organizers in learning new scientific information.
For example, the concrete analogy of electrical conduction as
a chain of falling dominoes influenced subsequent learning.
Similarly, White and Mayer (1980) analyzed the concrete
models used by physics textbooks. For example, Ohm's Law is
described in terms of water flowing in pipes, a boy pushing a
heavy load up an inclined street, or an electron flow in a
circuit. Recent results by Cook and Mayer (1980) show that
when concrete analogies are embedded in a technical text,
novices tend to perform best on recalling these familiar
models and tend to recognize the information related to the
models.

DuBoulay and his colleagues (DuBoulay and O'Shea, 1976;
DuBoulay, O'Shea and Monk, 1980) have distinguished between
two approaches to learning computer programming. In the *black
box* approach, the operations of the computer are hidden to the
learner so that the learner has no idea of what goes on inside
the computer. In the *glass box* approach, the user is able to
understand the changes that occur inside the computer for each
statement. Although the description need not, indeed should
not, be on a machine language level, DuBoulay, et al. (1980)
suggest two properties for making the hidden operation of a
computer language more clear to the novice: (1) *simplicity* -
there should be a "small number of parts that interact in ways
that can be easily understood"; and (2) *visibility* - novices
should be able to "view selected parts and processes of this
notational machine in action." DuBoulay, et al. have implemented these suggestions in an instructional course in LOGO,
since each statement is related to a concrete model called
"the LOGO machine." However, there is yet no empirical test
concerning the effects of the LOGO machine on learning.

D. *Research of Concrete Models.*

1. *Transfer.* In order to provide some information concerning the role of models on learning computer programming, a
series of studies was conducted (Mayer, 1975). In the studies, subjects were either given a concrete model of the computer (such as shown in Figure 1, see pp. 131) or not; then,

all subjects read a 10 page manual describing seven BASIC-like
statements (see Table 1). Following reading, subjects took a

TABLE 1

SEVEN STATEMENTS USED IN BASIC-LIKE INSTRUCTIONAL BOOKLET

Name	Example
READ	P1 READ (A1)
WRITE	P2 WRITE (A1)
EQUALS	P3 A1 = 88
CALCULATE	P4 A1 = A1 + 12
GOTO	P6 GO TO P1
IF	P5 IF (A1 = 100) GO TO P9
STOP	P9 STOP

test that consisted of six types of problems (as shown in
Table 2). For "generate" problems, the subject had to write a
program; for "interpret" problems, the subject had to describe
what the program would do.

   The proportion correct response by type of problem is
given in the top of Table 3. As can be seen, the control
group performs well on problems that very much like the material in the instructional text, e.g., generate-statement and
generate-nonloop. However, on problems that require moderate
amounts of transfer -- e.g., generate-loop and the shorter
interpret problems; the model group excels. The difference in
the pattern of performance suggests that models enhance transfer performance but not simple retention of presented material. Apparently, the model provided an assimilative context
in which novices could relate new technical information in the
booklet to a familiar analogy. This assimilative process
resulted in a broader learning outcome that supported moderate
transfer.

TABLE 2

EXAMPLES OF SIX TYPES OF TEST PROBLEMS
FOR A BASIC-LIKE LANGUAGE

Generation-Statement

Given a number in memory
space A5, write a state-
ment to change that num-
ber to zero.

Interpretation-Statement

A5 = 0

Generation-Nonloop

Given a card with a num-
ber on it is input, write
a program to print out
its square.

Interpretation-Nonloop

P1 READ (A1)
P2 A1 = A1 * A1
P3 WRITE (A1)

Generation-Looping

Given a pile of data
cards is input, write
a program to print out
each number and stop
when it gets to card
with 88 on it.

Interpretation-Looping

P1 READ (A1)
P2 IF (A1 = 88) GO TO P5
P3 WRITE (A1)
P4 GO TO P1
P5 STOP

2. *Locus of the Effect.* One problem with the above
study is that the model subjects receive more information than
controls. Therefore, another series of studies was conducted
(Mayer, 1976a) in which all subjects read the same BASIC-like
manual, but some subjects were given the same model after
reading the manual.

The proportion correct response by type of problem for
the two groups is shown in the bottom of Table 3. As in the
previous study, the *before* group excels on creative transfer
to new situations but the *after* group excels on simple retention of the presented material. Thus, as predicted by assimi-
lation theory, the model serves as an assimilative context for
learning only if it is available to the learner at the time of
learning.

TABLE 3

PROPORTION CORRECT ON TRANSFER TEST BY TYPE OF PROBLEM FOR MODEL VS. CONTROL GROUPS AND BEFORE VS. AFTER GROUPS

	Generation			Interpretation		
	Statement	Nonloop	Looping	Statement	Nonloop	Looping
Model vs. Control						
Model	.63	.37	.30	.62	.62	.09
Control	.67	.52	.12	.42	.32	.12
Before vs. After						
Before	.57	.50	.20	.47	.63	.17
After	.77	.63	.13	.27	.40	.17

Note: For model vs. control, n = 20 per group; interaction between treatment and problem type, p ∨ .05.

For before vs. after, n = 20 per group; interaction between treatment and problem type, p ∨ .05.

3. Recall. The above studies used transfer tests as measures of what is learned under different instructional treatments. In a follow-up study (Mayer and Bromage, 1980), subjects read the manual and were given a concrete model of the computer either before or after the reading as in the previous study. However, as a test, subjects were asked to recall all they could about certain portions of the manual.

In order to score the protocols, the information in the manual was broken down into idea units. Each idea unit expressed one major idea or action. There were three kinds of idea units in the manual: (1) *conceptual* idea units related to the internal operation of the computer; (2) *technical* idea units gave examples of code; and (3) *format* idea units gave grammer rules. Table 4 gives examples of each type of idea unit.

Table 5 shows the average number of idea units recalled from each category by the two groups. As can be seen, the *before* group recalls more conceptual information while the *after* group excels on recall of technical and format information. This pattern is consistent with the idea that good retention requires recall of specific code, but good transfer requires understanding of conceptual ideas. Also, the before group included more intrusions about the model and other sections of the manual, suggesting they integrated the information more broadly.

4. Different Language. Although the above results are consistent and were obtained in a long series of studies, their generality is limited by the fact that just one type of language was used. Thus, a follow-up study was conducted (Mayer, 1980a) in which subjects learned a file management language (Gould and Ascher, 1974) either with or without a concrete model. Table 6 lists the eight statements that were described in the instructional manual. Figure 3 shows the concrete model that was used: long-term memory is represented as a file cabinet; the sorting function is represented as an in-basket, out-basket and save basket; temporary memory is represented as an erasable scoreboard; executive control is represented as a list of pointer arrows; output is represented as a message pad. After instruction, all subjects took a transfer test including simple retention-like problems (sort-1) and problems that required putting all of the learned commands together in a novel way (compute-1 and 2) (see Table 7).

TABLE 4

EXAMPLE OF CONCEPTUAL, FORMAT,
AND TECHNICAL IDEA UNITS

Type	*Idea Unit*
Technical	READ is one kind of statement.
Format	The format is READ ( ).
Format	An address name goes in the parenthesis.
Conceptual	An address name is a space in the computer's memory
Conceptual	There are 8 memory spaces.
Technical	The spaces are called A1, A2, . . .
Technical	An example is, READ (A2).
Conceptual	First, the computer checks the number from the top data card.
Conceptual	Then, that number is stored in space A2.
Conceptual	The previous number in A2 is destroyed.
Conceptual	Then the data card is sent out of the computer.
Conceptual	This reduces the pile of data card by 1.
Conceptual	Then, go on to the next statements.

Table 8 gives the proportion correct response by type of problem for the two treatment groups. As in the previous studies, the control group performs best on simple problems like those in the manual, but the model group excels on longer problems that require creative integration. Thus, previous results and conclusion seem to generalize to this new domain.

TABLE 5

AVERAGE NUMBER OF RECALLED IDEA UNITS FOR THE BEFORE AND AFTER GROUPS

| | Idea Units | | | Intrusions | | |
	Technical	Format	Conceptual	Inappropriate	Appropriate	Model
Before	5.0	1.9	6.6	1.5	1.3	3.1
After	6.0	2.9	4.9	2.5	.8	.5

Note: $N = 30$ per group; interaction between treatment and type of score, $p < .05$.

TABLE 6

EIGHT STATEMENTS USED IN FILE MANAGEMENT LANGUAGE BOOKLET

Name	*Example*
FROM	FROM *AUTOMOBILE*
FOR	FOR *WEIGHT* IS CALLED *3000 OR MORE*
AND FOR	AND FOR *COLOR* IS CALLED *GREEN*
OR FOR	OR FOR *MAKE* IS CALLED *FORD*
LIST	LIST *NAME*
COUNT	COUNT
TOTAL	TOTAL *CURRENT VALUE*
LET	LET *TOTAL* ÷ *COUNT* BE CALLED *AVERAGE*

5. *Ability*. The pattern of result described above tended to be strongest for low ability subjects (Mayer, 1975) were ability is defined in terms of mathematics SAT scores. Apparently, high ability learners already possessed their own useful "models" for thinking about how a computer works, but low ability students would be more likely to lack useful prerequisite knowledge.

6. *Text Organization*. The pattern of results described above also tended to be strongest when material was poorly organized (Mayer, 1978). Apparently, the model is more useful when material is poorly structured because it helps the reader to hold the information together.

7. *Evaluation*. These results provide clear and consistent evidence that a concrete analogical model can have a strong effect on the encoding of new technical information in novices. These results provide empirical support to the claims of DuBoulay and O'Shea (1976, 1978) that allowing novices to "see the works" allows them to encode information in a more coherent and useful way. When appropriate models are used, the learner seems to be able to assimilate each new statement to his or her image of the computer system. Thus,

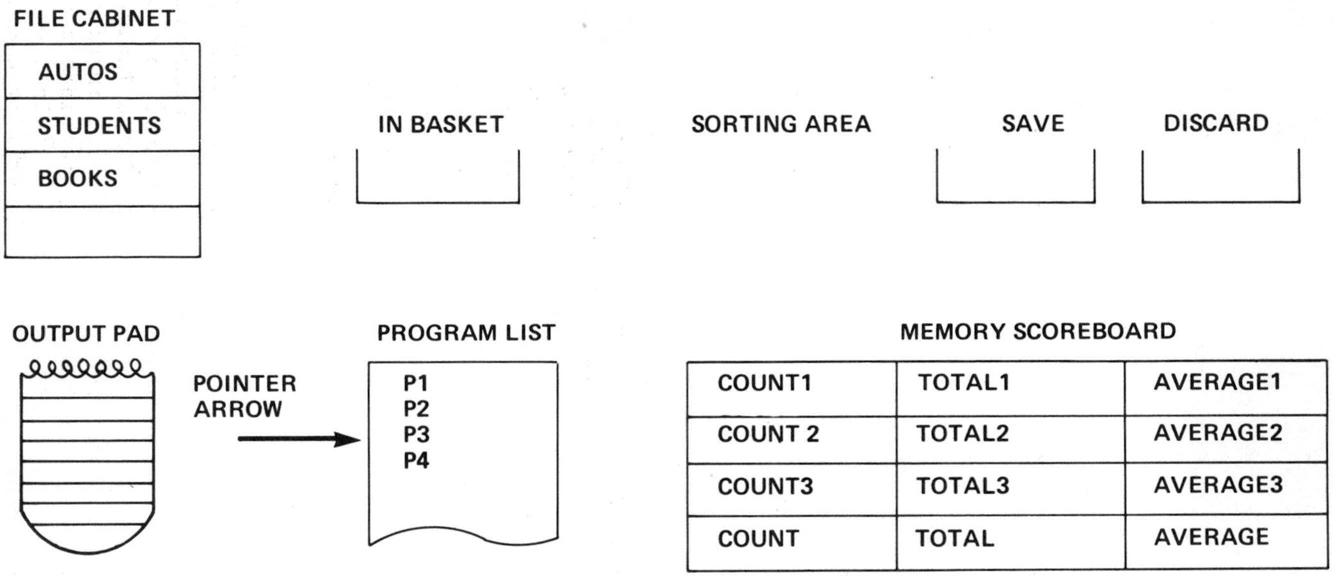

FILE CABINET

| AUTOS |
| STUDENTS |
| BOOKS |
| |

IN BASKET

SORTING AREA

SAVE

DISCARD

MEMORY SCOREBOARD

COUNT1	TOTAL1	AVERAGE1
COUNT 2	TOTAL2	AVERAGE2
COUNT3	TOTAL3	AVERAGE3
COUNT	TOTAL	AVERAGE

PROGRAM LIST

P1
P2
P3
P4

POINTER
ARROW

OUTPUT PAD

Figure 3. A concrete model of the computer for a file management language.

TABLE 7

EXAMPLES OF TEST PROBLEMS FOR A FILE MANAGEMENT LANGUAGE

Sort 1

List the owners' names for all cars weighing 3000 pounds or more.	FROM *AUTOMOBILE* FOR *WEIGHT* IS CALLED *3000 OR MORE* LIST *NAME*

Sort 2

List the owners' names for all late model green Fords.	FROM *AUTOMOBILE* FOR *YEAR* IS CALLED *1976 OR MORE* AND FOR *COLOR* IS CALLED *GREEN* AND FOR *MAKE* IS CALLED *FORD* LIST *NAME*

Count

How many cars are registered in Santa Barbara County?	FROM *AUTOMOBILE* FOR *HOME COUNTY* IS CALLED *SANTA BARBARA* COUNT LIST *COUNT*

Compute 1

What is the average current value of all cars?	FROM *AUTOMOBILE* COUNT TOTAL *CURRENT VALUE* LET *TOTAL* ÷ *COUNT* BE CALLED *AVERAGE* LIST *AVERAGE*

Compute 2

What percentage of 1977 cars are Chevrolets?	FROM *AUTOMOBILE* FOR *YEAR* IS CALLED *1977* COUNT LET THIS BE CALLED *COUNT 1* AND FOR *MAKE* IS CALLED *CHEVROLET* COUNT LET THIS BE CALLED *COUNT 2* LET *COUNT 2* ÷ *COUNT 1* BE CALLED *AVERAGE* LIST *AVERAGE*

TABLE 8

PROPORTION CORRECT ON TRANSFER TEST FOR MODEL
AND CONTROL GROUPS -- FILE MANAGEMENT LANGUAGE

Type of Test Problem

	Sort-1	Sort-2	Count	Computer-1	Computer-2
Model	.66	.66	.63	.58	.45
Control	.63	.44	.43	.33	.22

*Note. N = 20 per group; treatment x problem type interaction,
p < .07.*

one straightforward implication is: if your goal is to
produce learners who will not need to use the language crea-
tively, then no model is needed; if your goal is to produce
learners who will be able to come up with creative solutions
for novel problems, then a concrete model early in learning is
quite useful. More research is needed in order to determine
the specific effects of concrete models on what is learned,
and to determine the characteristics of a useful model.

II.   ENCOURAGE LEARNERS TO "PUT IT IN THEIR OWN WORDS"

A. *Statement of the Problem*

A second technique for increasing the meaningfulness of
technical information is *elaboration* -- encouraging the
learner to explain the information in his or her own words and
to verbally relate the material to other concepts or ideas.
Elaboration techniques may influence meaningful learning
because they encourage the activation of existing knowledge
that is relevant for comprehending the presented material --
i.e., elaboration may affect the activation process as indicated by the arrow "c" in Figure 1.

B.   *Example*

For example, in our own research, we have taught subjects a simple file management language as described in the previous section (see Tables 6 and 7). In order to encourage subjects to elaborate on the material, we presented questions after each page of the instructional booklet. Table 9 gives examples of "model elaboration questions" which ask the learner to

TABLE 9

EXAMPLE OF THE ELABORATION EXERCISE
IN THE PROGRAMMING TEXT

Model Elaboration

Consider the following situation. An office clerk has an in-basket, a save basket, a discard basket, and a sorting area on her desk. The in-basket is full of records. Each one can be examined individually in the sorting area of the desk and then placed in either the save or discard basket. Describe the FOR statement in terms of what operations the clerk would perform using the in-basket, discard basket, save basket, and sorting area.

Comparative Elaboration

How is the FOR command like the FROM command?

How is the FOR command different than the FROM command?

relate the material to a familiar context, and "comparative elaboration questions" which ask the learner to relate one part of the material to another.

C.   *Background*

There is some evidence that asking subjects to put ideas into their own words during learning can enhance their breadth of learning. For example, Gagne and Smith (1962) found that

subjects who were required to give a verbal rationalization
for each move as they learned to solve a new problem resulted
in longer learning time but better transfer performance than
nonverbalizers. Results by Seidel and Hunter (1970) suggest
that verbalization *per se* may not significantly enhance computer programming performance.

More recently, Wittrock (1974) has proposed the "generative hypothesis" -- i.e., learning occurs when the learner
actively generates associations between what is presented and
what he or she already has in memory. For example, when
school children were asked to generate a one-sentence summary
for each paragraph in a prose passage, Wittrock (1974) found
that recall was nearly double that of a control group. Apparently, when students are encouraged to actively put information in their own words, they are able to better connect new
information to existing knowledge.

Elaboration techniques have long been used to enhance
learning of paired associates. For example, when students are
asked to actively form images or sentences involving word
pairs, paired associate recall is greatly enhanced (Bower,
1972; Paivio, 1969). More recently, elaboration techniques
have been used in school curricula (Dansereau, 1978; Weinstein, 1978). Several researchers have argued that students
should be given explicit training in "learning strategies" --
i.e., how to actively process new material (O'Neil, 1978).

1. Transfer. In a typical study, (Mayer, 1980a) subjects read the instructional booklet covering a simple file
management language, with some subjects having an elaboration
page after each page in the booklet (model elaboration) and
others not (control). A second study followed the same procedure but there was a comparative elaboration page after each
page for half the subjects.

On a subsequent transfer test, using problems described
in Table 7, the control groups performed well on simple retention problems but the elaboration groups (both model and
comparative) perform better on problems requiring creative
transfer. Table 10 shows the proportion correct by type of
problem for four treatment groups. Thus, there is evidence
that requiring the learners to put technical information in
their own words through relating the material to a familiar
situation or through making comparisons, results in broader
learning.

TABLE 10

PROPORTION CORRECT ON TRANSFER TEST BY TYPE OF PROBLEM FOR
MODEL ELABORATION VS. CONTROL GROUPS AND
COMPARATIVE ELABORATION VS. CONTROL GROUPS

Type of Test Problem

	Sort 1	Sort 2	Count	Computer 1	Computer 2
Model vs. Control					
Model Elaboration	.65	.58	.64	.64	.45
Control	.66	.64	.41	.38	.27
Comparative Elaboration					
Comparative Elaboration	.90	.90	1.00	.75	.55
Control	.90	.90	.65	.65	.25

Note. *For model elaboration vs. control, n = 20 per group; treatment x problem type interaction, p ❮ .05. For comparative elaboration vs. control, n = 13 per group; treatment x problem type interaction, p ❮ .05.*

2. Recall. In order to access the generality of these
findings, the studies were replicated using recall as the test
(Mayer, 1980a). For scoring, the manual was divided into idea
units. Some idea units described how the computer operated
(conceptual idea units) and others emphasized the grammar and
technical aspects of each statement (technical idea units).
Table 11 shows the average number of idea units recalled by
type for model elaboration, comparison elaboration, and control groups. As can be seen, the control group tends to

TABLE 11

AVERAGE NUMBER OF RECALLED IDEA UNITS
FOR MODEL ELABORATION, COMPARATIVE ELABORATION
AND CONTROL GROUPS

	Type of Idea Units	
	Technical	*Conceptual*
Model Elaboration	5.3	13.9
Comparative Elaboration	9.4	14.1
Control	7.5	7.5

*Note. N = 20 per group; treatment x type interaction,
   p $<$ .05 for low ability.*

recall equal amounts of both types of information, but the
elaboration groups tend to emphasize recall of conceptual as
compared to technical information. This pattern is consistent
with the idea that conceptual emphasis is likely to support
transfer performance.

3. Notetaking. In order to provide further generality,
an additional series of studies was conducted (Peper and
Mayer, 1978) using a different language (a BASIC-like lang-
uage) and a different elaboration activity (note-taking).
Subjects watch a 20 minute videotape lecture describing seven
BASIC-like statements similar to the manual described earlier.

Some subjects were asked to take notes by putting the basic information in their own words. Others simply viewed the lecture without taking notes. As a test, some subjects were given transfer problems and some were asked to recall portions of the lesson.

As in previous studies, there was a pattern in which note-taking improved performance on transfer problems but not on simple retention problems. Similarly, there was a pattern in which note-takers performed better on recall of conceptual information but not technical information. These patterns were observed for subjects scoring low in mathematics SAT, but not for high ability subjects. Presumably high ability learners already possess strategies for putting new information into their own words.

4. Evaluation. Unfortunately, there is no fool-proof way to design elaboration activities. However, it is important to keep in mind that the goal of elaboration is to help the learner be able to describe the key concepts in his or her own words, using existing knowledge. Emphasis on format or grammatical details, and emphasis on errorless verbatim recall of statements will not produce the desired effects. The learner should be able to describe the effects of each statement in his or her own words.

III.   ASSESS AND BUILD ON LEARNERS' INTUITIONS

A. *Statement of the Problem*

Learners come to the learning situation with certain existing expectations and intuitions about how to interact with computers. For example, since students have experience with conversations in English, they are likely to try to view computer conversations in the same way (Miller and Thomas, 1977; Sackman, 1970). Similarly, since most users are familiar with calculators, they may view interactions with computers in the same way (Mayer and Bayman, 1980; Young, 1980).

B. *Example*

For most users, calculators represent the first exposure to interacting with a computational machine. Thus, intuitions that are established may be important for later learning of

computer programming languages. For example, consider the
keystrokes:

    7 + =

If subjects have a conception of incrementing internal regis-
ters, they might suppose that this sequence would result in 14
being displayed. However, less sophisticated intuitions might
predict that the display would show 7 or 0.

C. Background

There is a growing interest in using words and logical
structures that are similar to everyday English. For example,
Ledgard, Whiteside, Singer and Seymour (1980) found that text
editing systems that use "natural language" are easier to
learn than those that use "computerese" for commands. Similarly, Shneiderman (1980) reports that meaningful or mnemonic
variable names may affect programming performance. Finally,
there is evidence that branching structures used in BASIC are
not as intuitive or as easy to learn as other branching structures (Green, 1977; Mayer, 1976b; Sime, Green and Guest, 1977;
Sime, Arblaster and Green, 1977).

More recently, Young (1980) has developed "mental models"
of calculators -- i.e., representations of the internal components that a learner needs to understand. Scandura, Lowerre
and Veneski (1976) have interviewed children who learned to
use calculators through "hands-on experience." Many develop
bizarre intuitions even though they can use the calculator to
solve routine problems. Thus, in order to build on the learners' intuitions, and modify them as needed, one must assess
what those intuitions are. In other words, the instructor
should have techniques for determining the learner's "mental
model."

D. Analysis of Users' Intuitions of Calculator Operations

A series of studies was conducted (Mayer and Bayman,
1980) in order to determine the intuitions that novice and
expert users have concerning how pocket calculators operate.
The novices were college students with no experience with
computers or computer programming, while the experts were
intermediate-level computer science students. Each subject
was given a 4-page questionnaire with 88 problems. Each
problem listed a series of key presses and asked the student
to predict what number would be in the display, assuming a
standard four-function calculator was being used.

The subjects differed greatly with respect to when they thought an expression should be evaluated. For example, consider the problems,

2 + 3

2 + 3 +

2 + 3 + 7

2 + 3 + 7 =

Some subjects behaved as if an expression was evaluated only when an equals was pressed; thus, the answers were 3, 3, 7, 12. Others behaved as if an expression was evaluated as soon as an operator key was pressed, yielding answers of 3, 5, 7, 12. Finally, some subjects behaved as if an expression was evaluated as soon as a number was pressed, giving answers of 5, 5, 12, 12. Results indicated significant differences between experts and novices, with most experts opting for second approach while novices were fairly split among all three approaches. There also were important differences concerning how to evaluate a chain of arithmetic such as 2 + 3 x 7 =, and how to handle non-standard sequences such as 2 + = + =.

1. Evaluation. We are just beginning to develop techniques for describing users' intuitions, e.g., users' mental models of computational machines. However, as techniques become available, teachers may use them to diagnose whether students have acquired useful intuitions, and to remediate where needed.

IV. PROVIDE TRAINING IN CHUNKING

A. *Statement of the Problem*

One technique for making storage of information easier is to form meaningful chunks of schemas (Bransford, 1979). Within the context of computer programming, this means that learners should develop the ability to view a cluster of statements as a single unit that accomplishes some nameable goal.

B.   Example

For example, Atwood and Ramsey (1978) suggest that
experienced programmers encode a segment such as,

SUM = 0

DO 1 1 = 1, N

   SUM = SUM + (1)

1 CONTINUE

as "CALCULATE THE SUM OF ARRAY X."

C.   Background

There is some evidence that experts and novices in a
particular domain differ with respect to how they organize
information in memory, with experts using more efficient
chunking techniques (Larkin, McDermott, Simon and Simon,
1980). In recent reviews of research on how to teach people
to become better problem solvers, Greeno (1980) and Simon
(1980) conclude that good problem solving performance requires
that the user has large amounts of domain-specific knowledge
organized into chunks. For example, Simon (1980) estimates
that a person needs 50,000 chunks of domain-specific knowledge
(e.g., such as the example given above) to become an expert.

In a classic study, Chase and Simon (1973) asked subjects
to view briefly presented chess board configurations and
then try to reconstruct them. Chess masters performed better
than less experienced players in reconstructing positions from
actual games, but the advantage was lost when random board
positions were presented. In an analogous study reported by
Shneiderman (1980), experienced and inexperienced programmers
were given programs to study. The experts remembered more
than the novices when actual programs were presented but not
for random lines of code. These findings suggest that experts
have a large repertoire of many meaningful chunks, i.e., ways
of grouping many lines of code into a single meaningful unit.
More recently, Mayer (1979c, 1980b) has suggested that highly
used chunks, such as looping structures, should be explicitly
taught and labeled as part of instruction. For example,
frequent looping structures in BASIC include "repeating a
READ," "waiting for a data number," "waiting for a counter,"
and "branching down."

V.   PROVIDING TRAINING IN ANALYSIS OF STATEMENTS

A.   *Statement of the Problem*

What does it mean to "understand" a statement? In many psycholinguistic theories, comprehension involves relating a statement to its underlying case grammar (see Kintsch, 1974).

B.   *Example*

In a previous paper (Mayer, 1979c), I have suggested a possible case grammar for BASIC. Each statement may be described as a list of transactions. A transaction consists of an action applied to some object at some location in the computer. For example, the statement, LET X = 5, consists of six transactions.

   1.   *Find the number indicated on the right of the equals.*

   2.   *Find the number in the memory space indicated on the left of the equals.*

   3.   *Erase the number in that memory space.*

   4.   *Write the new number in that space.*

   5.   *Go on to the next statement.*

   6.   *Do what it says.*

C.   *Background*

An implication of the "transaction" approach is that the same statement names may actually refer to several different types of transactions. For example, we have shown that a counter set LET such as LET X = 5 is different from an arithmetic LET such as LET X = 10/2 (Mayer, 1979c, 1980c). Explicit naming and describing of different types of statements with the same keyword may become a useful part of computer literacy curricula. More recently, this approach has been successfully applied to the analysis of commands in "calculator language" (Mayer and Bayman, 1980) and text editor languages (Card, Moran and Newell, 1980).

VI.   CONCLUSION

This paper has provided five tentative recommendations, listed in the introduction, for increasing the meaningfulness of computer concepts for novices. Reviews of cognitive research indicate that there is qualified support for the first two recommendations, and that active research is needed concerning the latter three recommendations.

REFERENCES

Atwood, M.E. and Ramsey, H.R. (1978). "Cognitive Structure in the Comprehension and Memory of Computer Programs: An Investigation of Computer Programming Debugging." ARI Technical Report TR-78-A210. Englewood, CO: Science Applications, Inc., August.

Ausubel, D.P. (1960). "The Use of Advance Organizers in the Learning and Retention of Meaningful Verbal Material," *Journal of Educational Psychology,* Vol. 51, pp. 267-272.

Ausubel, D.P. (1963). *The Psychology of Meaningful Verbal Learning.* New York: Gruene and Stratton.

Ausubel, D.P. (1968). *Educational Psychology: A Cognitive View.* New York: Holt, Rinehart & Winston.

Bower, G.H. (1972). "Mental Imagery and Associative Learning," in L. Gregg (Ed.) *Cognition in Learning and Memory.* New York: John Wiley & Sons, Inc.

Bransford, J.D. (1979). *Human Cognition.* Monterey, CA: Wadsworth.

Bransford, J.D. and Johnson, M.K. (1972). "Contextual Prerequisites for Understanding: Some Investigations of Comprehension and Recall," *Journal of Verbal Learning and Verbal Behavior,* Vol. 11, pp. 717-726.

Brownell, W.A. and Moser, H.E. (1949). "Meaningful vs. Mechanical Learning: A Study in Grade III Subtraction. In *Duke University Research Stuties in Education, No. 8,* Durham, NC: Duke University Press, pp. 1-207.

Card, S.K., Moran, T.P., and Newell, A. (1980). "Computer Textediting: An Information Processing Analysis of a Routine Cognitive Skill, *Cognitive Psychology,* Vol. 12, pp. 32-74.

Chase, W.G. and Simon, H.A. (1973). "Perception in Chess," *Cognitive Psychology,* Vol 4, pp. 55-81.

Cook, L. and Mayer, R.E. (1980). "Effects in Shadowing on Prose Comprehension and Problem Solving," *Memory and Cognition,* Vol. 8, in press.

Dansereau, D. (1978). "The Development of a Learning Strategies Curriculum," in H.F. O'Neil, Jr. (Ed.), *Learning Strategies,* New York: Academic Press.

Dooling, D.J. and Lachman, R. (1971). "Effects of Comprehension on the Retention of Prose," *Journal of Experimental Psychology,* Vol. 88, pp. 216-222.

du Boulay, B. and O'Shea, T. (1976). *How to Work the LOGO Machine,* Edinburgh: Department of Artificial Intelligence, Paper No. 4.

du Boulay, B., O'Shea, T., and Monk, J. (1980). *The Black Box Inside the Glass Box: Presenting Computering Concepts to Novices,* Edinburgh: Department of Artificial Intelligence, Paper No. 133.

Gagne, R.M. and Smith, E.C. (1962). "A Study of the Effects of Verbalization on Problem Solving," *Journal of Experimental Psychology,* Vol. 63, pp. 12-18.

Gould, J.D. and Ascher, R.M. (1974). "Query by Non-Programmers," *Paper presented at American Psychological Association.*

Green, T.R.G. (1977). "Conditional Program Statements and their Comprehensibility to Professional Programmers," *Journal of Occupational Psychology,* Vol. 50, pp. 93-109.

Green, T.R.G. and Arblaster, A.T. (1980). "As You'd Like It: Contributions to Easier Computing," U.K.: MRC Social and Applied Psychology Unit, Memo No. 373.

Greeno, J.G. (1980). "Trends in the Theory of Knowledge for Problem Solving," in D.T. Tuma and F. Reif (Eds.) *Problem Solving and Education: Issues in Teaching and Research,* Hillsdale, NJ: Erlbaum.

Holtzman, T.G. and Glaser, R. (1977). "Developing Computer
    Literacy in Children: Some Observations and Suggestions,"
    Educational Technology, Vol. 17, No. 8, pp. 5-11.

Kintsch, W. (1974). *The Representation of Meaning in Memory,*
    Hillsdale, NJ: Erlbaum.

Larkin, J., McDermott, J., Simon, D. and Simon, H.A. (1980).
    "Expert and Novice Performance in Solving Physics Prob-
    lems," *Science,* Vol. 208, pp. 1335-1342.

Ledgard, H., Whiteside, J., Singer, A., and Seymour, W. (1980).
    "The Natural Language of Interactive Systems," *Communi-
    cations of the ACM,* Vol. 23, in press.

Mayer, R.E. (1975). "Different Problem-Solving Competencies
    Established in Learning Computer Programming With and
    Without Meaningful Models," *Journal of Educational Psy-
    chology,* Vol. 67, pp. 725-734.

Mayer, R.E. (1976a). "Some Conditions of Meaningful Learning
    for Computer Programming: Advance Organizers and Subject
    Control of Frame Order," *Journal of Educational Psychol-
    ogy,* pp. 143-150.

Mayer, R.E. (1976b). "Comprehension as Affected by the Struc-
    ture of Problem Representation," *Memory and Cognition,*
    Vol. 4, pp. 249-255.

Mayer, R.E. (1977). "Different Rule Systems for Counting Be-
    havior Acquired in Meaningful and Rote Contexts of Learn-
    ing," *Journal of Educational Psychology,* Vol. 69, pp.
    537-546.

Mayer, R.E. (1978). "Advance Organizers that Compensate for
    the Organization of Text," *Journal of Educational Psy-
    chology,* Vol. 70, pp. 880-886.

Mayer, R.E. (1979a). "Can Advance Organizers Influence Mean-
    ingful Learning?" *Review of Educational Research,* Vol.
    49, pp. 371-383.

Mayer, R.E. (1979b). "Twenty Years of Research on Advance
    Organizers: Assimilation Theory is Still the Best Pre-
    dictor of Results," *Instructional Science,* Vol. 8, pp.
    133-167.

Mayer, R.E. (1979c). "A Psychology of Learning BASIC," *Communications of the ACM,* Vol. 22, pp. 589-594.

Mayer, R.E. (1980a). "Elaboration Techniques for Technical Text: An Experimental Test of the Learning Strategy Hypothesis," *Journal of Educational Psychology,* Vol. 72, in press.

Mayer, R.E. (1980b). *Ten Statements Spiral BASIC: From Calculator to Computer.* Encino, CA: Glenco Publishing Co.

Mayer, R.E. and Bayman, P. (1980). "An Information Processing Analysis of Users' Knowledge of Electron Calculators," Technical Report No. 80-1, University of California, Santa Barbara: Department of Psychology.

Mayer, R.E. and Bromage, B. (1980). "Different Recall Protocols for Technical Text Due to Sequencing of Advance Organizers," *Journal of Educational Psychology,* Vol. 72, in press.

Mayer, R.E., Larkin, J.H., and Kadane, J. (1980). "Analysis of the Skill of Solving Equations," *Paper presented at the Psychonomic Society.*

Miller, L.A. and Thomas J.C. (1977). "Behavioral Issues in the Use of Interactive Systems," *International Journal of Man-Machine Studies,* Vol. 9, pp. 509-536.

O'Neil, H.F. (1978). *Learning Strategies,* New York: Academic Press.

Paivio, A. (1969). "Mental Imagery in Associative Learning and Memory," *Psychological Review*, Vol. 76, pp. 241-263.

Peper, R.J. and Mayer, R.E. (1978). "Note Taking as a Generative Activity," *Journal of Educational Psychology,* Vol. 70, pp. 514-522.

Resnick, L.B. and Ford, S. (1980). *The Psychology of Mathematics Learning.* Hillsdale, NJ: Erlbaum.

Royer, J.M. and Cable, G.W. (1975). "Facilitated Learning in Connected Discourse," *Journal of Educational Psychology,* Vol. 67, pp. 116-123.

Royer, J.M. and Cable, G.W. (1976). "Illustrations, Analo-
    gies, and Facilitative Transfer in Prose Learning,"
    Journal of Educational Psychology, Vol. 68, pp. 205-209.

Sackman, H. (1970). "Experimental Analysis of Man-Computer
    Problem-Solving," *Human Factors,* Vol. 12, pp. 187-201.

Scandura, A.M., Lowerre, G.F., Veneski, J., and Scandura, J.M.
    (1976). "Using Electronic Calculators with Elementary
    School Children," *Educational Technology,* Vol. 16, No. 8,
    pp. 14-18.

Seidel, R.J. and Hunter, H.G. (1970). "The Application of
    Theoretical Factors in Teaching Problem-Solving in Pro-
    grammed Instruction," *International Review of Applied
    Psychology,* Vol. 19, pp. 41-81.

Shneiderman, B. (1980). *Software Psychology: Human Factors
    in Computer and Information Systems.* New York: Winthrop.

Sime, M.E., Arblaster, A.A. and Green, T.R.G. (1979). "Reduc-
    ing Programming Errors in Nested Conditionals by Pre-
    scribing a Writing Procedure," *International Journal of
    Man-Machine Studies,* Vol. 9, pp. 107-118.

Simon, H.A. (1980). "Problem Solving and Education," in D.T.
    Tuma and F. Reif (Eds.) *Problem Solving and Education:
    Issues in Teaching and Research,* Hillsdale, NJ: Erlbaum.

Spilich, G.J., Vesonder, G.T., Chiesi, H.L., and Voss, J.F.
    (1980). "Text Processing of Domain-Related Information
    for Individuals with High and Low Domain Knowledge,"
    Journal of Verbal Learning and Verbal Behavior, Vol. 18,
    pp. 275-290.

Weaver, F. and Suydam, M. (1972). "Meaningful Instruction in
    Mathematics Education," *Mathematics Education Reports.*

Weinstein, C. (1978). "Elaboration Skills as a Learning Stra-
    tegy," in H.F. O'Neil (Ed.) *Learning Strategies,* New
    York: Academic Press.

Wertheimer, M. (1978). *Productive Thinking.* New York: Har-
    per & Row.

White, R.T. and Mayer, R.E. (1980). "Understanding Intellec-
    tual Skills," *Instruction Science,* Vol. 9, pp. 101-127.

Wittrock, M.C. (1974).   "Learning as a Generative Process,"
     Educational Psychologist, Vol. 11, pp. 87-95.

Young, R.M. (1980).   "Surrogates and Mappings: Two Kinds of
     Conceptual Models for Pocket Calculators," *Paper pre-
     sented at conference on Mental Models,* La Jolla, CA.

DISCUSSANT REMARKS

John Seely Brown

Xerox Palo Alto Research Center

SUMMARY

- *Mental models of how complex (computer) systems work are important to teaching a set of procedures for using the systems.*

- *Mental models of a system plus a set of guessing strategies provide the user a sense of control over the technology.*

- *It is essential that computer systems be designed to be forgiving thereby encouraging users to experiment with it and thereby expand their understanding of the system.*

- *Cognitive science can help us refine and exploit formative evaluations of a system.*

- *Psychological experiments help raise issues, not necessarily settle them.*

- *We need to attempt to create metaphors for a construct of a computer language that match the learners' experience and the particular intellectual construct to be learned. Attempts to prove that language A is inherently more learnable than language B, where A and B are syntactically incomparable, are probably misguided since the availability of appropriate metaphors swamp other considerations.*

John Seely Brown

NARRATIVE

I want to broaden the scope of cognitive science beyond
the issues addressed in Mayer's paper. I have three basic
topics: the why, the how, and some of the mind-bugs of using
cognitive science that follow-up on some of the ideas expressed
in Mayer's paper. The main topic that is of interest to both
of us is the role of creating mechanistic mental models of how
computer systems work or, more generally, how complex mechanistic systems work. I can't tell you with any kind of preci-
sion what a mental model really is or why such models seem to
enhance our understanding. Yet, we do know that they are kind
of a neat thing to have and we all feel that we understand
computer systems by somehow envisioning, at some procedural
level, how they do function. To the casual user, these
mental models enable his/her procedural skills for using a
piece of equipment or computer subsystem to become more robust
thereby helping him/her to handle a wider variety of unusual
circumstances or "casualties." Furthermore, these mental
models play a crucial role in allowing the casual user to
reconstruct the procedural skills s/he had previously mastered
while using a given system or performing a given task. This
ability to reconstruct partially forgotten procedural skills
is especially important for the mathematical or computational
skills that we so laboriously teach school children -- skills
that often go unused for long periods of time given the near
omnipresence of handheld calculators.

Let us elaborate on the above point. In a somewhat over
simplified fashion, we claim that the back-to-basics movement
has focused on drilling into students rote, computational
procedures. By and large, these procedures have been designed
to optimize *computational efficiency* often at the cost of
semantic transparency. That this is so is not too surprising
since there is no well developed theory of what makes one
procedure more semantically transparent than another procedure. The more semantically transparent the procedure is, the

better chance there is that one can reconstruct it when parts
of it have been forgotten through lack of use. So, for various systems -- be they mathematical, office or machine related
systems -- it is likely that if we had a theory of how to
construct semantic models for requisite procedural skills, we
could use these models to help reconstruct the knowledge about
how to use the particular system at hand.

Now how do semantic or mental models relate to the crucial issues of computer literacy? I believe that one of the
most important issues in computer literacy has to do with
providing everyone a sense of control over the technology at
the user's disposal. The unexpected always happens when using
a piece of high technology. If the user feels that the only
way to cope with that unexpected situation is to reach for the
system's manual and do a rote scan on how to circumvent that
situation, you can be sure that after a while, the user is
going to end up resenting that system. His/her constantly
needing to search for and apply some rote method to get out
of his/her current jam or to ask for help leaves the user feeling that s/he is not in control. One way to try and get
around this is to try to provide the user some kind of a
mental model of how the system works, plus a set of *guessing
strategies* on how to handle this new, bizarre situation.
However, in order to exploit the user of such mental models
and associated guessing strategies, we must make very sure the
computer system itself is very forgiving. That is, the system
should encourage users to experiment by guaranteeing that
anything a user does can necessarily be *undone*. Almost no
system on the market today has that property.

How might cognitive science actually be of some help in
our being able to build more "friendly" and useful high technology systems? For one, it might encourage us to focus our
attention not on the standard evaluation of systems, but
rather on formative evaluations. In particular, we must come
to terms with the fact that technology is moving ahead so fast
that our own intuitions about how people will use and respond
to novel, complex systems are really shot. One way around
this dilemma is to build, in a quick and dirty fashion, a
prototype of the intended system and put it in the field and
evaluate it. But this evaluation must go beyond just determining if the system wins or loses. It must determine why
those parts of the system that win actually win and vice
versa. Determining the whys rather than just the whats is
often, however, a tricky business. The AI/cognitive science
fields provide us some tools for this task. For example, we
now have tools for protocol analysis that enable us to look at
a user's responses and try to uncover much of the tacit knowl-

edge that s/he uses in successfully performing the task. One
of the things that we are finding out is that most of what
constitutes expertise is not what we *think*. Expertise rather,
has a tremendous tacit component to it that has been experi-
mentally learned and is difficult to formalize within the current meta-languages used to describe domain expertise.

Here are some potential mind bugs that are apt to arise
when researchers try to use cognitive science in this kind of
arena. First, I caution us all against the belief that experiments, no matter how well conducted, settle issues; they
don't. They help to raise issues, not necessarily settle
them. For example, all that one experiment on the pedagogical
effectiveness of simulations really shows, if anything, is
that we may or may not be very good at creating semantically
meaningful simulation models. Thus, we must be cautious at
over-interpreting some of the experimental results in Mayer's
paper.

One other point is that there are going to be a lot of
experiments coming along which try to show that language X is
better than language Y; system X is better than system Y.
This is an extraordinarily complex type of question. The
simple reasons why it is complex -- and we should keep these
in mind -- are that the quality of a language, the learnabil-
ity of a language, often have to do with, speaking metaphori-
cally, how the important constructs of that language have an
"impedance match" with the learner's head. It turns out that
if you look at a language like LOGO, on the one hand, it can
look very hard to learn. On the other hand, we can create
certain types of metaphors to explain the critical intellectual constructs of that language that map it onto, in a very
easy way, a learner's experience. In fact, we can create
metaphors for teaching recursion that make it seem more transparent than iteration. So, it is not really a question of
whether iteration is easier or harder to learn than recursion.
It is often a question of: Can we create metaphors for a
construct language that makes those metaphors have impact for
that particular learner on this particular intellectual construct?

At Xerox, we have a language called SMALLTALK. It is
very hard to learn at one level and another level is very easy
to learn. This is because it is based on a set of metaphors
which learners understand a lot easier than other types of
metaphors for standard procedural type languages. It has to
do with *message passing*. Students can understand how they can
be a member of a society of agents (people) and how they pass
messages off to each other. In some sense, that metaphor

makes understanding that important construct much easier than the function-calling construct found in most standard computer languages. This is not to say one language is better than another, but if we want to evaluate these things, we have to look at what are the supporting metaphors for those languages.

DISCUSSANT REMARKS

Joseph Lipson

National Science Foundation

SUMMARY

- *Working theoretical models for interpreting Mayer's data, and his and others' future studies is needed.*

- *We need to examine individual results to help us gain deeper insight into the learning process.*

- *The variable of emotion should receive greater attention in studies of computer-based education and an algorithm for determining which signals we will attend is needed.*

- *The creation of a theoretical model with a more comprehensive view of key variables and the way learning interacts with our whole life is strongly urged.*

Joseph Lipson

NARRATIVE

I would like to take this opportunity to mention that the National Science Foundation is supporting a variety of computer literacy projects and we would like to encourage more proposals in this area. Examples of relevant projects are:

1. *Computertown, USA -- Bringing Computer Literacy to the Entire Community.* Ramon M. Zamora, Principal Investigator, People's Computer Company, Menlo Park, CA;

2. *Interest Worlds: Precollege Mathematics in a Computer Culture.* Seymour A. Papert, Principal Investigator, MIT, Cambridge, MA; and

3. *High School Computer Science Education.* J.M. Moshell, University of Tennessee, Knoxville, TN.

These examples are in addition to the NSF support of projects conducted by HumRRO and MECC, the sponsors of this conference.

Throughout this conference it has been clear that the concept of computer literacy is evolving and no consensus definition exists at this time among the participants of the conference. This result is not unexpected. It takes time for the dimensions of a new idea to be agreed upon by a community of people.

The comments I am about to make in no way imply a lack of admiration and respect for the work of Dr. Mayer. I have long been a fan of his and believe that he has added significantly to our understanding of science learning. He has also made important methodological contributions to research in science education. Having said this let me engage my task of finding something to worry about. A concern I have with Dr. Mayer's

paper is that I cannot find any deep theoretical structure
behind it. My intuition is that, between the neurological
level and the ideas we use in teaching, there may be many
levels of representation that we must, like archaeologists,
dig through before we understand human learning. Thus, I
would like to see a kind of working theoretical model for
interpreting Dr. Mayer's data, and to guide his and others'
future studies.

Another issue is the way data are gathered and presented.
An examination of anomolous cases that go against the trend
may help us to gain deeper insight into the learning process.
The data presented by Dr. Mayer are group data. I advocate
looking beyond the aggregated data to examine individual results that may call into question our theories and explanations. For example, were there people who got the rote treatment but who, in fact, did very well on the transfer task?
Were there people who were given training to promote transfer
who, in fact, got worse in transfer? If unusual cases can be
found, what is the explanation for them?

Often in educational studies we arrive at results of no
significant difference. This may mean that we were not at-
tending to the correct variables, or that we weren't using the
correct model. For example, the University of Mid-America
conducted a number of studies comparing correspondence teaching *with* open broadcast television and correspondence teaching
without open broadcast television. The average grades of
those who completed the courses were about the same. However,
the *completion rate* for those who had access to television was
about double that of those who did not have access to television! Thus, if only scores on final exams had been measured,
a very strong effect with profound implications for distance
teaching would have been missing.

A variable that I propose for greater attention in studies of computer-based education is that of emotion in learning. I propose that it is almost impossible to learn without
some affective response. We are all bombarded by more signals
than we can process. Therefore, we need some mechanism, an
algorithm, for determining which signals we will attend. Our
emotional response to a stimulus is one of the three factors:
(1) direct sensory input; (2) memories triggered by a stimulus; and (3) emotional states that influences to what one pays
attention, what one remembers and, presumably, what one does.
Along this line, I recommend a study by Thomas Malone on what
makes things intrinsically interesting, what makes computer
games fun (Malone, 1980).

The final point to consider in studies such as the one conducted by Dr. Mayer is the following: A student will study differently depending upon what s/he envisions or anticipates as the outcomes. For example, if there is going to be a test, what makes a difference is the person's vision of the test. If the person expects a multiple-choice test s/he will prepare differently than if s/he expects an essay or open-ended problem test. It will make a difference, I would predict, if the person expects to have to make an oral explanation and presentation before an audience. And, if there is some intended personal use of the knowledge and skills being learned, what is the student's vision of that intended personal use?

The overall message that I am trying to suggest is that our model of instruction and learning may be too narrow. I advocate a theoretical model with a more comprehensive view of the variables that come into play and the way that learning interacts with our vision of life as a whole.

REFERENCES

Malone, T.W. (1980). *What makes things fun to learn? A Study of Intrinsically Motivating Computer Games;* Cognitive and Instructional Sciences Series, CIS 7 (SSL-80-11); Xerox Palo Alto Research Center, Cognitive and Instructional Sciences Group, Palo Alto, CA 94304; August 1980.

DOES COMPUTER PROGRAMMING ENHANCE PROBLEM SOLVING ABILITY?
SOME POSITIVE EVIDENCE ON ALGEBRA WORD PROBLEMS[1]

Elliot Soloway

Department of Computer and Information Science
University of Massachusetts at Amherst

Jack Lochhead
John Clement

Department of Physics and Astronomy
University of Massachusetts at Amherst

I. INTRODUCTION

There is a common intuition among those in computer science education that programming encourages the development of
good problem solving skills. Papert (1971) and the LOGO project were early proponents of this view; they developed a
method to teach geometry by way of computer programming. Underlying their view is a recognition of the importance of
"doing," of activity, and of procedure. Educators from Dewey
to Piaget have emphasized that students need to take an
active role in order to understand a concept.

This pedagogical intuition needs to be investigated
empirically so it can be articulated more precisely. A step
in that direction was made recently by Howe, O'Shea, and Plane
(1979) in a series of experiments based on the following

[1] This research was supported in part by NSF Grant SED 78-22043
in the Joint National Institute of Education -- National
Science Foundation Program of Research on Cognitive Processes
and the Structure of Knowledge in Science and Mathematics.
This research was also supported in part by a grant from the
U.S. Army Research Institute for the Behavioral and Social
Sciences, ARI Grant No. DHC-19-77-G-0012.

paradigm: a course in mathematics was taught in the standard way without incorporating computer programming, and simultaneously, the same course was taught with computer programming. Students' mastery of the subject matter was then compared across the two groups. In such experiments Howe et al. obtained a consistent effect in favor of computer programming.

The above work might be characterized as experiments on the "macro" level; in contrast, the work reported here was focussed on the "micro" level. That is, we have attempted to develop *tools* which would enable us to isolate specific, critical factors contributing to the above results. Rather than studying an entire course, we have focussed on single problems. Results concerning the surprisingly poor performance of college students on two ostensibly simple algebra word problems are presented in Section II. These results suggest several hypotheses. One is that errors resulted from the students' failure to give a *procedural* interpretation to the algebraic equation. A second set of experimental results (see Section VI) provides significant, new support for this hypothesis. Namely, students do significantly better on certain algebra word problems when they occur in a traditional, algebraic (non-programming) context. Based on analyses of group test data, and on video-taped student interview data, we suggest several factors involved in programming which could account for the way in which this activity fosters a more active interpretation of algebra by students. We conclude this paper with a discussion of the implications of this work for education.

II. EXPERIMENTS WITH WORD PROBLEMS IN A TRADITIONAL ALGEBRAIC SETTING

In a previous study, Clement, Lochhead, and Monk (1980) uncovered several types of ostensibly simple problems which gave students great difficulty. In Table 1 we list two of of these problems and typical performance results. Among engineering students, 37% missed the first problem while 73% missed the second! In their experiments, Clement, Lochhead and Monk (1980) were able to eliminate algebraic manipulation and "tricky wording" as sources for the errors.

The errors made on problems 1 and 2 were largely of one kind: most were "reversals": $6S = P$ instead of $S = 6P$ and $4C = 5S$ instead of $5C = 4S$. The consistency of these error

TABLE I

Problem 1.

Write an equation using the variables S and P to repre-
sent the following statement: "There are six times as many
students as professors at this University."   Use S for the
number of students and P for the number of professors.

Sample Size	*% Correct*	*% Incorrect*
150	*63*	*37*

Problem 2.

Write an equation using the variables C and S to repre-
sent the following statement: "At Mindy's restaurant, for
every four people who order cheesecake, there are five people
who ordered strudel."   Let C represent the number of cheese-
cakes and S represent the number of strudels.

Sample Size	*% Correct*	*% Incorrect*
150	*27*	*73*

Problem 3.

Spies fly over the Norun Airplane Manufacturers and re-
turn with an aerial photograph of the new planes in the yard.

They are fairly certain that they have photographed a
representative sample of one week's production.   Write an
equation using the letters R and B that describe the relation-
ship between the number of red airplanes and the number of
blue airplanes produced.   The equation should allow you to
calculate the number of blue planes produced in a month if
you know the number of red planes produced in a month.

Sample Size	*% Correct*	*% Incorrect*
34	*32*	*68*

patterns argues against the idea that they were caused simply by carelessness, and suggest that they stem from a common conceptual bug.

III.   INTERPRETATION OF ALGEBRA EXPERIMENTS

How is it possible for students with such weaknesses to survive high school and college science courses? It appears that these students have developed special purpose translation algorithms which work for many textbook problems, but which do not involve anything that could reasonably be called a semantic understanding of algebra. Many word problems are constructed so that they can be solved through a trivial word-to-symbol matching algorithm. Others, such as physics problems, are given in a highly restricted context, where there are only two or three pre-taught equations to choose between. This choice can be made either by picking the one equation which contains all of the given variables or through units analysis. While these techniques may be partially successful in many classroom situations, they are too primitive and unreliable to be trusted in any but the most routine applications.

In order to pursue the source of these errors, we conducted audio and video-taped interviews with 20 students who were asked to think out loud as they worked these and other related problems. On the "Students and Professors" problem we were able to identify two strategies which led to the reversal error. In the first, the student simply assumed that the order or contiguity of key words in the English language problem statement mapped directly into the order of symbols appearing in the algebraic equation. Weaknesses in this type of direct translation strategy have previously been analyzed by Paige and Simon (1966).

On the other hand, in a second incorrect strategy, students acted as if they did not use an accurate representation of the meaning of the problem. However, reversal errors appeared to arise because of confusion about the semantics of the algebraic equation. For example, one subject wrote '6S - 1P' and explained:

> *"There's six times as many students, which means it's six students to one professor and this (points to 6S) is six times as many students as there are professors (points to 1P)."*

When asked to draw a picture to illustrate his equation, the student drew from right to left one circle with a 'P' in it, an equal sign, and six circles with "S's" in them. Subjects such as the above seem to use an accurate model of the practical situation, but they still fail to symbolize that understanding with the correct equation.

   Apparently such subjects interpret the reversed equation, '6S = P', as stated that a large group of students are associated with a small group of professors. To these students the letter "P" stands for "a professor" rather than "the number of professors" and the *equal sign expresses a comparison or association rather than an equivalence.* The fact that the "S" side of the equation has a "6" on it indicates that it is larger than the "P" side which has no modifier. Thus, there appear to be more S's than there are P's. Thus, the student attempts to write the algebraic equation '6S = P' as a "figurative" statement, describing a *passive picture* in which relative sizes of the entities are represented.

   This contrasts to the correct equation 'S = 6P', which needs to be viewed as expressing an *active operation* being performed on one number (the number of professors) in order to obtain another number (the number of students). The correct equation, S = 6P, does not describe sizes of the groups in a literal or direct manner. Rather, it describes an equivalence relation that would occur if one were to make the group of professors six times larger. In other words, the equation S = 6P is not a direct description of the actual situation, but rather, it represents the hypothetical state of affairs which would result after performing the operation of multiplying the current number of professors by 6. The key to fully understanding the correct translation lies in viewing the number six as an *operator* which transforms the *number* of professors into the *number* of students. For example, one subject who correctly wrote S = 6P said:

   "If you want to even out the number of students to the number of professors, you'd have to have six times as many professors."

The equation is thus interpreted in a procedural manner as an instruction to *act.*

IV. COMPUTER PROGRAMS VS. ALGEBRAIC EQUATIONS: EXPERIMENTAL RESULTS

On the basis of the foregoing analysis, we developed the following hypothesis: if students were placed in an environment which could induce them to take a more active, procedural view of equations, then the error rate on these problems should decline. One clear candidate for such an environment is that of computer programming. That is, a computer program is a definite prescription for *action*; it is a set of commands which produce some result. Below, we present empirical tests of this hypothesis; in Section V we shall present our analysis of these results.

A. *Experiment 1*

In this experiment, our subjects were primarily freshmen and sophomores in a course on machine and assembly language programming. Half the class was given Problem 1 in Table 2, while the other half simultaneously was given Problem 2 in Table 2. The only difference in the questions is that the latter requests a computer program while the former asks for an algebraic equation. As indicated in Table 2, significantly more students could solve Problem 1 than could solve Problem 2. Probability of these results on the assumption that errors on each problem were equally likely is $p < .05$.

B. *Experiment 2*

The above experiment explored the *writing* of computer programs or equations. However, Clement, Lochhead and Monk (1980) observed that *reading* equations also gave students a great deal of trouble. That is, many students failed to write a correct explanation of the relationship expressed by the equation. Following the hypothesis outlined above, we wanted to compare the results of students reading and explaining an equation embedded in a computer program, with students reading and explaining an equation, which stood alone. The two questions in Table 3 were given as part of an 11 question test to 87 freshman, engineering students. The difference between the groups which answered one correctly but the other incorrectly is quite interesting. Namely, the group of students who answered the computer problem correctly (Problem 2, Table 3), but the equation problem incorrectly (Problem 1, Table 3) was more than 3 times as large as the group who answered the equation problem correctly, but missed the computer problem.

TABLE 2

Problem 1.

Given the following statement:

   "*At the last company cocktail party, for every 6 people who drank hard liquour, there were 11 people who drank beer.*"

   Write a computer program in BASIC which will output the number of beer drinkers when supplied (via user input at the terminal) with the number of hard liquour drinkers. Use H for the number of people who drank hard liquour, and B for the number of people who drank beer.

Sample Size	% Correct	% Incorrect
52	69	31

Problem 2.

Given the following statement:

   "*At the last company cocktail party, for every 6 people who drank hard liquour, there were 11 people who drank beer.*"

   Write an equation which represents the above statement. Use H for the number of people who drank hard liquour, and B for the number of people who drank beer.

Sample Size	% Correct	% Incorrect
51	45	55

Probability of these results on the assumption that errors on each problem were equally likely is p $<$ .05.

TABLE 3

Problem 1.

    Write a sentence in English that gives the same information as the following equation:

$$A = 7S$$

A is the number of assemblers in a factory.
S is the number of solderers in a factory.

Problem 2.

```
Program Kayak
Input I
K = I * 2
Print K
End
```

    For the above computer program describe in English the mathematical relationship which exists between I, the number of Igloos, and K, the number of Kayaks.

Comparison of Problem 1 and Problem 2

a. Number of people who got 1 correct, but 2 incorrect   5
b. Number of people who got 2 correct, but 1 incorrect   18

Probability of these results on the assumption that case a and b were equally likely is $< .005$.

This difference is significant at the .005 level. Here again, we see that the programming environment facilitated the students' understanding.

TABLE 4

PRELIMINARY HYPOTHESIS:
WHY PROGRAMMING FACILITATES PROBLEM SOLVING

1. *Unambiguous Semantics of Programming Language Construc-
    tions.* While various mathematical symbols (e.g., the
    equal-sign) are often open to a variety of interpreta-
    tions in mathematics (Kaput, 1979b), programming lang-
    uages require that only one interpretation be associated
    with each symbol. This fact is usually emphasized in
    programming language instruction. For example, the
    meaning of '=' in 'I = I + 1' is explicitly defined as an
    act of replacement, i.e., the value of the right side of
    the equation becomes the new value of the variable on the
    left. Also, the interpretation of variables is clear,
    i.e., they stand for *numbers* which are acted on by opera-
    tors.

2. *Explicitness Required by the Syntax of Programming
    Languages.* The fact that one must write '6*S' rather
    than simply '6S' might serve to prompt one to view that
    expression operatively as meaning "six times the number
    of students" rather than falling into the error of
    viewing it descriptively as "six students".

3. *Viewing an "Equation" in a Programming Language as an
    Active Input/Output Transformation.* That is, the right
    hand side of the equation (the input) is *operated* on to
    produce a value for the left hand side (the output).

4. *The Practice of Debugging Programs.* While students may
    not be encouraged to "run their equations" in typically
    mathematics courses, this concept of actual number
    testing is an integral part of programming and program-
    ming education.

5. *The Practice of Decomposing a Problem into Explicit
    Steps.* A number of students solved the computer program
    problem by writing down a two step sequence of opera-
    tions.
        X = B/6
        B = 11*X
    One interpretation for this phenomenon might be that
    students "saw" partial results "produced" on the way to
    the solution.

V.   WHY A PROGRAMMING CONTEXT DECREASES REVERSAL ERRORS: SOME HYPOTHESES

Based on the experiments described earlier, we developed a set of hypotheses (see Table 4) that could explain the performance difference discussed above. Other researchers have commented that they felt that hypothesis 4 was the key reason for the performance difference. That is, they felt that "checking one's answer by substituting numbers" was the factor that enabled students to write the correct equation. This technique -- writing a program down, and "running it" with test data for verification -- *is* emphasized in programming courses. Moreover, if the "checking" hypothesis were correct, then the contribution of the programming environment *per se* would be minimal; one *could* "run" straight algebraic equations, though this technique is not stressed in instruction.

In order to better understand the factors involved, we employed the same technique that had provided valuable insights in the algebra study (Clement, Lochhead, and Monk 1980), namely, video-taping students as they solved problems. The same written test discussed in Experiment 2 above was given to students who were taking a second course in computer programming. We selected for video-taping, 5 students who missed the algebra version of the problem on the written test. During the video-taping session, we asked each student to solve 4 problems of the type discussed earlier. Half of these students were given the problems in the following order: an algebra version, a programming version, an algebra version, and a programming version. The other half started alternating with the programming version. Of the 5 students interviewed, 3 "flip-flopped" on their answers at least once, i.e., they got the algebra wrong and the programming correct (or the programming correct and the algebra wrong), and some did this more than once. In some cases, the opposing solutions appeared within 30 seconds to 1 minute of each other, with the student's written work appearing on the same piece of paper. It is interesting to note, though, that all 3 students did answer the last (fourth) problem correctly.

In the video-taped interviews with these students, we did *not* see any indication that number checking/substitution was the main factor contributing to a correct program solution. It appeared that other factors in the programming environment were more important. For example, the students regularly and systematically put a READ statement at the top of the program. This appeared to "trigger" the concept of input, which in turn, triggered the concept of variable, i.e., a place that holds a value, a number. Thus, they were less likely to fall into the misconception of thinking of S as a *label* for "a student."* As they wrote the program, or after it, the students repeatedly gave "qualitative" explanations for their correct answer. For example, one subject said:

> *Slightly more bought hamburgers than bought sand-*
> *wiches . . . so I knew 6/7 wouldn't quite work so*
> *it must have been 7/6 . . . I knew the ratio of*
> *people getting hamburger to sandwich is just a lit-*
> *tle bit more than one so I was looking for a frac-*
> *tion using the numbers in the problem which would*
> *be slightly more than 1.*

After the correct equation was written down, we did see some students checking the equation with numbers: however, this came *after* the students appeared quite confident with their equations, as evidenced by explanations such as the above.

At this point our analyses and conclusions (e.g., the five hypotheses in Table 4) are in flux. We are, for example, investigating the hypothesis that students have different "spheres" or "frames" of knowledge for algebra and programming. When asked to solve a problem using a program, the student may be switching to a new knowledge base, somewhat independent of the algebra knowledge base. We are currently analyzing more video-tape data in order to evaluate and refine our hypotheses.

VI.   IMPLICATIONS FOR EDUCATION

The data of Clement, Lochhead, and Monk (1980) show that it is particularly important to distinguish between the math courses a student has taken and the knowledge of mathematics the student actually possesses. If one defines mathematical literacy as the ability to translate back and forth between problems in the world and mathematical descriptions, then there is good reason to question whether mathematics instruction has promoted such literacy.

*By "labels" we mean that students appeared to treat "S" and "P" as they would "feet" and "yards" in the following rela-tionship "3 feet = 1 yard."

This is not merely an academic question. Recent surveys suggest that Russian college students are at least two years ahead of their American counterparts in the level of their mathematics coursework. Like the missile crisis of the 1960's, this information could spur a major national effort to catch up. But, if Russian math courses are no more effective in teaching students how to think mathematically than are our own, we may only be competing to see who can get further behind. We do not mean to belittle the potential threat of a math-gap. On the contrary -- we see it as a very critical issue which must be studied seriously and quickly.

Based on our work, we can make two proposals which might facilitate "problem-solving literacy." The first is obvious; integrate a course(s) on programming into the mathematics curriculum. The assumption underlying this recommendation is that "transfer" will occur -- the skills learned in the programming course will resurface in the mathematics courses. While our data does not conclusively show transfer, we have results which are consistent with that hypothesis. In particular, recall that all students who were interviewed on videotape did eventually solve the test problems correctly. Whether this was a practice effect or a true transfer is unclear. We are currently planning a series of experiments to further explore the "transfer" question.

Our second proposal is more radical: redefine much of the early "mathematics" curricula *to be programming-based*. That is, teach algebra as an integral part of programming. Clearly, the students would learn the same symbol manipulation skills that they develop in the algebra course. In addition, they would be in a better position to develop problem-solving literacy, the goal of the former courses. Transfer would be less of an issue, since algebra and programming would be integrated at the start! We believe that this approach would help students develop a much deeper understanding of the concepts of variable and function, and a much greater facility with mathematical modelling in practice situations. Clearly, this suggestion is not new; it has been put forth, in various forms, by Papert (1979).

A. *A Cognitive Appropriate Programming Language*

If programming should be included in the curricula, the question of "which language" to use arises. Here again, the style of research employed in the above studies could play a key role. That is, with the precious little empirical research into the cognitive factors involved in programm (Seidel and Hunter, 1970; Mayer, 1979; Miller, 1976; Ledgard, 1979), and with the current push in the direction of more "formality" in programming, programming languages are in danger of becoming like mathematics, i.e., developing a notation system that students can learn, but only with difficulty, and can manipulate, but without any real understanding. We have begun an empirical study, using the group testing and individual video-taping techniques described above, to explore how students learn to program in Pascal, a programming language which has recently gained wide acceptance.

Our preliminary results are quite unsettling (Soloway, et al., 1980). We conducted a pilot study of students in a summer school course on introductory Pascal programming. During the course, we collected "on-line protocols" of students as they interacted with the Pascal system in order to solve homework assignments, and we administered a group test at the end of the school semester. Based on an analysis of this data, we found, for example, that students were confused in many ways about the basic iteration constructs in Pascal. They did not seem to understand -- or trust -- the complex functions which the "for," "while," and "repeat" constructs perform. Students either made explicit those functions which are implicitly performed (e.g., loop-end testing, index-variable incrementing) or they assumed that more actions would be performed than actually are (e.g., incrementing the index variable in the "while" construct). Since we believe that one of the primary benefits of programming is that students are required to make each step explicit, we are suspicious of the blind initial use of sophisticated constructs which have many explicit operations. We speculate that, in fact, students do not have mental models of the primitives which compose these higher level constructs. This suggests that they should be taught iteration first using the primitives, and then graduate to the complex constructions, as was often done in teaching BASIC and FORTRAN.

VII.   CONCLUDING REMARKS

We have attempted to empirically explore the contribution of programming to problem solving in the context of ostensibly simple word problems. Our general hypothesis was that programming does enhance problem solving, because programming encourages the needed procedural view. We have carried out a number of studies on this question (Clement, Lochhead, and Soloway, 1980), many of which are reported here. To date, all of these studies support our initial hypothesis. Clearly, however, *much* more needs to be done. In particular, our work has focussed on a limited context, and issues such as transfer must be further explored. Nonetheless, we are encouraged by the results of these studies, and are planning further experiments in order to broaden and deepen our hypotheses. Finally, based on this research, we have put forth two suggestions which call for the "wedding" of mathematics and programming. While many questions remain to be researched, we have before us the exciting prospect of uncovering new modes of instruction many times more powerful than those we now employ.

REFERENCES

Clement, J., Lochhead, J., and Monk, G. (1980). "Translation Difficulties in Learning Mathematics," *American Mathematical Monthly,* in press.

Clement, J., Lochhead, J., and Soloway, E. (1979). "Translating Between Symbol Systems: Isolating Common Difficulty in Solving Algebra Word Problems," COINS Technical Report 79-19, Department of Computer and Information Science, University of Massachusetts, Amherst.

Clement, J., Lochhead, J. and Soloway, E. (1980). "Positive Effects of Computer Programming on Students' Understanding of Variables and Equations," *Proceedings of the National ACM Conference,* Nashville.

Howe, J.A.M., O'Shea, T., and Plane, J. (1979). "Teaching Mathematics Through LOGO Programming," DAI Research Paper 115, Department of Artificial Intelligence, University of Edinburgh.

Kaput, J. (1979a). Personal communication.

Kaput, J. (1979b). "Mathematics and Learning: Roots of Epistemological Status," *Cognitive Process Instruction* (J. Clement and J. Lochhead, eds.), Franklin Institute Press, Philadelphia, PA.

Ledgard, H., Whiteside, J., Singer, A., and Seymour, W. (1979). "Report on an Experiment on the Design of Interactive Command Languages," COINS Technical Report 79-21, Department of Computer and Information Science, University of Massachusetts, Amherst.

Mayer, R.E. (1979). "A Psychology of Learning BASIC," *Comm. of the ACM,* November.

Monk, G.S. (1979). Personal communication.

Paige, J. and Simon, H. (1966). "Cognitive Processes in Solving Algebra Word Problems," *Problem Solving Research, Method and Theory* (B. Kleinmutz, ed.), John Wiley and Sons, New York.

Papert, S. (1971). "Teaching Children to be Mathematicians versus Teaching about Mathematics," MIT AI Lab Memo 249, Cambridge, MA.

Papert, S. (1979). "Computers and Learning," *The Computer Age: A Twenty-Year View,* (M. Dertouzos and J. Moses, eds.), The MIT Press, Cambridge, MA.

Seidel, R.J. and Hunter, H.G. (1970). "The Application of Theoretical Factors in Teaching Problem-Solving by Programmed Instruction," *International Review of Applied Psychology,* April, Vol. 19, No. 1.

Soloway, E., Bonar, J., Barth, J., and Woolf, B. (1980). "Conceptions and Misconceptions in Students' Understanding of Basic Programming Issues," in preparation.

DISCUSSANT REMARKS

Gary M. Olson

University of Michigan

SUMMARY

- *Empirical research on computing and cognitive systems should be encouraged.*

- *Cognitive and developmental psychology are important to the implementation of computer literacy goals.*

- *It is necessary to do careful, systematic research on the cognitive, motivational, and social foundations of a phenomenon for any innovation: (1) foundations of involved skill; (2) small-scale implementation plans; (3) evaluation of large scale implementations.*

- *Soloway's research is flawed and incorrect due to a variety of factors including insufficient theory, lack of experimental control.*

- *We need careful research before we can conclude that there is a transfer from computer programming to algebra.*

Gary M. Olson

NARRATIVE

I have a different perspective from most of the participants in this conference since I am a newcomer to the topic of
computer literacy. I have not done research in the area nor
have I given it the kind of systematic thought that most of
you have. However, I have had a personal interest in the
topic: I have been concerned with my own literacy, with the
literacy of my research assistants and graduate students, and
now as a father of elementary school children with their developing literacy. And from the perspective of an interested
newcomer, a couple of things about this conference have struck
me. On the one hand, I have been impressed with the enthusiasm, interest, and insight that I've seen in the discussions
here. The topic is important, with many major social and
educational implications, and it is reassuring to find so many
people working on it and worrying about it. On the other
hand, as an empirical scientist, I've been struck by the
nature of these discussions. They have been based primarily
on informal observation, anecdotes, opinions, biases and
briefs. Almost no research has been discussed and I find this
very disturbing.

Thus, in the context of what I've been hearing it is
refreshing to find in Elliot Soloway's paper the kind of
empirical research on psychological aspects of computing that
is highly relevant to the broader issue of computer literacy.
This kind of work is exceedingly important, for without knowledge of the cognitive system to be made literate it is going
to be difficult to know how to proceed. I definitely want to
give Elliot all the encouragement I can to be patient and continue to conduct research. There is a tendency to draw strong
conclusions early in a program of research, to plunge ahead
with generalizations and implications before the empirical
foundation is firm. I'll return to this theme a bit later.

But first I want to say some general things about the connec-
tions between psychology and computer literacy.

There are two broad aspects to computer literacy. The
first is establishing and justifying goals. For the most
part, these are determined by factors extrinsic to psychology.
In a society where computers are becoming an everyday fact of
life some degree of literacy is desirable for citizenship in
general, and certainly considerable amounts of literacy are
required for many career paths. There facts alone justify the
need for literacy. Soloway offers an interesting justification for literacy that psychology has a lot to say about,
namely, that knowledge of certain aspects of computing could
have indirect effects, leading to improved intellectual performance in other domains. I'll return to this in a moment.

What should computer literacy consist of? This is a
question largely determined by the goals of literacy, and
again is a question of policy for which psychology has little
to say. We have been hearing a lot about this topic here,
especially in connection with the HumRRO and Minnesota projects. Clearly these are not easy matters to settle.

The second aspect of literacy, of course, is the implementation of the goals. Here cognitive and developmental
psychology are much more relevant. However, there are some
important lessons to be learned about the implementation step
by examining how this has worked in a number of other areas.
Time and time again, premature implementation of what seemed
to be promising educational innovations have shown how costly
it can be to fail to do the required research. I'm thinking
particularly of such things as the new math, discovery learning, open classrooms, and so on. For any particular innovation, it is necessary to do very careful and systematic research on the cognitive, motivational, and social foundations
of the phenomenon. In fact, three types of research are
needed. First, research on the foundations of the skill involved. What are the skills like, and how do they develop?
Second, small-scale development research on possible plans for
implementation. And third, evaluation research on preliminary
large-scale implementations. All of these are needed because
it is not the case that cognitive or developmental theory is
yet well enough specified so that guidelines for the implementation in any particular area can be drawn from such theory.
Cognitive and developmental theory can be suggestive, they can
lead to hypotheses about how things could be implemented. But
these suggestions or hypotheses have to be examined and researched, they can't be assumed.

An example of this comes from Piagetian theory. There
has been a lot of research in the last 20 years on Piaget's
theory (e.g., Brainers, 1978). Not surprisingly, Piaget seems
to have been right about some things but not about others.
For instance, it is generally agreed that there is an order to
the acquisition of the various cognitive skills. Children of
different ages know different things, represent the world in
different ways, and thus treat their experiences in very
different manners. There is a lot of quibbling in developmental psychology about when these things happen and whether they
happen with discontinuities that imply some kind of stage has
been achieved. But all of that quibbling aside, I think that
everyone would agree that much of Piaget's basic description
is correct. However, it is also agreed that the translation
from statements about the order of acquisition of general
cognitive competencies to particular domains is exceedingly
complicated. Thus, particular kinds of competence can be
achieved earlier in certain domains than others, and there are
all kinds of influencing factors. So, within any particular
domain, such as computers or any of the aspects of computer
literacy, there is no obvious translation from even a reasonably well-affirmed theory like Piaget's to what you should do.
The bottom line is that to know what to do in a particular
case, you have to study it.

Let me now return specifically to Soloway's work. His
research focuses on the topic of transfer. At least since the
Greeks there has been interest in the extent to which learning
of certain subject matters like logic or mathematics leads to
improvement of thinking in general. Classical education, with
its Trivium of grammar, logic, and rhetoric, and modern educational movements that emphasize basics, are rooted in the
philosophy that learning certain basic skills will have good,
indirect effects in many specific domains.

However, the general picture from research on problem
solving and thinking is that the conditions under which transfer occurs from one domain to another are subtle and limited.
In fact, more often than not one is more impressed by the
extent to which transfer doesn't occur. Now, I think some of
the comments John Seely Brown made about interpreting negative
results are relevant here. While we may have strong intuitive
reasons to believe that transfer occurs from one domain to
another. At least so far, the research suggests that it is
far from universal and you cannot assume *a priori* that it is
going to occur. It is encouraging and impressive that someone
like Elliot is working on a problem as important as this.
It's intuitively plausible to think that there ought to be

transfer from computer programming to algebra. But it cannot
be assumed, and before we can conclude that such transfer
occurs, we must see a lot of careful research that deals with
the many factors that are involved.

To reemphasize my initial point: one has to be patient
about drawing conclusions in an area like this. Elliot presented in his paper a couple of studies that examined this
issue, and if this were a psychological convention instead of
the kind of meeting that it is, my role really would be to
raise the following two criticisms. First of all, there is
not enough theory. What kinds of psychological mechanisms are
being examined? What are the skills, the relevant knowledge?
How do the processes work? Under what condition does transfer
occur and when doesn't it? And so on. This is a common
criticism in psychological research, but very important.
Without clear theory we cannot advance. The second critical
task would be to review his experiments in detail, showing how
he forgot to counterbalance for this or control for that.
This too is an important exercise, for only through experimentation and critical evaluation can we make empirical progress.
But this is not the appropriate forum for doing this. It
tends to emphasize too much the negative rather than the
positive of what Elliot is doing. I want to stress, however,
that these kinds of exercises are not trivial, that they are
very important to the entire issue of how research is conducted and how good research gets done. Elliot's studies are
flawed and incomplete. They represent important first steps
in a program of research. But a number of issues need to be
cleared up before there is an adequate empirical foundation
for his claims.

Broad conclusions about things that are important like
this really require, first of all, not just a few preliminary
studies, but a broad program of thoroughly critiqued research.
This is a point that John Seely Brown made as well. Don't
jump to conclusions on the basis of preliminary research,
whether the conclusions are negative ones or positive ones.
There are simply too many examples of the high cost of impa-
tience. I understand there are a lot of reasons to be impa-
tient in the field. It's a fast-developing field, with rapid
technological change and incredible social pressure for education. But the history of social policy decisions based upon
research suggests that virtue will be rewarded in the long
run, and that it is too costly to make some of the mistakes
that have been made in the past.

REFERENCES

Brainerd, C.J. (1978). *Piaget's Theory of Intelligence*.
    Prentice-Hall, Englewood Cliffs, NJ.

DISCUSSANT REMARKS

Thomas Dwyer

University of Pittsburgh

SUMMARY

- *The term "problem solving" has a broader and deeper meaning than its educational association with mathematics implies. Computer environments make it possible for students to experience some of the deeper ideas that underlie a correct understanding of what "human problem solving" entails.*

- *Students learn best in settings where they can move from the empirical to the theoretical and back again freely. This coincides with the way real problem-solvers function.*

- *Low-cost microcomputers make it possible to incorporate these ideas into mathematics curricula as well as into new courses in Computer Science and Computer Literacy.*

Thomas Dwyer

NARRATIVE

The term "problem solving" has been used a great deal in recent discussions of the potential of computers in education. This is an exciting idea, especially when one considers that the concept of problem solving has been synonymous with human endeavors of the best possible kind -- with the mastery of the physical, social, and intellectual worlds we live in. Unfortunately, when used in educational writings, the term is often narrowed to the point where it is equated with a subset of school mathematics. In particular, we seem to have confused the teaching of symbol manipulation in high school algebra with the teaching of the broad-based strategies from which these symbolic representations arose.

The problem is, of course, that there is insufficient time for anyone to revisit all the experiences of the past. One could even argue that the symbols of any discipline are a codification of that experience, and that teaching the symbols does, in fact, teach the experience. From a practical point of view, there is the further advantage that it is a lot easier to define a curriculum in terms of manipulative skills than in terms of inventive learning.

I am not arguing that this is a bad thing. Symbolic manipulative skills are the culmination of a great heritage that should be passed on. Our problem as educators is that we are forced to skip over the experiences that created this heritage. The problem is further compounded by the time limits in school, and the fact that most teachers are not practicing professional mathematicians or scientists. The result is that we tend to dilute the symbolic information, and then try to compensate by inventing "problem solving exercises" that are anything *but*. I believe this is why students today encounter difficulties with math and science; their innate intelligence tells them something is wrong, but they have no idea what it is.

What can we do about this situation? Well, it is obvious that we can't develop some sort of magic box in which to place students where they can live through the thousands of years of experience that have led to modern mathematics and science. We can't do it literally, that is; but perhaps we can create environments using computers, where some of that experience can take place in new forms and at new levels. The machinery will not do this by itself, but with the right combination of teachers and interactive computing we can go a long way in moving students into the role that people have historically played in "discovering things." I agree with those who argue that the discovery approach by itself is never going to work unless we couple it with some structure and discipline. But it is nevertheless a very important factor. This is one of the reasons I find the potential of interactive computing in the school exciting. It promises an environment where students work with significant problems *before* learning to abstract their experiences -- to work much in the same way that the great minds we associate with problem solving have always worked.

The most important thing is that students learn to be empirically inventive, even if at times their ideas miss the power of symbolic ideas. At some point after they have "fooled around" and learned that with the magic of the computer they can spew out results by the ton, the teacher can show the student that s/he really doesn't have to spend hours doing this. Students will learn -- much to their delight in my experience -- that by knowing some of the secrets developed by those who took the time to conceptualize ideas in abstract form, one can do some amazing things with pencil and paper.

It's interesting to note that the progression I am arguing for (lots and lots of real computing prior to learning to deal with and understand generalizations) is the route followed by most professionals in the field of computer science. One finds that in general, the more experienced a computer scientist is, the less likely it is that s/he will run to a computer when first attacking a problem. In fact, the ratio of compute-to-think-time seems to approach zero the further one goes up the professional ladder.

We ought to seriously ask why we don't use this model as the basis for educational innovation in general, and for the introduction of Computer Literacy courses into the schools in particular. It's the beginner who should be given the full power of interactive computing. The success we have in capturing the promise of "Computer Literacy for all" will be dependent on how well we understand this lesson. (Editor's

Note: An example of recent work in exploring the use of microcomputers to support this model can be found in Dwyer, T. (1981), "Multi-Micro Learning Environments: A Preliminary Report on the Solo/NET/works Projects," *Byte*, January, pp. 104-114 and in Dwyer, T. (1982), "Multi-Computer Systems for the Support of Inventive Learning," *Computers and Education*, Vol. 6, pp. 7-12.)

AUTHOR REBUTTAL

(Soloway)

Essentially, I agree with the criticisms of Olson and
Dwyer. (1) having patience for research and the need for
developing cognitive theory; and (2) being less expansive
about interpreting to the entire domain of problem solving
when working only on one or two pages (e.g., algebra). There
are two other related points: (a) allowing a broader definition of a computer programmer, and (b) cautioning us in drawing conclusions about general problem solving when working
with a particular programming language.

Rich Mayer talked about giving the people the primitives.
When doing this, it is important to be careful in the choice
of language. To be useful, the programming language itself
should mirror the metaphor which students use to represent the
problem on which they are working. If the languages are
mathematical and students have difficulty with mathematics,
then they will have difficulty mastering problem solving
constructs in such a language (e.g., PASCAL, and looping). It
would be nice if the programming language mirrored, to some
level, some degree, the plain language, and the metaphor that
they are using to solve the problem. In PASCAL, for certain
classes of problems, they have to introduce extra kinds of
constructs to get the problem right and it does not match the
student's metaphor.

With this and related kinds of issues, more and more
research has to be done. But there is a contrary trend in
computer science. The notion of a programmer is very narrowly
defined as a person who participates in a 100-man programming
team to build the MX missile system. A programmer, unfortunately, is not defined as someone who drives Big Track (the
programmable toy). Programming is, according to the computer
scientists, for people who are very serious and mathematically
sophisticated. What is the implication of this? Proofs of
correctness or that kind of philosophy is behind the development of large programs. It is also behind the development of
languages.

It doesn't take a genius to predict that if languages
look more and more like mathematics, and people have difficulties learning mathematics, then these same people are
going to have difficulties in learning those languages.

What are people going to do about programming? Somehow,
people have to have an input into the design of programming
languages. Proofs of correctness might be right for the 100-
man team, (which I don't agree with), but for somebody who
wants to program Big Track, who wants a program of graphics,
simple graphics -- those languages aren't going to work. We
have to be aware of the trend and remember there are a lot of
people who aren't working on 100-man programming teams.

AUDIENCE COMMENTARY

● Transferability, while an interesting finding, is not relevant to teaching computer literacy. We don't justify teaching skills in language because it makes people perform better in math, and we don't do the reverse. In fact, to test whether or not people have acquired what we think is good about language is a language test. A math test tests what was done in math. And, in the end, a computing test will test what was done in computing.

Computing is one way of representing what we think we know. Languages are a means of representing knowledge and mathematics is another highly distilled way of representing certain kinds of things we know. Computing is worth knowing because it provides yet another way to think about things and how to represent them.

● Are there games for children that would be useful for teaching computing, before children got involved with computing and while they were actually involved in learning computer languages? Why do languages use the words that they do? And since Mayer analyzed BASIC in a kind of way, how can BASIC be reworked. Instead of having a word like "read," how about something like "get an erase" or another phrase?

● One point not discussed sufficiently is how we evaluate. Often our evaluations results show nothing much has happened. The fact of the situation is a lot has happened but we don't know much about how to evaluate or measure it. That's a very major concern. Let's be very careful that we're not killing ourselves off by deciding in advance what it is we are going to measure to find out what the students have learned. We find out "yes" the student has or has not increased or improved on those measures, but we still don't know what they have learned. At the end of his paper, Rich Mayer was making a useful distinction, and it's one we should be very, very careful about. Particularly, we need to help school people, teachers, school administrators, educators, be aware of these kinds of issues, too. The whole LOGO environment goes a long

way to meeting a lot of the kinds of considerations that Mayer
was talking about providing students with concrete models.
The Turtle is a kind of concrete model. All the other issues
Mayer mentioned -- the five issues very thoughtfully, carefully, and explicitly built into the LOGO programming environment -- are not naturally and thoughtfully built into the
BASIC programming environment. It is something we should be
very thoughtful about as we promote computer literacy -- e.g.,
what kinds of programming environments?

●   We seem to have gotten off here through Rich's paper into
some discussion on how to teach programming and that's certainly a component of computer literacy. There is quite a
variety of alternate tactics for getting into teaching programming, some of which have not come out in this discussion
at all. Many of us tend to think in what might be called
textbook or grammatical mode. There is a variety of quite
different tactics. One is to start with examples -- to some
extent, some of the teaching of LOGO has done that. This,
also, has been done heavily many years ago with FORTRAN, and
more recently, with PASCAL. The advantage of examples is the
capability to deal with an individual student's background,
interest, and needs. Another quite different tactic is the
ten-finger approach. Here the student is put into a control
discovery mode entirely. The student is interacting with the
machine, and there is some print pages; the first print page
may say 2+3, the student types 2+3, and this strange beast
comes back 5. Nothing is told to the student. It is all
coming in a discovery mode, but one that is carefully guided.
That's the amount of time we find students take to get into
APL with that sort of strategy. Another quite different
approach, an old one that has never got much attention, is
through intelligent editors; that is, editors who know a lot
about the programming languages.

●   Most of our focus has been on students in schools. The
two things which seem to be key here are concrete models and
mass communication. When I look at successful models I want
to replicate, I think about watching the *Cosmos* series by Carl
Sagan. This is a subject that is abstract, and difficult to
understand. One of the things we see is the ability to take
incredibly difficult abstract concepts and concretize them
into the kinds of models that people are sitting down and
talking about over lunch. "Did you see that program," "I can
see that and I can grasp that now." We are missing the boat
if we only try to deal with what we can do with students in
schools, and not recognize that the awareness of our society
is going to make the jobs of educators, teachers, NSF, and

everybody much easier if our society is saying, "This is
something I can understand, I can get a handle on, and I think
my students ought to be getting more of this, and I think we
ought to be doing that." We ought not to forget about television. Broadcast television today has the ability to do
things much more quickly than we could do in the schools with
a very limited number of micros and resources. We have to put
a lot of emphasis on coming up with quality materials that are
really going to be able to create that awareness in large
numbers.

● Models are something that are perceived and understood by
students based on their background. A film in Chemistry tried
to explain equilibrium by putting two Florence flasks with
gold fish in each and a stop cork in the middle of one. When
all the fish were in equal number in both flasks, equilibrium
was obtained. Students thought equilibrium meant equal numbers. Despite the fact that the film emphasized that it was
the rate and that the other factors were involved, the iconic,
visual image came through so clearly that the students carried
away just as many wrong concepts as they did right ones. If
we're going to use concrete models we have to have teachers
who are well enough educated to probe their students to find
out the things that are meaningful to them, and to construct
those concrete models based on metaphorical reasoning gleaned
from student behavior and from what students tell us.

WORKING GROUP II*

DEVELOPMENTAL SEQUENCE OF COMPUTER LITERACY
FOR GRADES K-12

QUESTIONS

1. Is there a necessary hierarchy of computer literacy
    objectives?

2. As one point of departure, critique K-8 scope and se-
    quence matrix proposed in the HumRRO project from a
    developmental standpoint, i.e., should there be a K-12
    recommended sequence? K-6? 7-9? 10-12?

    Do cognitive science and related research provide any
    guidelines for design and development and implementation
    of computer literacy curricula?

    Recommend research that needs to be done in order to
    answer questions such as above.

3. Where does computer awareness fit in a computer literacy
    approach?

4. Should there be an independent computer literacy course?
    What topics should it include? At what grade levels?

5. At what age (if ever) should children learn how to write
    computer programs in general purpose programming lang-
    uages such as BASIC or PASCAL? Should child-appropriate
    languages be developed?

*<u>Participants</u>: Kay Morgan, Jerry Bracey, Bob Seidel, Tom
    Hansen, Dick Rickett, Ken Brumbaugh, Andy Molnar, Gary
    Olson, and John Seely Brown.

6. Recommend research that needs to be done in order to
    answer questions such as above.

7. Is there any empirical basis for recommending particular
    pedagogical strategies such as "discovery learning," for
    computer literacy?

HIGHLIGHTS

- Sequencing of computer literacy curricula
  must fit the student's cognitive and personal
  development.

- Conceptual frameworks for the sequencing of
  computer literacy curricula suggested were:
  a special developmental approach (simple to
  complex and concrete to abstract); supermarket model (modules selected by teacher/stu-
  dent); and tree structure (links and prerequisites).

- Identified areas of needed research included:
  data on how computer concepts and processes
  relate to development stages; user friendly
  languages; interaction of computer literacy
  skills and other curricula and skills.

- Values and ethics in computing as a separate
  abstract topic should be left to 7th and 8th
  graders; at earlier grades it should be
  introduced as part of the on-going student
  activities in existing curricula.

WORKING GROUP II

DEVELOPMENTAL SEQUENCE OF COMPUTER LITERACY
FOR GRADES K-12

This group was concerned with the sequencing of computer literacy curriculum in K-12. The issues addressed were:

- *Is there a necessary hierarchy of computer literacy objectives?*

- *Should computer literacy be taught as a separate subject or integated into other curricula?*

- *At what age should children learn how to write computer programs and with what language?*

- *Is there any empirical basis for recommending particular pedagogical strategies (e.g., discovery learning) for computer literacy?*

- *Does cognitive science research provide any guidelines for the design, development and implementation of computer literacy curricula?*

In addition, the group addressed the ethics and values issues.

The discussion on sequencing dealt with three major questions:

1. *What must be done before something else (i.e., prerequisites)?*

2. *What order is easier or more convenient for the teacher or school system (given the present state of affairs)?*

3. *What order is best for the student due to developmental*
    considerations?

Underlying the first and third question was the issue of
whether computer literacy skills involve a long developmental
period or whether they can be acquired over a short period of
time. This issue addresses the question of whether computer
literacy should be a separate course or integrated into the
entire K-12 curriculum. Another side of this question is
whether computer literacy is to be taught by one teacher or
all teachers -- clearly the latter approach means a great deal
more teacher training.

It was agreed that the sequencing of computer literacy
curricula must fit the cognitive and personal development of
the student. For example, it was pointed out that children
like to do certain activities at certain ages, e.g., stacking
things when they are around 3, or drawing and painting when
they are about 7. There may be age/stages when they would be
particularly receptive to word processing or information
retrieval concepts. On the other hand, the LOGO project
suggests that providing even very young kids with simple but
powerful computers makes learning geometry possible.

One argument for introducing the computer as early as
possible is that it creates awareness. Thus, simply playing a
game on the computer arouses an interest in, and familiarity
with, computers upon which teachers can then build. The
computer literacy curriculum ought to match the "microworlds"
or dominant metaphors of the student, i.e., it ought to have
relevance to their current interests or concerns. For example, when kids get interested in libraries and book selection
is an appropriate time to teach about computer libraries or
information retrieval.

A number of different metaphors were discussed as possible conceptual frameworks for the sequencing of computer literacy curricula. One was a spiral metaphor in which the sequence involves increasing elaboration or differentiation of
earlier computer concepts. This might encompass concrete to
abstract, simple to complex, and familiar to unfamiliar developments (consistent with Piagetian developmental stages). The
early curricula would be relatively general "awareness,"
whereas the later curricula would be specific (e.g., computer
programming). Another metaphor was the supermarket model in
which many computer literacy modules would be defined but it
would be up to the teacher/student to determine which ones to
select. Another metaphor is a tree structure with explicitly
defined links and prerequisites.

A number of research areas were identified as part of the working group's discussions. One of these was the need for data on how computer concepts and processes mapped onto developmental stages (e.g., Piaget). Another research area was the design of "friendly languages" -- what makes a language easy or difficult for kids, and at what ages? Also needed is research on how computing literacy skills interact with present curricula and skills. For example, what does word processing skills have to do with English skills?

On the question of values and ethics, it was felt that values probably should be left until about 7th or 8th grade when kids fully understand the concept of responsibility. Earlier, values should be handled in terms of a code of ethics relevant to all activities.

SECTION IV

COMPUTER LITERACY AND CURRICULUM DEVELOPMENT

Presentations were made by HumRRO and MECC on their alternative approaches for curriculum development in computer literacy. Their remarks focused on their major development projects: Computer Literacy Instructional Modules (CLIM), and instructional materials for grades K-8. This section also includes papers on computer literacy and the mathematics, sciences, and social studies curriculums as well as a point paper on computer literacy in 1985. They focus attention on computer literacy needs and pre-college curricula. Computer literacy curriculum and instructional programs within mathematics, social sciences, and science were discussed in Working Groups III, IV, VII, VIII, and IX.

THE MINNESOTA EDUCATIONAL COMPUTING
CONSORTIUM (MECC) PROJECT ON COMPUTER
LITERACY INSTRUCTIONAL MODULES (CLIM)

Ronald Anderson

MECC

The Minnesota Educational Computing Consortium (MECC),
with funding from the National Science Foundation, has
launched a project to develop instructional modules for
computer literacy. This project, Computer Literacy Instructional Modules (CLIM), is engaged in the design, development,
and testing of a loosely integrated set of student learning
modules for science, mathematics, and social studies courses
in the secondary schools. The project is based on the premise
that computer literacy consists of a broad understanding of
the role of computer in society as well as the ability to
communicate with computers. The learning packages will be
based upon a set of learning objectives that reflect these
areas. The materials will be written for students entering
junior high school, although many students at other grade
levels will probably find the materials suitable to their
needs.

This project builds upon several computer literacy
research projects at MECC. One of these projects was a
survey of 3,576 high school teachers of mathematics, science,
and business education in the state of Minnesota. One important finding of this survey was that there is considerable
diversity of goals and activities with respect to computer
utilization in the classroom. This implies that materials
should be designed for a wide variety of situations with
varying degrees of computer access and teacher training.

From the teacher survey we were able to assemble a list
of over 2,600 high school courses in Minnesota where the
computer was being used either as a teaching tool or as the
subject of the course. Most of the courses utilized the

computer as an instrument for drills, simulations, games,
etc. However, 38 percent of the courses reportedly included
computer programming. Some courses were strictly programming
courses; other included data processing and/or introduction to
computer science. Many courses took a comprehensive approach
by including both computer programming and material on the
role of computers in society. Minnesota may have more instructional computing than most states, but these findings do
suggest that there are already a great many existing high
school courses moving in the direction of computer literacy
instruction.

While there are many existing pre-college computer
courses, no large assortment of curriculum materials yet
exists. Our MECC project on Computer Literacy Instructional
Modules (CLIM) is designed to begin to fill this void of
teaching aids. The CLIM modules are designed to be added as
supplementary units to the usual science, social studies and
mathematics courses in junior and senior high school. Since
many teachers have also expressed a desire for materials for
an entire course in computer literacy, the modules will be
written such that they can be used in sequence as a course.

Each learning package will include background material,
student activities, text materials, visual aids, instructions
for computer-based learning and other activities. Each
package will also have an accompanying teacher's guide containing instructions, objectives, an overview of student
activities, test items, and other materials. The packages
will contain computer-based learning activities, designed to
run on an APPLE II and other selected microcomputers, that
will help students understand computer capabilities and uses.
These activities will significantly enhance learning but in
some cases will be optional because not every classroom has
access to microcomputers. Accompanying the entire set of
learning packages will be a curriculum guide, which will aid
teachers and administrators in the adoption and use of either
selected learning packages or the entire set. The learning
packages will be classroom tested and evaluated, and the
results will be made available to interested teachers and
researchers.

In addition to the materials in each package, a guide to
the entire set will be provided as an aid for curriculum
planning and implementation. In this regard, we will rely
heavily upon the products and experiences of the HumRRO
computer literacy project. Alternative methods of incorporating the CLIM materials into the programs of a school or

district will be suggested. In addition, ways of sequencing the modules to form a one-semester course will be suggested, as well as ways of incorporating the individual modules into existing courses.

While this plan is fairly concrete, there are a number of additional considerations that are yet to be totally resolved. Foremost among these are the problems of implementation by the teacher in the classroom environment. Some of these general instructional design issues include:

I.   INDIVIDUALIZATION

Because the teaching of computer literacy is not highly institutionalized within the schools, it is prudent to develop modules for traditional delivery. Traditional as opposed to individualized delivery is also more readily accepted by teachers and administrators. Even though we are not individualizing the modules, the students will be able to many of the activities on their own.

II.   EXPERIENTIAL LEARNING

We will attempt to strike a comfortable balance between active and passive learning. We believe in the principle of learning by doing but sometimes learning by digesting is also necessary. Our many computer-based activities will be designed to foster many experiences which will solidify the impact of the instruction, but we must also provide expository materials for students and teachers in order to provide direction and build a foundation for a well-rounded literacy in computing.

III.   CURRICULUM INTEGRATION

The computer literacy modules will be designed to be integrated into existing course structures as supplementary units. In the field of mathematics this infusion is not so unusual; however, to have it occur widely in other disciplines may require special effort. There is a difficult trade-off between an investment in the design of materials for computer-resistant courses as opposed to courses where computing is already likely to be taught.

IV.   HIERARCHY OF INSTRUCTION

The modules will be designed to be largely independent of each other. The question of a recommended path through all of the modules has not been resolved and will require very careful attention. During the design phase, any prerequisite relationships or apparent hierarchy will be dealt with so that the teacher who chooses to utilize a series of modules can capitalize on this implicit structure.

V.   COST

At least in certain domains of computer literacy, the use of computers is essential. A major concern is how to make this usage as economically feasible as possible. Also, the cost of the eventual course material is a design consideration.

VI.   TEACHER READINESS

The question of how prepared teachers are to deliver instruction about computers has been raised many times. Since teacher readiness, both affective and cognitive, is a major factor determining the success or failure of any new instructional materials in the classroom, certain assumptions about their knowledge and motivation must be designed into the materials from the beginning.

VII.   STUDENT READINESS

Because computer literacy is not a universal course offering, students will have different entry skills depending on individual exposure to the subject. The course materials will take into account this variability in student motivation and entry level knowledge and skills.

VIII.   THE COMPUTER ENVIRONMENT

Not only do we have to make assumptions about what computing equipment is most likely to be available for stu-

dent access, but we must make assumptions about the availability of various languages and operating system features.
The conceptualization of the programming instruction is such
that languages other than BASIC might be taught within the
same structure. Due to limitations in resources, we do not
intend to develop extensive instruction in programming languages. Across the various models and configurations of computers, especially microcomputers, there are many areas of
incompatibility. In particular, there are differences in
BASIC syntax and in operating system commands which must be
taken into account in designing computer literacy modules.

CONCLUSION

     Despite these complex design questions, the MECC computer
literacy project is proceeding to develop modules. The
schedule is to design and develop the modules during 1981 and
to evaluate and test them during 1982. These materials will
be released by MECC sometime in 1982.

     In the process of initiating this project we have iden-
tified important questions facing anyone who is contemplating
the development of computer literacy. Comments, suggestions,
and ongoing dialogues about issues are most welcome.

COMPUTER LITERACY CURRICULUM FOR
GRADES K-8

Beverly Hunter

Human Resources Research Organization

I encourage people to precede their advocacy of strategies for implementation with some statement of where they
imagine the strategy will lead. So, I will summarize very
briefly my own vision of where I think we are headed. My
focus is on computer literacy in schools, and in particular,
in grades K through 8. I will then summarize our approach to
getting to that visionary state, the reasons for that approach, and important problems encountered in this approach.

I envision that at some time in the future, perhaps
around the year 2000, schools will, in fact, exist. The
buildings may be smaller due to high energy costs of trans-
porting children to large, distant schools. The schools will
be, in some respects, microcosms of the larger society, and
will reflect the information-handling characteristics of the
culture. Students and teachers will have the tools -- intellectual and physical -- that they need in order to operate in
this culture. They will learn such skills as formulating
requirements for information they need in order to solve problems; knowing where and how to access that information; knowing how to use the information they get. I envision students
and teachers having access to many different kinds of data
bases, software systems for structuring information, and
systems for organizing and communicating their ideas to
others. They will have both the intellectual and technological tools for analyzing data, and will know why they are doing
this. They will have many aids to learning. They will have,
for example, drills to use when they need to memorize something. More importantly, students will be able to very simply
build their own aids to learning. They will have lots of
media-based materials in libraries, and be able to access what
they need when they need it. Students will have computer-

based tools to aid them in studying much more complex problems
than are assigned to them today. There will be much communication among students, not only within a building but around
the world.

Built into this information/communications culture will
be a culture of social responsibility. There will be rules
for how we share information, build systems, and communicate
with each other. We will have learned better how to respect
privacy and at the same time share and cooperate, and children
will naturally learn this as part of the culture.

Those then are some fragments of my vision of where we
are headed. The strategy that we are formulating for implementation of computer literacy derives from that image of what
computer literacy will be about in schools. Before I describe
our strategy, I want to point out that nationally we need to
be pursuing several strategies simultaneously. First, we need
some far-out models, some exciting places that may not now
affect the masses of children but point the way to where we
may be headed. At the same time, we need the short-term
approaches that will affect the majority of people very
quickly, such as the eighth grade computer literacy course
that was mentioned earlier by Arthur Luehrmann and Sylvia
Charp.

Our strategy is a long-term strategy that addresses the
problems of universal computer literacy. The way I characterize this strategy is with the phrase "modesty of aims."

Even though the long-term vision may not be modest, we
must be very humble about the short-term implementation. If
we were to consider all the goals for computer literacy that
all of us in this room, and others around the world have right
now, it would be a very large set. Then, if you consider what
is actually happening in schools today, that's also a very
large set of events and activities and ideas -- but there is
not a lot of overlap between the first and second sets.
Thirdly, consider the set of learning materials and devices
available to support computer use for learning, teaching and
thinking in schools. Clearly, we are developing very rapidly
a large set of both programs and devices, but this set does
not overlap very much with our goals for computer literacy or
with current school curricula.

So the little triangle on *Figure 1* represents the domain
we are addressing in our current project. We are taking a
modest set of computer literacy goals that are achievable now,

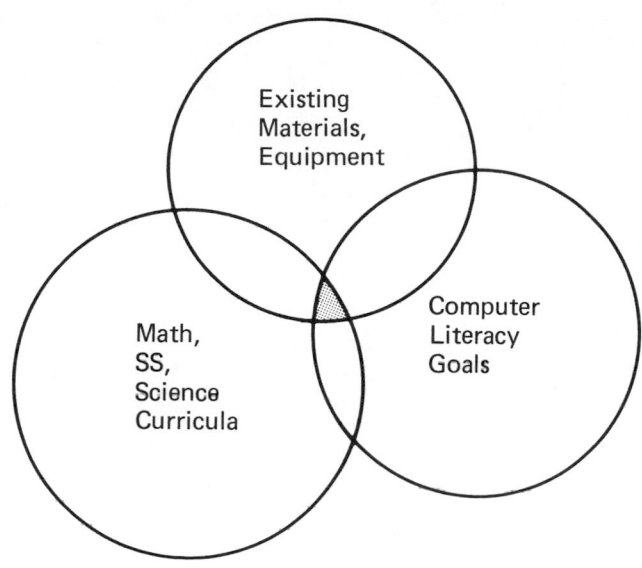

Figure 1.   Modesty of Aims.

and that are integratable, in the minds of today's educators,
with their curricula. I do not have time to describe that set
of objectives now. The four main areas covered by these
objectives are:

- *using computer programs*
- *procedural thinking*
- *computer applications*
- *social and values implications of computer/communications
  systems*

We are trying to infuse these objectives into the curriculum, grades K-8. This implies a developmental sequence of
objectives. We are basing the developmental sequence on both
an interpretation of Piagetian ideas of children's cognitive
development and upon the practicality of existing school
curriculum sequences. I will give an example of a developmental sequence in one of the four main areas -- *computer applications*.

The objectives in the applications area are *not* to have
students be aware that computers are used in various ways by

various people and organizations. Rather, the purpose is to
provide the student with the skills and concepts s/he will
need whenever there is a need to learn about any particular
application or system. That is, the student learns to think
in terms of the systems, including users, uses, output, input,
control, data bases, processes and communications. The student learns about specific applications as a concrete vehicle
for developing these more abstract concepts.

In the applications sequence of objectives, the student
learns first about applications that are close to personal
experience and then proceeds to learn about applications that
are more distant, in much the same way that social studies
curricula typically proceed from kindergarten to grade 8.
Along another dimension, what is learned about the applications becomes more detailed and complex as one goes through
the sequence. By the end of this sequence, the student would
be able to trace the flow of information and control through a
fairly complex system, indentifying people, communications
links, data bases, equipment and processes involved.

These applications are not learned, in our view, through
textbook descriptions or lectures or even field trips and
films -- although those can supplement the basic experience.
The applications and systems are learned primarily through
experience. Thus, the student will be first *using* an information retrieval system for his/her own work and study, and
then, or concurrently, learning how a journalist or a lawyer
or a scientist uses similar systems.

So, for example, in the sixth grade if you take all the
strands together, the student would be using an information-
retrieval system to do a term paper. S/he would also be
learning about other IR applications in the bigger world.
Also, in terms of fundamental concepts of computer systems,
s/he would be learning about mass storage. In the impact of
society area, s/he might be learning and discussing problems
of restricting access of data bases, some of the impacts on
different groups in society. So the objectives in the strands
are not really separate fragments -- but, rather are interrelated. And the purpose of strands is because people tend to
think about different computer literacy ideas in these different categories -- using computers, computers in society, etc.

The advantages that we argue for the infusion approach
are first of all that we are addressing universal computer
literacy. The argument is that if you wait until high school
to give a programming course and students don't have use of
computers earlier then many, many students will not be reached.

I think more importantly we look down toward the bottom of
this list -- relevance to intellectual work in the content
context. It doesn't make any sense to have a child sitting
for 7 years working out long division, with paper and pencil,
and memorizing a bunch of stuff, then all of a sudden in
eighth grade, they're learning that they can use a calculator
or an information retrieval system to get that same information. In other words, it's building the culture in the early
years. Building computer use into the intellectual work of
people begins in grade K, just the way using pencils and books
and papers begins in the early years. Now, we also argue that
the infusion approach could minimize the teacher training
problem in this sense -- that an individual teacher need not
be fully educated in a total set of everything that we're
trying to do. The individual teacher is responsible, say at
the fifth grade, for a very limited understanding -- perhaps
the preceding objectives, and the following objectives -- but
not the entire scope of everything that students have to
learn.

I.   LIMITATIONS AND PROBLEMS TO THIS APPROACH

     To even attempt to infuse computer literacy into the
total curriculum, you're implying something that's institu-
tion-wide, that is, within a school district or perhaps an
even larger entity. You need some top-down commitment for
doing that kind of a thing. It involves a lot of people and a
lot of coordination, and that means somebody to make that
coordination happen at a time when school districts have fewer
central staff to perform such coordination functions. The
people in a school district who would perform these coordination functions and infusion functions themselves are not very
computer literate, so they don't really understand very well
how to go about this process. They need to be educated. We
don't have enough materials available for children to support
this, particularly in science. It's just awful. How do
children use the computer to learn science? The materials
just aren't there. There are plenty of books on basic programming but how to use those tools in learning about any
scientific phenomenon just isn't there. What about books in
the existing curriculum -- some are there. We're starting to
get a glimmer of it but some is not clear yet. We also need
infusion into other disciplines besides the scientific ones.
And, we're only addressing the science, math, and social
studies.

COMPUTER LITERACY AND THE MATHEMATICS CURRICULUM

Jane D. Gawronski

Department of Education
San Diego, California

In April, 1980, the National Council of Teachers of Mathematics presented AN AGENDA FOR ACTION -- Recommendations for School Mathematics of the 1980's. These curriculum recommendations were based on studies funded by the National Science Foundation, the mathematics assessments of the National Assessment of Educational Progress, and a survey of both lay and professional opinions. The survey data were obtained from the Priorities in School Mathematics (PRISM), a project conducted by NCTM and funded by the National Science Foundation. These objective data, as well as the expertise of a task force of professionals, provided the basis for the eight recommendations. These are:

1. *problem solving (should) be the focus of school mathematics in the 1980s*

2. *basic skills in mathematics (should) be defined to encompass more than computational facility*

3. *mathematics programs (should) take full advantage of the power of calculators and computers at all grade levels*

4. *stringent standards of both effectiveness and efficiency (should) be applied to the teaching of mathematics*

5. *the success of mathematics programs and student learning (should) be evaluated by a wider range of measures than conventional testing*

6. *more mathematics study (should) be required for all students and a flexible curriculum with a greater range of options be designed to accommodate the diverse needs of the student population*

7. *mathematics teachers (should) demand of themselves and their colleagues a high level of professionalism*

8. *public support for mathematics instruction (should) be raised to level commensurate with the importance of mathematical understanding to individuals and society*

The use of computers and computer literacy could be a component of implementation of any one of these recommendations. Recommendation 3 has particular relevance for computer education. It states that "mathematics programs must take full advantage of the power of calculators and computers at all grade levels." This implies that students must have access to computers and that computers be integrated into the core mathematics curriculum. This demands curriculum materials that integrate and require the use of computers be available for teachers and students.

In addition, for implementation of this recommendation, NCTM has suggested that "A Computer Literacy course, familiarizing the student with role and impact of the computer, should be a part of the general education of every student."

This recommendation and these recommended actions are not passive acceptance of the inevitability of the use of computers in the classroom. They are aggressive advocacy of the use of current technology to enhance the teaching and learning of mathematics.

This aggressive advocacy is also seen in Recommendation 6 which calls for requiring more mathematics study and designing a flexible curriculum with a greater range of options. Implementation strategies for this recommendation are relevant to computer use and computer literacy also. One recommended action states that "All high school students should have work in computer literacy, and the hands-on use of computers, and the applications of computers where possible and appropriate throughout their mathematics program." Courses in computer literacy and computer applications are ways of increasing course options and providing a more flexible curriculum for students.

A mathematics curriculum that focuses on problem-solving requires the integrated use of computers. Numerous opportunities to practice and use newly acquired problem-solving skills in imaginative and real life applications are needed and can be provided by computer use. Computer programming is virtually a microcosm of what we know about problem-solving and provides practice in problem-solving. Parameters and protocols reflecting local adaptations to problem-solving settings are possible with appropriate computer programming but are often too costly or too dangerous otherwise. Computer literacy or computer curriculum projects must be sensitive to and provide for these applications and integrated uses in the mathematics curriculum.

COMPUTER LITERACY IN THE SOCIAL STUDIES CLASSROOM

Richard A. Diem

The University of Texas at San Antonio

The social studies constitutes both a subject area of the elementary and secondary school curriculum and a field of study concerned with people individually in groups, past and present, and in a variety of relationships and settings. Its content, concepts, and methodologies are drawn primarily from history, geography, political science, economics, sociology, psychology, anthropology, and philosophy, with attention to the arts and humanities.

The primary purpose of social studies programs is to provide learning experiences for students that will lead to the acquisition and development of the knowledge, attitudes, processes, and competencies essential for self-development, positive human relationships, and participation in a democratic society. Within this context social studies programs can, and should, provide computer literacy competencies in four distinctive areas:

1. *Social Responsibility and Values*
2. *Decision Making Skills*
3. *Use of Information in a Democratic Society*
4. *Impact of Technology, Historically, and in the Future*

Presently, there are no classroom textual materials extant in these areas that include computers and computer literacy as part of their subject matter. There have been several recent journal articles in *Social Education* and in *The Social Studies* that describe the impact of technology and the energy crisis but these do not deal with computer literacy even tangentally. Instructional materials are desperately needed in these areas.

Of particular importance is the development of case study materials. A case study allows students to interact with concrete examples and to make decisions based on factual analysis. These types of thinking skills are a necessary adjunct in developing computer awareness and literacy. Materials such as these are readily programmable and could be put on small or large computer systems enabling students to use the computer while studying its possible effects.

If our society is to become computer literate, a significant component of its computer education must be a critical evaluation of the uses of the computer and its impact on the values of the society. The social studies classroom, provided it has the tools, is the arena for this to take place.

GETTING COMPUTER LITERACY INTO THE PRE-COLLEGE CURRICULUM IN SCIENCE

Phyllis R. Marcuccio

National Science Teachers Association
Washington, D.C.

"Getting Computer Literacy into the Pre-College Curriculum" through the science curriculum on any significant scale will be a formidable task at the elementary school level. Some critics say that science teaching is in a worse position than it was before the Soviet Union launched Sputnik in 1959. Many of the data available today on science education supports the comment that science is declining and suggests implications for incorporating computer education into the school curriculum. For example, we know that:

1. *The knowledge that teachers have about science is declining.* This condition is due in part to the fact that in many states for teacher certification a student need not take more than one course in science for graduation from a teacher training institution. You can not teach what you do not know. Also, science teaching methods courses tend to concentrate on styles of teaching with only superficial treatment of science content, and nothing at all in computer education. Will the necessary background in computer literacy come from the teacher education courses in mathematics? From in-service training?

2. *Enrollment in science courses beyond the junior high school is declining.* Students can meet the requirements for graduation from high school without taking a science course beyond one year of biology. The lack of interest by females in mathematics beyond the fifth grade is also documented by National Science Foundation studies. Consider for a moment the science and mathematics taught to children in other countries and reflect upon the possible impact for these nations

and ours over the next 10 years in the fields of science and technology.

3. *Test scores from the National Assessment of Educational Progress (NAEP) show that children's knowledge in science is declining at all levels with only a slight gain for 17-year olds in biology.* Interesting to note here is that one of the purposes for the formation of the NAEP was to assess children's progress in science, then mathematics. Do you know that in the next round of assessments, science is not included?

4. *There is a "crisis of confidence in science" alerts Donald McCurdy, President of the National Science Teachers Association.* Dr. McCurdy warns that Americans have lost faith in science's ability to find answers to the problems plaguing modern man; and in fact, science is being blamed for causing many of society's difficulties. When this kind of doubt in the "cause and effect" nature of science occurs, the public turns to pseudo-sciences, cults, and exotic philosophies for direction. In the classroom, this trend suggests that "their science"; e.g., *Star Wars* vs. *Cosmos.* A lesson for computer education is that when building and implementing a curriculum, remember to deal with the social impacts of contemporary questions of society.

5. *School budgets are lower for science than ever before.* This trend will probably continue for all non-basic subject areas.

6. *Less "hands-on" science is being taught and teachers are returning to the less threatening styles of textbook and lecture teaching.* These techniques increase second-hand learning and are not productive for either effective science or computer education. There is also less time for teaching science than for other subjects. Children can experience personal success in science activity and very probably in computer learning experiences as well. The value of science in the development of self-esteem and personal satisfaction to a child has yet to be explored in educational research. The opportunity for no penalty "trial and error" make these fields appealing as non-threatening learning experiences for children.

7. *There is less time for teaching science than other subjects.* According to the recent National Science Foundation studies an average of 20 minutes per day is spent on science in the elementary school as compared to an average of 44 minutes on mathematics and 86 minutes on reading. Almost three years has passed since these data were collected. With the continued decline, the situation is probably more dramatic

today.   The National Science Teachers Association has been
compiling a list of elementary and middle schools nationwide
which have had sustained science programs offering science at
every grade for at least an hour and a half a week for the
past five years.   We hope to identify and nurture these
schools.   To day, about 300 have been named.   Interestingly,
about 25 percent of them are private schools.   Perhaps one of
the best prospects for launching a computer literacy curriculum would be in schools such as these where a commitment to
science is evident.

Compounding these complex problems facing science education are the predicted science teacher shortages, the pres-
sures from fundamentalist groups with curriculum alternatives,
and a need to reform the training of science teachers.   In
addition, science must serve all disciplines as well as the
more recent science-related areas of concern -- environmental
education, energy education, science career education.   Time
in the science classroom is therefore very precious and must
be utilized to its maximum.   Computer literacy is one of the
priorities.

COMPUTER LITERACY: 1985

Kenneth E. Brumbaugh

Minnesota Educational Computing Consortium

First, fast, and informative: that was the ABC November, 1980 election night coverage theme. How many Americans know and understand how the television networks program and use computers to obtain information for immediate presentation to millions of people? Is the use of computers interpolating and extrapolating election results beneficial to the electorate as a whole? The use of computers is analyzing pre- and post-election data is just one of the many ways that computers indirectly and directly affect every citizen of our country. Questions such as the above indicate that more and more Americans should become computer literate if we are to maximize our problem solving abilities and be more productive in our daily lives. And this is 1980. What will be required of Americans in 1985 regarding computer literacy? The computer is in our lives and will be even more so in 1985. By then the computer will be expected to:

- enable individuals to save energy resources and costs
- allow governments to operate by handling the necessary data
- enable individuals to travel more efficiently and effectively
- enable doctors to verify all prescriptions for medication
- enable individuals to do all banking tasks without travel
- allow commercial establishments to lower costs
- allow offices to improve the quality of work and life

What about instructional uses of computers in 1985? To be more specific, what about instruction in schools in 1985?

What will be the classroom size and shape? What will be the
student/teacher ratio? Will the students continue to be
assigned to classes with teacher supervision? Finally, will
there be a computer in every classroom? The answers to questions such as these will influence the extent and method by
which computer literacy programs are incorporated into schools
and colleges. As society makes more use of computers, so will
schools; thus, it is essential to develop a school curriculum
which includes a computer literacy component.

I.   COMPUTER LITERACY: A DEFINITION

What is meant by the term *computer literacy*? How often
is this term adequately defined? Most individuals, including
those who are in the computer field, are not comfortable and
confident of their definition of computer literacy. A definition of this concept might be as follows. To be computer
literate, one must be able to define, demonstrate, and/or
discuss:

- how computers are used
- how computers do their work
- how computers are programmed
- how to use a computer
- how computers affect our society

I have not listed the different computer literacy components
in any particular order for it is difficult, if not impossible, to get consensus on such ordering. Perhaps the biggest
issue being discussed today is whether computer programming
should be a requirements in computer literacy curricula. If
computer programming is not a requirement, then hands-on
experience using a computer device most certainly is.

II.   INSTRUCTIONAL COMPUTING: 1985

In 1985, my children will be into the 'elementary' school
as we know it today. Will their school have instruction which
utilizes appropriate computer technology? Will their teachers
have a fundamental knowledge and understanding of how and when
to incorporate the computer into instruction? Will their
school have acquired the necessary computing resources to
permit timely and regular computing activities? The answer is
yes, provided that a critical mass of instructional computing

materials and methods exist. The agents which develop and distribute curricula to schools and colleges must make a high quantity of quality materials available so that individual teachers and schools can choose what they deem to be best for them. In order for this to happen, numerous curriculum development projects must begin so that the conduits being established by the commercial publishers for instructional computing materials are filled and being to flow.

The computer literacy component designed for 1985 schools and colleges should have as their primary focus individualization of instruction. The content should be so designed to include topics to which the student can personally relate. Such topics could include training in particular skills, financial assistance, work assistance, entertainment, utility, and hobbies. If students are prepared for the advancing technology, they will be able to understand how power, skill, control, intelligence, and policy can be influenced and used properly. Many individuals today are concerned about the introduction of new technology, such as computers, into the classroom. They are apprehensive about privacy, misuse, attitudes, and automation in general. The way to eliminate these concerns in 1985 is to develop curriculum materials which relate to the individual. Students are individuals; this fact often gets overlooked. During an average class period a student receives very little, if any, individual attention. On the contrary, by its own nature the computer can provide high amounts of individualization for the student. Individualized instructional materials developed for the computer should take into consideration that students are different. Some are motivated and poor. Some are from rural America, while others like art. Thus, emphasizing cognitive subject matter is necessary, but new curricula materials must focus on the affective domain by incorporating numerous student options, and appropriate instruction and help options.

III.   COMPUTER LITERACY GUIDES

A set of computer literacy materials for students (elementary, secondary, and higher education versions), for teachers, and for community members should be prepared and disseminated to the fullest extent. These materials should be text-based and authored such that individuals from each group could utilize them *without* the tutelage of an instructor. Individuals in 1985 who use such materials may not be in a conventional school or student-teacher setting. Furthermore, the required computer-based component should be written in the

BASIC programming language and provide for the existing most popular computers. In all cases, the individual using these literacy guides should not be required to have any in-depth subject matter background in the discipline being studied.

The Human Resources Research Organization (HumRRO) and the Minnesota Educational Computing Consortium (MECC) have both received National Science Foundation (NSF) grants to develop computer literacy materials. HumRRO's computer literacy guide will be aimed at promoting instructional computing in the elementary school and will establish a scope and sequence for learning outcomes by grade level, subject matter, and topic. HumRRO will also provide suggested supplemental activities, resources, and training for teachers to consider. The NSF-MECC computer literacy project will produce twenty-five student learning modules, including background material, student activities, text material, and visual aids. Some of the modules will contain computer-based learning activities designed to run on selected microcomputers. The HumRRO and MECC computer literacy projects will benefit the instructional computing community by establishing a classification scheme for computer literacy objectives and by providing a model set of computer literacy materials.

However, both HumRRO and MECC in their NSF computer literacy project planning seem to be tied to 1980 methods and materials for classroom instruction. Less emphasis should be placed on *student and teacher* materials. In 1985, individuals should be given *learner-based* materials, which they could use without a teacher, or outside of the conventional classroom. The modules being planned by MECC are perhaps aimed more at computer awareness than at computer literacy. I fail to see how the hands-on use of a computer could be considered optional in a computer literacy instructional module. If schools and colleges cannot afford a computer, costing as little as $199.50, they have no right proposing to teach computer literacy. Computer literacy is a knowledge and feeling about computers. How can you feel something without touching it?

IV. SUMMARY

There is a need for computer literacy now, and by 1985 that need will be exponentially greater. Every person associated with the field of instructional computing should have a definition for computer literacy. Individualization will be a major instructional need in 1985 and instructional computing methods and materials can and should address that need. Com-

puter literacy materials should be developed for students at
all levels of education, for teachers, and for community
members. All of these materials should be learner-based, not
requiring the aid of an instructor, nor requiring any significant amount of subject matter knowledge or experience. There
is a need for local, state, and national funds for the development of computer literacy materials. Funded projects should
focus on the development of products, not research, which can
directly facilitate individual learning at school and at home.
If the critical mass of worthwhile instructional computing
materials is developed and distributed to schools and colleges, we will have a computer literate student population in
1985.

SUGGESTED READINGS

Billings, K. and Moursund, D. (1979). *Are You Computer Lite-
    rate?* Dilithium Press, Portland, OR.

Creative Computing magazine, (1980), September, Vol. 6, No. 9.

Department of Management Information Systems (1980). "Compu-
    ters in the Classroom: A Plan for the Use of Computer
    Technology in the Anchorage School District: January
    1980-June 1982," Anchorage School District, Anchorage,
    Alaska.

Doerr, C. (1979). *Microcomputers and the 3 R's: A Guide for
    Teachers,* Hayden Book Company, Inc., Rochelle Park, NJ.

Hodges, P. (1980). "Fear of Automation," *Output* magazine,
    August, Vol. 1, No. 6.

Human Resources Research Organization (1980). "Curriculum
    Guide for Computer Literacy: Project Brief," Alexandria,
    VA.

Minnesota Educational Computing Consortium (1980). "A Study
    of Computer Use and Literacy in Science Education: Final
    Report," St. Paul, MN.

Rawitsch, D.G. (1978). "The Concept of Computer Literacy,"
    MAEDS Journal of Educational Computing, Summer, Vol. 2,
    No. 2.

Tri-County Goal Development Project (1979). *Course Goals in
    Computer Education, K-12,* Portland, OR.

WORKING GROUP III*

COMPUTER LITERACY LEARNING MATERIALS
FOR GRADES K-8

QUESTIONS

1. *Suggest existing (or soon to be available) learning materials to support the HumRRO proposed K-8 curriculum in computer literacy.*

2. *What information retrieval systems exist that are suitable for use by children? Could national or regional data bases be made accessible to school children?*

3. *Recommend to curriculum developers and publishers priorities for materials development (topics, objectives, media, etc.).*

4. *Should child-appropriate programming languages be developed?*

5. *Recommend characteristics or standards for materials development and evaluation.*

6. *How should (or will) computer literacy materials be packaged? How should they be integrated with textbooks in math, science, social studies?*

7. *Should separate guides be developed for administrators? What should they contain?*

*Participants: Dan Klassen, Karen Billings, Carol Hargan, Joyce Hakansson, Beverly Hunter, William Kraus, Sue Moats, Jean Rice, Gary Shelly, and Rachelle Heller.

239

8.   *How, when, and by whom will needed materials be devel-*
      oped? What should be the role of the federal government?
      State governments? Publishers?

HIGHLIGHTS

- *Some type of programming languages should be taught from grades K on up.*

- *Computers should be in each classroom in the lower elementary grades whereas central laboratories should be adequate in junior high or upper grade levels.*

- *Elementary school children should develop a computer awareness, a readiness and ability to use computers as tools via school computing environments.*

- *Each classroom should have a computer or terminal and students should obtain hands-on experience.*

- *Computer-based tools/software that allow students to use the computer in ways that are real, appropriate, and meaningful should be developed.*

- *Students should be taught to program or construct/instruct a computer to do something that is meaningful to them.*

WORKING GROUP III

COMPUTER LITERACY LEARNING MATERIALS
FOR GRADES K-8

Should computer literacy be integrated into the curriculum, or should it be treated as a separate entity? In relation to this question, three different approaches were discussed. The first was simply to use computers as a delivery system for CAI. The second approach considered was to use computers as a student tool (e.g., using or writing programs to solve problems, using simulation and other openended type programs). The third approach discussed was to provide direct instruction designed to meet computer literacy objectives.

The group agreed that the first two of these are particularly important in the elementary grades. However, when we discussed materials, there appeared to be better materials for the third than for the first grade, and particularly for the second grades. In the lower elementary grades, there is an apparent need for a computer(s) in each classroom. In the junior high or upper level grade levels, however, there would be certain situations where a central location or a computer lab might be more useful.

We discussed the placement of programming in the elementary grades and determined at least three levels of programming. One was to use programmable toys like Big Tracks; the second level would use LOGO or LOGO-like languages or programs; and the third would use BASIC. The discussion of BASIC raised a number of issues, the most important of which was simply how should we stress good programming techniques, particularly in the early grades, and how to encourage good techniques without restricting experimenting and creativity that we really want to foster in the lower grades.

It was suggested that LOGO creates a good environment for programming, and encourages good programming techniques.

However, BASIC shares these as well as other characteristics including availability and versatility. We reached no consensus on the subject of programming languages, although it was clear that the group did favor some type of programming at most grade levels, K on up.

We believe that elementary school children should develop an awareness of computers and computing, and a readiness and ability to use computers as tools as individuals and members of society. Schools should provide computing environments that allow this goal to be achieved.

As guidelines to those responsible for implementing computing in the elementary schools, we recommend:

1. *A computer or computer terminal be placed in each classroom;*

2. *Students should use the computer or computer terminal, i.e., hands-on experience(s);*

3. *Computer-based tools/software that allow students to use the computer in ways that are real, meaningful and appropriate to them be developed, i.e., simple word processing systems, data handling tools, etc;*

4. *Children should be taught to program or construct/ instruct a computer to do something that is meaningful to them;*

5. *Educational agencies, for example, schools or departments of education, local school districts, state education agencies, should implement programs, courses, and workshops, both in-service and pre-service, designed to ensure that all K-8 educators become computer literate; and*

6. *Another conference or task force be commissioned to carry on and build up what has begun here.*

These recommendations reflect the most immediate pressing needs and other more specific guidelines need to be prepared.

WORKING GROUP IV*

COMPUTER LITERACY LEARNING MATERIALS
FOR GRADES 7-12

QUESTIONS

The following questions relate to the MECC project on Instructional Materials for Computer Literacy (IMCL):

1.   *What are the high priority content objectives for 7-9, 10-12?*

2.   *How will the IMCL fit into the traditional course sequences?*

3.   *How will the IMCL be evaluated? By whom?*

4.   *What roles (e.g., drill, simulation, tutorial, testing, etc.) should the computer play in the design of IMCL? What percent of IMCL will be computer delivered?*

5.   *How individualized and teacher independent will the IMCL be?*

6.   *What micros will the IMCL be implemented on? APPLE II, TRS-80, Atari? What minimum configuration will be assumed?*

7.   *To what extent will the alternative computer implementations take advantage of unique features of a particular machine?*

*Participants: Thomas Liao, Ron Anderson, Wes Fasnacht, Barbara Kurshan, Stephen Lewis, Robert Taylor, Cheryl Weiner, and Wayne Welch.

HIGHLIGHTS

- *The creation of teacher or machine materials depends, in part, on the school environment (e.g., suburban vs. urban).*

- *Materials created as a separage program as opposed to those created as "plug-ins" are needed and each will directly affect teacher training.*

- *MECC should focus at the national level on the issues of teacher training and the integration of computer literacy into the school curriculum.*

- *Publishers should be actively involved in the problems of dissemination.*

WORKING GROUP IV

COMPUTER LITERACY LEARNING MATERIALS
FOR GRADES 7-12

Our group was charged with the topic of computer literacy learning materials of grades 7-12 focusing on the MECC project. We decided to focus on 3 major concerns that we felt would relate to developing a set of curriculum materials.

1. *How does one slice up the computer literacy pie? There are many dimensions to this umbrella concept of computer literacy.*

2. *What type of learning environment does one put together in the curriculum package, and does it depend on whether it is teacher or machine-centered, or the type of hybrid system developed?* A lot depends on where you are going to use the materials. Suburban schools would be very different from urban schools. In many city schools, the number one problem is discipline and security, and those issues dominate schools. If something new is introduced in the curriculum, it is important to convince the teachers and administration that the students are going to be in an environment where those concerns will only worsen. Moreover, these concerns might be important in some environments, but not as important in other.

3. *Another concern of the group was that it is important to decide on what the implementation strategy is going to be before curriculum materials are developed. For example, do you want to try to implement the materials across the board? Or, do you want to let people choose, and if the materials are appropriate they will use them?* The group focused on this issue most of the time. For example, a dichotomy that developed concerned MECC's need to make a priority decision -- whether they are going to work with a curriculum that will be integrated into the existing curriculum such as science, math, social studies, etc.

Or, is MECC going to develop materials that teachers can put together into a single course?

Currently, the trend seems to be that MECC is moving towards the former and is attempting to develop materials that can be integated into the existing curriculum. But, if that is the final decision, then the materials will have a very different type of composition. In other words, it is quite different if a separate course is developed than if materials are developed that plug into different components of an existing curriculum. Also, the whole area of teacher training takes on a completely different look dependent upon the chosen approach.

The group consensus is that we need both. We need to have materials that teachers can easily fit into existing curriculum that do not disrupt the curriculum too much from the point of time and/or resources that are used. On the other hand, there are certain things that we can do simply by plugging in these materials. We may need materials that are specifically for a course.

The group felt the MECC enjoys some special advantages in Minnesota in terms of an existing framework and dissemination that other computer literacy programs won't have and that MECC itself won't have at the national level. We wanted to raise some issues that we felt were important in that broader national context.

Twin issues that we considered very important are how to get computer literacy into the curriculum and how to train the teachers who will teach computer literacy. We recognize the conference is well aware of these issues, but we weren't certain if it was aware of how moot the other issues will be if these aren't resolved.

We want to emphasize the importance of dissemination strategies to MECC in terms of national impact, and to the conference with regard to other programs as a whole. We think, for example, that NSF should entertain proposals for training teachers because it is the key to further development. We believe conferences should think about ways to communicate to "outsiders" who know and care a lot less about computers than the conference participants. We find that computer journals aren't in the ERIC network although that wouldn't be difficult to accomplish. We suggest that some proposals to NSF concerning computer literacy involve opening up bids to publishers immediately upon approval of the proposal rather than after development, either partial or com-

pletion of the project, as a new and different way to attack
the problem of dissemination.

Regarding MECC's specific objectives for computer literacy, we suggest there is probably more than can be handled by
any school right now. An important step in establishing
priorities is to approach schools with these objectives and
topics to validate different levels of interest in the topics
by teachers. Some additional brief descriptions of each
objective would be useful in allowing the developers to get a
good feeling for what areas teachers are most interested in
and what parts of the curriculum these objectives can be
integrated. After having done this at the national level,
MECC could develop high-priority areas somewhat more fully,
and go back to the schools for continued input.

WORKING GROUP VII*

COMPUTER LITERACY IN THE MATHEMATICS CURRICULA

QUESTIONS

1. *React to the integration of computer literacy into the K-8 math curriculum as proposed in the HumRRO K-8 scope and sequence.*

2. *How and where does study of computers and computer applications fit within math curricula K-12?*

3. *What is or should be the relationship of computer literacy to problem-solving in math curricula? K-6? 7-9? 10-12?*

4. *Suggest existing materials, programs, texts, etc., to support the HumRRO K-8 objectives.*

5. *What existing curriculum materials in math might serve as a model for computer literacy?*

6. *How might computer literacy objectives and activities support or reinforce existing curricula in math?*

7. *How can the NCTM and other organizations to which teachers belong support or enhance the computer literacy of teachers?*

8. *What are likely roles of established textbook publishers in disseminating computer literacy materials and curricula?*

*Participants: *Jane Gawronski, Joseph Caravella, Henry Hamburger, John Haugo, Laurette Lipson, Richard Mayer, Carol Muscara, Elliot Soloway, and Martha Torn.*

9. *How should the various disciplines cooperate in order to achieve computer literacy goals?*

10. *What is the responsibility of the math teacher in the computer literacy movement?*

11. *List rules of legal and ethical behavior that students and teachers should adhere to in using computer and information systems.*

HIGHLIGHT

- *The mathematics curriculum should include standards in algorithms and programming beginning at the elementary levels. Mathematics can be studied using procedure-oriented languages very early with higher level languages taught later.*

- *Mathematics must be viewed as part of an integrated whole rather than fragmented or isolated from other disciplines. The use of computers can facilitate this.*

- *The mathematics curriculum should take advantage of high technology capabilities, such as computer graphics and word processing.*

- *The mathematics curriculum should include the use of strategy games in a planned, systematic fashion, to develop critical thinking and reasoning skills.*

- *Mathematics instruction should include self-study and small group projects involving computer work.*

- *The role of the mathematics teacher should include serving as a resource consultant to students working on problem applications in other disciplines.*

- *The math teacher should spend less time on less functional areas; e.g., long division and related computational skills, and use this time-saved to teach computer literacy and programming skills.*

- *NCTM should play a lead role in helping to achieve computer literacy in teachers.*

- *Finally, computers in mathematics should be an available course option in the secondary schools. Computer studies or computer science courses should be options for those secondary school students who have low level computer literacy and are interested in continuing their studies. This could conceivably involve data processing courses.*

WORKING GROUP VII

COMPUTER LITERACY IN THE MATHEMATICS CURRICULA

Computer literacy should be viewed as more than a concern exclusively for the schools. The home and community are involved and must contribute as well to developing computer literacy skills. In view of this, it is recommended that computer-based curriculum materials should be made available and sold to the public the same way that electronic toys are sold. These materials should be oriented to the home market if they are to have an impact on computer literacy in the community as a whole. Also, home movie and video media should be explored as a means of promoting interest in computer education and computer. *COMPUTERTOWN, USA!* is a project with the goal of computer literacy for the whole community. It is recommended that both MECC and HumRRO include objectives and develop materials that can be used in the home and in community agencies as well as the school.

Computer-based systems such as word processing equipment should be used in instruction. This equipment should be compatible and networked with equipment in other departments to facilitate inter-departmental cooperation and integrated curriculums. Consideration must be given to getting the best, though inexpensive, devices. The use of the computer and computer-based systems may foster more integration of the mathematics curriculum in other curriculum areas. Mathematical applications are often relevant to the social studies and science curricula. When mathematical models are embedded in computer programs, teachers can more readily convey the results as well as the concepts.

The development of personal values and ethics must be a part of the student's instructional program. Values and ethics are personal issues and personal commitments that can be expressed in codes of behavior. Students must be helped to develop their own ground rules of behavior with respect to the use of computers.

There are some areas of the curriculum where teachers are spending excessive amounts of time, e.g., long division and related computational skills. By spending less time in less functional areas, teacher time can become available to teach computer literacy and computer programming skills. The recent study of priorities in school mathematics which included a survey of attitudes towards the use of calculators and computers, found that there was strong parental support for introducing computers and computer literacy in the mathematics curriculum. In fact, there was more support for computer use than for calculator use in the mathematics curriculum. Educators, too, supported increased computer utilization in the curriculum.

The mathematics curriculum should include separate strands in computer literacy, which includes programming. Presently there are strands such as geometry, computational skill, and problem solving. Problem solving strands in particular can include computer units since the computer is a very powerful problem-solving tool and the writing of programs embodies processes of problem solving. The act of writing programs actually provides practice in problem solving. Problem solving is taught in other disciplines, although it is often described as critical thinking. There is a natural link between mathematics and computer science, and that natural link is in the area of algorithms and programming. The logical structure of mathematics will not change, but some problems within the discipline of mathematics lend themselves to computer technology and others do not. The challenge is being able to identify those.

Existing curriculum materials and computer programs indicate an abundance of curriculum support material, but there is very little quality control or quality assurance about the material. A mechanism is needed for gaining that assurance. Elementary teachers need courseware that is appropriate, useful, and "friendly" to use (e.g., user-oriented). Modules need to be developed that not only use the computer but provide teachers with activities and discussion guides. NCTM provides software review and facilitates dissemination of information about support materials. However, a major effort of NCTM should be in helping teachers to become computer literate. Contacts and joint activities with other organizations are also needed. The National Association of School Boards, National Association of Elementary School Principals and Secondary Principals, and other associations should work together to gain the kind of curriculum change needed and to assist teachers and administrators in becoming computer literate.

WORKING GROUP VIII*

COMPUTER LITERACY IN THE SCIENCE CURRICULA

QUESTIONS

1. *React to the integration of computer literacy into the K-8 science curriculum as proposed in the HumRRO K-8 scope and sequence.*

2. *How and where does study of computers and computer applications fit within science curricula K-12?*

3. *What is or should be the relationship of computer literacy to problem-solving in science curricula? K-6? 7-9? 10-12?*

4. *Suggest existing materials, programs, texts, etc., to support the HumRRO K-8 objectives.*

5. *What existing curricula materials in science might serve as a model for computer literacy?*

6. *How might computer literacy objectives and activities support or reinforce existing curricula in science?*

7. *How can the NSTA and other organizations to which teachers belong support or enhance the computer literacy of teachers?*

8. *What are likely roles of established textbook publishers in disseminating computer literacy materials and curricula?*

*Participants: Dave Johnson, Dorothy Deringer, Tom Dwyer, Greg Kearsley, Kent Kehrberg, J.C.R. Licklider, Arthur Luehrmann, Wayne Moyer, and Phyllis Marcuccio.

9.   How should the various disciplines cooperate in order to
     achieve computer literacy goals?

10. What is the responsibility of the science teacher in the
     computer literacy movement?

11. List rules of legal and ethical behavior that students
     and teachers should adhere to in using computer and
     information systems.

HIGHLIGHTS

- The computer should be considered a science
  in its' own right, in the same sense as
  mathematics.

- Science teachers and students should think
  about computers as tools of the trade in the
  same way as microscopes and thermometers.

- High school science teachers should be able
  to assume students already know how to use a
  computer, so that they can get on with the
  job of using it in their science class rather
  than teaching computing as such. A major
  implication of this position is that it
  shifts responsibility of teaching computer
  use to the K-8 grades.

- Computers should be used (a) as the way to
  learn about the processes of science, such as
  model building, theory formation, and data
  analysis; (b) to learn the content; and (c)
  to understand the science in society and its'
  interaction.

- Science teachers should be instructed in the
  need for and the benefits of using computers.

- Computers provide an opportunity for scientific research, experiences, however, they
  should not be conceptualized as a replacement
  for "real" laboratory experiences.

WORKING GROUP VIII

COMPUTER LITERACY IN THE SCIENCE CURRICULA

A six-point manifesto is offered for computer literacy and science:

1.   The computer should be considered a science in its' own right, in the same sense as mathematics.

2.   Science teachers and students should think about computers as tools of the trade in the same way as microscopes and thermometers.

3.   High school science teachers should be able to assume students already know how to use a computer, so that they can get on with the job of using it in their science class rather than teaching computing as such.   A major implication of this position is that it shifts responsibility of teaching computer use to the K-8 grades.

4.   Computers should be used (a) as the way to learn about the processes of science, such as model building, theory formation, and data analysis; (b) to learn the content; and (c) to understand the science in society and its' interaction.

5.   Science teachers should be instructed in the need for and the benefits of using computers.

6.   Computers provide an opportunity for scientific re-search, experiences, however, they should not be conceptual-ized as a replacement for "real" laboratory experiences.

Computer literacy may not solve existing problems in science education. For example, teachers are better prepared to indoctrinate than they are to teach discovery.

Another problem is the lack of enough time allocated to science instruction. More time is needed to explore ideas and experimentation. Will computer impact these problems? The answer is yes, but the extent of the impact can not be estimated at this point in time.

Computers should be introduced in schools as a basic skill like writing or mathematics and computer science should be taught as a science subject in its own right.

On the ethical questions, it is the responsibility of the teacher to make it clear what the appropriate rules of conduct are regarding computers, but not to try and teach ethics *per se*. There are many ways to reduce ethical dilemmas. For example, illegal copying of diskettes can be minimized by giving students as many resources and meaningful activities as they want.

A key ingredient in getting teachers to use and teach about computers is to spark their interest by getting them to see the potential in the science classroom as opposed to just giving them machines. There are a number of ideas on how to motivate teachers:

1. Science teachers should be convinced that to be a scientist today you must be computer literate. The argument of job security is also valid. The consensus of the group was that the solution to computer literacy in science is not to totally overhaul existing science curricula, but to introduce it as a new subject in its' own right, such as English and biology.

2. National teachers associations can serve an important role in promoting computer literacy by making the subject prominent in conferences and journals.

3. Frustration with computer systems can be minimized by providing more computer resources and meaningful science activities.

WORKING GROUP IX*

COMPUTER LITERACY IN THE SOCIAL STUDIES CURRICULA

QUESTIONS

1. *React to the integration of computer literacy into the K-8 social studies curriculum as proposed in the HumRRO K-8 scope and sequence.*

2. *How and where does study of computers and computer applications fit within social studies curricula K-12?*

3. *What is or should be the relationship of computer literacy to problem-solving in social studies curricula? K-6? 7-9? 10-12?*

4. *Suggest existing materials, programs, texts, etc., to support the HumRRO K-8 objectives.*

5. *What existing curricula materials in social studies might serve as a model for computer literacy?*

6. *How might computer literacy objectives and activities support or reinforce existing curricula in social studies?*

7. *How can the NSTA and other organizations to which teachers belong support or enhance the computer literacy of teachers?*

8. *What are likely roles of established textbook publishers in disseminating computer literacy materials and curricula?*

*Participants: Don Rawitsch, Richard Diem, James Fridie, Beverly Hunter, Ken Laudon, Linda Roberts, James Sanders, and John Sonquist.

9. *How should the various disciplines cooperate in order to achieve computer literacy goals?*

10. *What is the responsibility of the social studies teacher in the computer literacy movement?*

11. *List rules of legal and ethical behavior that students and teachers should adhere to in using computer and information systems.*

HIGHLIGHTS

- *Computer related activities should be used to broaden existing social studies curricula -- to avoid, in part, the computer being studied in isolation.*

- *Students can utilize the computer through simulation programs, for example, to learn about the social world.*

- *Teachers should focus on integrating computers into existing curricula.*

- *Issues such as privacy, transborder data flow, computer crime, ethics, and morality are all issues that should be raised in social studies courses and materials.*

WORKING GROUP IX

COMPUTER LITERACY IN THE SOCIAL STUDIES CURRICULA

Computer related activities can broaden the existing curricula rather than be introduced as a new subject. The social studies curriculum needs to include the social uses of information and how people in society use information. Using the computer as part of a research effort in the social studies area is a good way to develop literacy. In addition, computer simulation can be used to teach the process of making decisions as well as taking actions and taking responsibility.

Problem solving in social studies areas is more complicated than in the physical sciences. The act of programming as a problem solving solution doesn't lend itself to the kinds of problems that exist in social studies education. Simulation programs are needed to solve certain kinds of problems, and statistical or data base packages are needed to solve other problems. Subject matter areas need to relate to teacher experience and interest. The fundamental idea is to learn about problem solving in a computer-enhanced setting that represents a microcosm of the social world. Students will learn to use what they learn about computing in ways that are microcosms of the computer utilization outside of school.

Computers shouldn't be studied in isolation, but should be integral parts of larger social systems. An interesting implementation of this would be to have outsiders come to the school to talk about the ways they use information.

Our last focus is on teachers. They are not extensively trained in the social sciences, and secondary school teachers tend to be content area specialists. Teachers want and need a complete cookbook approach to the applications of computing. On the other hand, studies of teachers show that social science teachers are among the highest in motivation to introduce computer technology. They are willing to change their curriculum. There is consensus that social studies teachers should

consider themselves professionally obligated to deal with
computer-in-society issues. The focus should be on integrating computers into existing materials and courses rather
than substituting new kinds of totally different courses.

Computer issues in this area parallel information issues
in general. For instance, problems of data accuracy relate to
all types of information. Many issues of rights and responsibilities in data access are relevant. Values such as privacy may conflict with other values such as lower crime rates.

What about ownership of data, trade secrets, patents, and
copyrights and the infringements thereon? Ethical issues
pertaining to computers should be dealt with in terms of
Kohlberg's work on moral development.

What about the professional obligations of computer science professionals? This could be brought into the study of
careers -- a sense of professional responsibility to do good
work and to keep the public good in mind.

Computer crime? How do professional groups decide what
sorts of things are ethical? How do they go about controlling
the ethical behavior of their members? For example, what is
the distinction between poor work and actually bad faith or
unethical behavior? Some software could be described as being
so bad that its release is unethical.

What kind of morality is associated with designers and
operators of systems? To design systems that don't injure
individuals and/or harrass them? What sort of morality is
associated with system users? In terms of the use of information for purposes other than that for which it was collected? In this sort of thing, it eventually becomes law and
then one has such things as contracts and obligations under
law. There is a large area of law and computers, and the law
has trouble keeping up with computers. For example, in a
search and seizure area you have to have a definition of the
premises. If you are going to go into a premise and search it
to obtain evidence, it usually is more than an address. But
in a computer network where a crime has been committed, how do
you decide where the premises are?

What about the morality question of showing or discussing
the technical facts of immoral computer use?

The question of values overlap and are hard to distinguish from ethical issues. For instance, should the society
develop things without deciding whether they should be devel-

oped? We should ask the converse: why are some technologies not developed when we know they would be good? There are ethical and value issues associated with the changes in society that relate to the power relationships between individuals and large organizations.

Ethics questions on computers correspond somewhat with ethics in general, but they also add new dimensions to old questions. There issues should be raised by activities and discussions in social studies classrooms.

SECTION V

ALTERNATIVE POLICIES AND IMPLEMENTATION
OF GOALS FOR COMPUTER LITERACY
DURING THE NEXT FIVE YEARS

Five panelists presented their thoughts on the various policies, goals, and strategies for their implementation in the public and private sectors. These papers suggest specific directions and national goals for computer literacy for a five-year period. Working Group V listed eleven major recommendations for the creation of national strategies for implementing computer literacy. They range in scope from suggestions for broad national policies to concerns over what available resources and support for adequate materials development and the need to provide adequate teacher training in computer literacy.

NATIONAL GOALS AND STRATEGIES FOR COMPUTER LITERACY

Nellouise Watkins

Bennett College

The rapid changes in the technology moving toward more interfacing of brands of computers, types of technologies (i.e., audio-video, communications, etc.) make predictions for the next five years very difficult. In fact, one of the goals for computer literacy should be to keep abreast of the changing nature of the field. The implementation of any dynamic force presents the difficulties of shooting at a moving target; nevertheless, there are some constants in the equation that we can zero in on. The student to be served, the organizational framework and the measurable competencies are three parameters possible for consideration.

The Students To Be Served

Students are defined as learners in:

> *Kindergarten to College*
> *Undergraduate Study*
> *Graduate Study*
> *Persons resuming study proceedings at any phase of life*

The Organizational Framework

Traditional:

> *Kindergarten*　　　　　　*Junior College*
> *Elementary School*　　　*College*
> *Junior High School*　　*University*
> *High School*

Other:

Continuing Education in Non-Traditional Environments

Competencies

The tools necessary for the pursuit of a productive, meaningful life in a technological age are considered competencies. New development in the technologies, of which the computer is a part, are occurring with such rapidity that guidance on "what information is essential," "how to acquire it," and "where can it be most effectively used" should not be left to chance.

Pertinent questions arise in regard to planning for the implementation of goals for computer literacy:

1. Should our educational information system continue to be free to our citizens?

2. What controls are necessary to prohibit costs from creating an elitist group within our society?

3. Government subsidy is a must but what role must government play in financing, coordinating, creating uniformity and implementing the benefits of interrelated technologies?

4. Are the current policies regarding open competition, already implemented by the FCC and legislation already under congressional consideration, in the best interest of improving computer literacy for all Americans?

5. Are we looking carefully at questions that have an impact on long range decision planning? Questions in this category are:

    a. What facilities and services could be offered? (satellite, terrestrial, cable, optic fiber, etc.)

    b. What methods of communications of information? (private, packet-switched, network, etc.)

    c. What forms of communication? (voice, data, television, etc.)

    d.   What means of transmission?
        (microwave, satellite, cable, etc.)

    e.   What factors for cutting costs?
        (quality of transmission, network control, etc.)

6. Does the technology offer opportunities for more exten-
    sive individualized education? Can we afford too much
    individualization and is it really good for our national
    goals?

7. Can we use individualization to address differences in
    learning patterns identified as ethnic, sexual and age
    related?

8. What is the new role of the teacher?

9. What kind of educational institutions will best meet the
    needs of the new era?

10. Will the traditional five days, eight hours, ages 6 to
    18, permissive requirements compliment or negate the
    effectiveness of computers, communication and audio-video
    technology?

    Right or wrong decisions on these and other pertinent
questions will have to be made in the next five years.

Comments

    Networks offer great promise for the effective and exten-
sive dissemination of knowledge as well as for amalgamation
and coordination of technological advances. Our universities -- because of resident expertise in both the technological and education principles -- must provide the leadership
for determining and implementing computer literacy. This
further implies that the federal government must provide the
funding incentives. Industry subsidy should be the rule because of the beneficial advancements that can be accrued for
it when vested interests are removed.

    The problem of shortage of software must be alleviated.
What better way to have educators invest the many hours necessary to produce effective software than to make the rewards at
least comparable to publishing books. This requires new,
improved laws to assure that the author is protected but at
the same time control software acquisition costs so that all
can profit.

The direction that some of the mini-computer companies took in providing author languages was excellent though not highly profitable for the company. This is not typical since different priorities are chosen when comparing profits in dollars rather than sociological benefits. These and other corporations (particularly the micro-computer corporations) should be encouraged to develop the 'authoring packages' so that the individualization of instruction can be tailored to the specific needs of the diverse users. The alternative, software developed by a combination of master teacher/programmer, will be a costly approach for some time to come.

Just as research in production of ways to improve the energy sources, federal emphasis should be directed to research in ways to increase the 'production' of a population capable of becoming scientists, engineers, economists, and in general, a population able to cope rather than merely exist in an information society. The consistent drop for the past 17 years, of SAT scores should impress upon us the urgency of action to save our greatest resource, people.

A NATIONAL COMMITMENT TO COMPUTER LITERACY

Ludwig Braun

State University of New York at Stonybrook

One of the things that seems to be absolutely imperative is that we have to develop somehow a national commitment to using computing in our educational system. Every other country in the industrialized world has a national commitment and we don't.

Part of the mechanism seems to be broadcast TV. England and Canada have done some very good jobs with TV programs that focus on these issues. The *Fast Forward* series done by Canadian TV as an example is an excellent one. We should be doing things of this sort.

Generating white papers by prestigious or compelling people to address school boards and administrators, and people where they live is another element of it. Teacher training is a critical national issue. We have megateachers out there who need to be trained and we need a multi-pronged approach to solve this problem. One element of it ought to be to identify the universities which have graduate programs already in place to do teacher training in computers and education. I don't think that there are very many who are doing this. They could probably be counted on the fingers of two hands and perhaps even one hand.

The federal government ought to establish a set of what NIH calls training grants, to provide fellowships for teachers to go to these universities to learn at a very high level how to teach computer literacy. I picture these fellowships as a source of master teachers. Some of those fellowships should go to the faculties of schools of education so they can go back and plant seeds in their own universities to provide training resources in a large way. The only way that this can possibly work is if we use all of the multiplier effects that we can possibly identify. These programs should not be one-year or two-year programs. They need to be five years. It would probably take at least this number of years to get the people we need to have.

We need to develop the standalone self-learning materials of the kind that Al Bork suggested. This needs to involve micro-computers, it needs to involve video-based materials, it needs to involve everything we know about how to provide self-teaching materials. The master teacher is an essential element of this because I don't think that people are going to learn much in isolation.

Another critical element is the development of courseware of all kinds. Provide the support for biology teachers, social studies teachers and math teachers, computer programming teachers, and teachers of all kinds of subjects in which computers can help kids.

Another ideal is to have a national contest for young course developers. I'm not sure who should fund this or how it should be organized. We could identify 20 or 50 or some relatively modest number of people out there who are talented, and I am thinking in terms of young being under 35. Maybe the federal government should be patrons to these people and just give them money to work on this kind of thing. Young people tend to not be able to write good proposals and they tend to be ignored by reviewers and therefore don't get funded even when they are creative and have good ideas -- basically because they don't know how to express themselves or don't know how to play the game.

I have been trying to push the *national centers* for some time now. Tom Downey, who is my local congressman, has introduced a bill in Congress twice and one which I hope he will introduce again in the spring, to establish several national centers for computers in education. I conceive a network where there are perhaps three to five national centers funded at something in the order of $2 million a year each, for some significant period of time, perhaps five years. Each of these national centers would serve a set of regional centers and there might be from 10 to 20 such funded at somewhere in the order of $.5 to $1 million each. These regional centers would serve a set of local centers. Local centers would be things like intermediate school districts or similar kinds of groups

in the hierarchy of educational systems. These local centers
would serve the school districts which in turn would serve the
schools.

In this network, an individual teacher who has a problem
can put a message out on the line that says something like,
"I've got a kid who can't understand blank, blank, blank," and
that goes up through the hierarchy until it gets posted on all
of the bulletin boards and this gets done through the computer
networks. Once up on the board perhaps someone will look at
it and come up with some sort of a solution and they can get
an answer on it within a day or two.

The school districts are already in place. The local
centers are already in place. Although not many of them have
enough adequate computer expertise, they are beginning to
realize that they need to have it. I have been in Michigan,
for example, where they have intermediate school districts,
many of which are very active in this area. Some of the BOCES
in New York are active as are lots of the local centers all
over the country are already in existence and are active.

I will describe the role of these local centers. First,
these centers should have representation in the community. In
addition to the university people who predominate in this
conference, there should be teachers and administrators,
citizens, business people, labor people, all of whom could
help to define the policies of the centers. The centers
should be a place where expertise is developed and maintained
on hardware and software and applications in the computer
learning environments. They should offer fellowships for one
week, one semester, one month or one year's duration for
school people, administrators, and teachers to come to learn
whatever it is they need. Courseware should be developed as
well as other kinds of learning materials. They should assist
local people in developing and using materials of all kinds.
They should identify and encourage non-school applications of
computers in learning. Applications include museums, libraries, the home, pizza shops, etc. There should be one national
center devoted to research. I like to think of it as the John
Seely Brown type center to characterize it as different from
other kinds of centers. There should be within that some kind
of support for annual conferences.

We discussed at some length last night the concept of an
industrial foundation to complement the National Science
Foundation and the National Institute of Education, to provide
the types of things that the federal government is precluded

from providing -- like permitting these national centers to
tell the truth about equipment. Federal agencies can not
support this kind of thing. The private foundation would be
supported by general industry and I don't imagine that this
would include Apple or Commodore or Atari but should include
General Motors and so on, to provide the kinds of general
unbiased view that needs to be provided.

PLURALYSIS IN/OF THE COMPUTER LITERACY MOVEMENT

Karl L. Zinn

University of Michigan

After nine hours of intensive discussion of national strategy for implementing computer literacy (Working Group VI), I felt the situation could best be summarized by Ecsher's drawing "Monestery Walk." Some of us were walking up, endlessly repeating the same steps; others continuously went downward, also never getting anywhere. Yet, people seemed to change from one circle of monks to the other!

Perhaps I made some progress toward consensus by listing multiple approaches to achieving goals, each suited to a different situation, resources or staffing. The problems faced by an expanded Working Group VI might be characteristic of the field presently, and were summed by the J.C.R. Licklider with the intriguing label "pluralysis."

Actually, the consistency in recommendations from two sets of Hearings before the House Committee on Science and Technology (1979, 1980) is encouraging: a large amount of quality material is needed for use in instruction; a major effort is required to train and assist teachers using new technologies.

Noting the many academics listed on the program, I came to this conference intending to appeal for work with the private sector. Computers and electronic games are being purchased, by families, if not by schools, with considerable potential for education uses. If the efforts of vendors and publishers to sell machines can be shaped by the market to provide better quality software and advice, all would benefit.

I.   NATIONAL STRATEGIES

As recorder for Working Group VI at this conference
(National Strategies for Implementing Computer Literacy), I
worked for consensus on a few recommendations. However, after
extended discussions of many sides of each issues, Steven
Gilbert and I decided to illuminate those issues rather than
constrain discussion striving for consensus.

A.   *Assessment of Needs*

The media will increasingly call attention to a crisis in
U.S. leadership in high technology. Whether or not public
discussion of a crisis is helpful to the advancement of computer literacy, it will result from journalistic initiatives.
Were any single event more dramatic, the effect would be that
of the launching of Sputnik in 1957: Hewlett Packard reports
the chips from Japan to be of consistently higher quality; the
new products list at the Consumer Electronics Show is domina-
ted by Japan; color computers from Radio Shack and Commodore
came from Japan. Perhaps the coordinated effort by the electronics industry in Japan will produce such an event within
the next three or four years, judging from Japan's national
plan for achieving an "information society" in this decade.

A national assessment of needs related to computer literacy could be very helpful at this time. Many sectors of
society are concerned about the impact of automatic and information systems on individual and national concerns: attitudes, coping skills, functional unemployment, national economy, and defense.

B.   *White Papers*

The requirements and opportunities for improved literacy
are significant enough to require a Presidential Task Force on
computing and education. But since a federal program may take
some years, we should look to the private sector for assistance. Dollars are needed to do the research; experts need to
collaborate on the interpretation; the documents need a credible endorsement and effective delivery. The initiative might
be taken by some manufacturers' association or professional
association. Useful data already will have been collected for
other purposes (employment, services, productivity); the
technology assessment on information technology in education
just started by the Office of Technology Assessment could be a
major contributor. The best interpretations should be distri-

buted by professional organizations, industry associations,
federal agencies and perhaps others. Such documents provide
moral support for local efforts, and can be referenced by them
in support of decisions favorable to the sound development of
literacy programs.

C.   Cooperation Between Public and Private Sectors

Recently, some conferences and symposia have given attention to the benefits of cooperation among educational institutions, public agencies, manufacturers and publishers. The
private sector is investing in educational products and mar-
keting, for better or worse. Over the long run, that which is
more educational will also be more profitable.

D.   Regional and National Centers

Already a few sites are providing significant training
and support functions, but the capacity is much too small to
meet the need. A number of national networks or "centers."
Among their functions are: (1) training for teachers, developers, support staff, and others; (2) assisting with the development of computer-related materials; (3) dissemination of
good information and materials; and (4) consultation on local
models for implementation. Lud Braun discussed this in his
presentation (see pp. 271).

E.   Update Government Regulations

National legislation regarding information technology and
education could do much to advance computer use and training.
Vendors and educational institutions can't wait for changes,
but a step in the right directions would help the spirit of
cooperative work. Some regulations are simply out-of-date,
having been established before computers, or before the small
and inexpensive computers. Others discourage cooperative work
at a time when it is very important to maximize the use of
available resources by both the industry and education. Some
of the money available for equipment is restricted to rentals
when stores want to sell rather than rent small computers.
Extension of subsidiaries are in order, as in "library book
rates" for electronic communications.

F.   Computing as a Science and a Language

The National Science Foundation and other government
agencies should give more attention to computing and information processing as a field of science as well as a tool in

other sciences, and as a language for communication as well as
a technology for instruction. Education about computers and
the use of computers in education and in other fields would
benefit greatly. These areas are in addition to the use of
computers as a technology for instruction.

G. A Dozen Approaches to Literacy

No single approach to providing literacy in computing
will best serve all audiences and situations. A single course
in computer studies is desirable, but diffusion of useful
computing concepts and skills throughout the curriculum is
also important. Materials which develop "awareness" and
"social issues" are valuable, but many learners also need
basic skills in automatic handling of information. Delivery
of instruction and information via mass media (perhaps through
something like the UK Open University) reaches many people,
but one-to-one tutorials and small group discussions in community centers and science museums are just as important for
their participants. A quality curriculum offered by two or
more publishers lends credibility and sets minimum standards,
but local adaptation or authoring of materials makes no less
important contribution to learning. These and other approaches should be supported.

H. Half a Dozen Approaches to Teacher Training

The different needs of individual teachers as well as the
different approaches to providing literacy justify some variety in teacher training. Many educators are learning on their
own, using self-instruction materials and courses offered by
vendors. Instruction provided through television (*Fast Forward, Adventures of the Mind,* and perhaps other) and regional
centers (Teachers College, SUNY, TERC, and others) should be
expanded. Perhaps courses suggestive of the UK Open University could be successful. In addition to a major increase in
offerings of schools of education, programs similar to the
Master of Arts Teaching will be very helpful. These and other
approaches to training, helping those now teaching as much as
those preparing to teaching, are much needed.

I. A Few Approaches to Support Services

One national approach is direct assistance to schools and
colleges. However useful it may be to distribute services
through regional centers, still more is needed. Local expertise needs to be developed in each school or other organizational unit. Furthermore, some national communications net-

work can be very effective in supporting local services and
moving good ideas around the circuit.

J.   Involve All Parties in Decision Making

The organizers of this conference attempted to get one or
a few representatives of most of the concerned and contributing parties: schools, colleges, universities, professional
associations, vendors, publishers, information technology
industries, etc. Apparently the organizers succeeded in samp-
ling the important areas since many attendees spoke about getting more participation for their sector. Many people have
roles to play in the development and delivery of effective
education related to computers, and all of them should be
involved in the planning and decision making at appropriate
levels. In addition to those involved in the production and
delivery of educational products, those using the computer-
related materials should be heard; not just traditional students but the elderly, homebound, and the minorities.

K.   Concerted Action

I began my remarks with a comment about the effectiveness
of our efforts as illustrated by an Escher drawing. I'd like
to conclude with an appeal for concerted action. The problems
caused by illiteracy regarding computers need to be allevia-
ted; the benefits of improved knowledge and skill regarding
computing and information systems need to be extended throughout our population. I urge each of you to consider the variety of useful approaches and help them along. We can all
endorse general recommendations, and encourage those specific
activities which appear to help, which each of us continues to
spend his or her time on those activities for which our individual skills and background are most appropriate.

NATIONAL GOALS FOR COMPUTER LITERACY

J.C.R. Licklider

Massachusetts Institute of Technology
Cambridge, Massachusetts

I. INTRODUCTION

This conference is on National goals for computer literacy. This talk is on *Some definite goals*.

In the process of thinking about the topic of the conference, I mentally scratched out literacy. The Reagan administration doesn't want literacy; it wants know-how. The kids
don't want literacy; they want know-how. So this is about
some definite national goals for computer know-how.

I was tempted to substitute information technology for
computer. What is important is not only computers; it includes telecommunications and also information *per se*. But
National goals for information technology know-how does not
scan.

The sense of national is not limited to the National in
National Science Foundation. It is a union of the United
States' private sector, electronics, chips, computers, communications, publishers, game makers. It is a meld of the education establishment, the school district, the counties, the
states, the national associations, the universities, the colleges, and the federal government, with its congressional com-
mittees and its National Science Foundation, its Department of
Education, and indeed, its Department of Defense, which has
great needs and concerns in this area.

The general context that I think it is essential to
assume, even if we have to engage in a deliberate suspension
of disbelief in order to assume it, is an overarching national

281

goal: to reverse the trend of decline of the United States
relative to its main competitors in productivity, prestige,
and leadership. We are going to be dedicated to reversing
that decline, and know-how in information technology is one of
the main keys to success in the endeavor. The general context
includes a recognition that economic and military strength and
the quality of life depend on the knowledge and skill and motivation of the people. It recognizes the essential role of
human resources and therefore of education and training. The
context recognizes the ascendancy of the information sector
and the crucial part played by information technology: digital computers, digital communications, information itself,
and, of course, semiconductors, optic fibers, and all the
stars in the technicological galaxy.

     The context includes, also, a new political orientation
that will influence the way education is evaluated. It may
not be harmful to education, on the whole, to assess its value
in terms of advantages it bestows in the domestic marketplace
and in the international theatres of economic and military
competition. Indeed, it may be positively helpful to recognize that education -- on the average, nationally, practical-
ly, economically -- is in seriously bad shape. In any event,
it is clear that, in the coming years, we are going to retool
our industry, and it should be made clear that we must, at the
same time, retool ourselves.

II. SOME DEFINITE GOALS

     Here are a few definite goals for education in computer
know-how. Again, these are not federal government goals; they
are goals appropriated for the concerted action of all the
players who should be in the game. And, of course, the bot-
tom-line goal is the orchestration of the concert.

A. *Interactive Computing*

     By 1990, 50 percent of high school students prefer in-
teractive computing to passive television. They routinely use
text editors, formatters, information retrieval systems, electronic message systems, and tutorial programs. They write
programs worth saving, save them, and use them. They emerge
from school with knowledge and skills that let them begin to
work productively in the information sector and take reasonable positions on information-related issues.

  1. Universal Access. By 1987, in 90 percent of the
school districts, each elementary and high school student gets
an hour a day at a console. The console is part of, or is
connected to, a well programmed computer, and the computer is
on a network that provides access to appropriate informational
resources. Equality of opportunity is part of this goal, and
there is in effect a regime of tutoring and helping that might
have been inspired by a phrase from the days of Presidente
Aleman in Mexico: To each who can read, the obligation to
teach; to each who cannot, the opportunity to learn.

  2. Teacher Training. By 1985, a systematic program of
teacher training under way, preparing teachers in 25 percent
of schools. Teachers selected on basis of interest and enthusiasm. Training time and expenses covered.

  3. National and Regional Networks. By 1984, a network
of national and regional educational resources organized.
This is an actual, electronic network, capable of transmitting
packets of information from one school (or clearinghouse or
software shop) to another. It is also an organization of all
the resources required to make an educational network meaningful: data bases, program libraries, computer wizards, and
so on. The network is, by 1984, interconnecting 30 percent of
the resource centers and 3 to 5 percent of the schools.

  4. Foci of Interest. By 1983, teacher-enthusiasts
identified in 75 percent of schools and made aware of regional
and national activities. It is clear that in many schools,
there is at least one teacher who, with or without the support
of the administration, is personally involved in the personal
computer movement. This goal is intended to give such teachers organized support and to increase their effectiveness.

  5. Steering and Fostering Organizations. By 1982, clarified roles and responsibilities for the national and regional
organizations that will see to it that all the other goals are
achieved. This may be the least realistic of the goals because much of the initiative and much of the support will have
to come from sources other than the federal government, and it
may take more time than there is between now and 1982 to work
out new ways and means. On the other hand, it appears that a
movement has formed and is gaining momentum, and one of the
main things it needs is an effective system of intercommunica-
tion among its very many small and local parts.

  6. Policy Issues Involving Information Technology. By
1987 -- going back to the longer time scale for this last
goal, which is a bit different from the others -- 25 percent

of students being graduated from secondary schools can deal
with major policy issues involving information technology at
levels beyond that's good and that's bad. They can understand
the concept of compromise, in its non-pejorative sense, with
respect to policy issues, and they look beyond the simplistic
formulations that now dominate discussions, for example, of
informational privacy and security.

III.   CONCLUSION

     The foregoing are some goals. I do not mean, of course,
to inflict my personal selection of goals upon this group or
upon the nation. It is just that I think it is important to
have some goals, and perhaps, by stating some, I can point to
the fact that there is no such list that represents a national
consensus, and I can urge that we should work toward the development of one. Let me suggest that as a metagoal.

     There should probably be some antigoals, too. Attention
should be paid to violation of rights of informational privacy, to creation of a brittle system liable to credit black-
outs and regional aphasias, and to the gross inequalities of
educational opportunity that might result if information technology entered the field of education mainly through the home
or through some new form of computer-based private school,
affordable only by the affluent.

     Finally, let me say that, in my experience, the world of
information technology has been a happy place, and the computer has been as much a motivator as a processor. The new
technology has opened so many fascinating paths and promising
frontiers that almost everyone involved in it feels that s/he
is doing an extremely important thing. I personally believe
that a lot of motivational charge comes from feeling that one
is being a pioneer, and I think that many students and many
teachers ought to experience it. The applications of information technology to education should be so diverse, so multi-
dimensional, that there will be opportunities for all to be
productively creative. I hope that there will be so much
space on the frontier that everyone will have a chance to be a
pioneer.

     In closing, I want to refer to the *Ten Commandments* pre-
scribing certain practices in the use of the computer in the
classroom, and I want to add one commandment: Thou shalt not
pollute the beautiful environment of interactive computing by
promulgating commandments that begin with *Thou shalt not.*

AUDIENCE COMMENTARY

● If you (researchers, academics, developer) teach us
(school administrators and teachers) how to use high technology, we'll teach you how to use low technology.

If education were a science that is being proposed, proposing would pose very few problems. However, it really isn't
a science, it is an art. Since it is an art we need to focus
in on people. Because people are education -- children,
teachers, administrators, etc. -- there are many intangibles
that go into the success or failure of the types of programs
that discussed at this conference. Intangibles aren't measurable -- they don't fit on diagrams. For instance, an intangi-
ble is, do teachers trust you? Do teachers trust academic
types? Do you trust teachers, do you listen to teachers when
they tell you what they need in the way of education?

Support at all levels for the programs for which we are
discussing is critical. Children need support from teachers
and their parents. Teachers need support from their local
principals. Principals need support from their upper level
management people. There isn't much talk about that kind of
support being provided. Workshops provide an initial spark
but beyond that there needs to be continued follow-up at
different levels. One of the most critical levels is the
school principal level. That is the level at which things
happen -- that is the real world. If you don't convince me
that computer literacy is valuable, then it won't get into my
school. If one of my teachers believes it is valuable and I'm
not convinced, the program will be sabatoged because it is a
threat to the administrator.

Commitment comes from people, it doesn't come from programs. If people are convinced there is a need then national
commitment will happen. The best program in the world can be
developed but if people really don't understand it and there
was no real effort to help people understand it, and there was
no real effort to give any support down the line, it will
fail.

There needs to be some courses set up around the country at key institutions for administrators and teachers. Not just workshops but courses where teachers and administrators can go for a week, two weeks, or three weeks, however long it takes and come away from that course feeling that competent to go back to our school districts and do something. Principals teach principals better because we are more credible to our own peers. The same thing applies to teachers. Don't give the teachers and administrators a program that is going to inhibit our abilities to survive or we'll drop it.

● Walking into this conference reminded me of meetings held in the late 1960's. The problems were the same, there seems to be no sense of the profound changes of the technology in computing, and as Dr. Licklider mentioned, information technology. It is no longer computers. Also, there seems to be not much sense of changing social environments. Schools are really in a different and a much more unsettled role, these days. This leads to my second point. The focus of this conference was announced to be Goals for National Literacy. During the first day of this conference, it was questioned whether the schools were even relevant. Let's reopen that question. The overall education budget of the United States, is maybe $140 billion, somewhere between that and $100 billion plus. The best numbers available for industrial education range between $50 and $100 billion. It is in the same order of magnitude and it's growing rapidly. The education budget is flat and is dropping. Rumor has it and it is a pretty good rumor, that well over $100 million is going to be dumped in public broadcasting system within the next year or so, to make an attempt to establish a real educational, nationwide, communication-based system. Schools may or may not be involved, if they are probably certification agents more than anything else. There is lots of alternative education popping up in this country and isn't unusual. This country has never viewed schools as the only source of education and training. So, in discussions about national literacy in any field, computers or reading, or writing, or whatever, the schools are only partial agents. It may well be that we are standing on the deck of a cruise liner deciding what port to land in next and the name of that liner is the Titanic. That's a rather apocalyptic view, but it's a view that has been expressed by superintendents, by boards of education, by teachers and principals.

There needs to be a focus on two important concepts. One is the continuing role of public education as the only outlet for large sectors of our society. The great battles of the minorities for access to public education may well end up with them winning a scorched earth and the middle class retreating from support of public education at the same time that these minorities groups finally get access to it. A lot of this alternate education is not necessarily accessible to those people.

Secondly, there's the human capital question that Dr. Licklider brought up. It is one that is going to be of great interest to this new (Reagan) administration and to this Congress.

What should the Federal Government do? There is not going to be a Commission on Educational Computing but there is a study at OTA. It's always true but is particularly true now, that if there is any case made for federal expenditures of anything of the order or magnitude that people are talking about now, a case is going to have to be made -- a hard, concrete case, not a case from the viscera. The needs assessment that Karl Zinn mentioned is key to that.

●   It is important for those of us who are representing the private sector to say thank you to HumRRO, NSF, and MECC for inviting us here. Also, for giving us the forum with which to discuss these kinds of ideas. These kinds of forums are critical. Not necessarily because of what the proceedings will say and who will read them, but because of the interaction, the proliferation of ideas, the papers that will undoubtedly result in the computer journals and possibly even in the *New York Times* and the *Wall Street Journal*. The multiplication of ideas, the multiplication function that we talked about will be the latent effect of the meeting. The continued involvement of these people is critical because of the kinds of comments that came out three weeks ago at the Harvard Conference on Microcomputers in Education. There the game industry basically came out and said, "we don't really care what cognitive psychology has to say about learning, we don't really care what learning theory has to say about gaming, we really don't care about education at all and what we do with kids. We're interested in selling a game or a toy that makes us money." The result of that is Big Track which is a tank that shoots missiles as opposed to a little mail truck that can run around and deliver messages. Conceptually the ideas are the same -- they are both interactive -- and yet we are building a metaphor among children. We're building a metaphor of how computing can be used.

Yesterday the term "meta-language" came out and I didn't know what it was. Talking to teachers about meta-languages will scare and intimidate them. One of the reasons that peo-

ple question why teachers weren't invited to this conference,
was because they would get intimidated, and would not be able
to talk or listen, and thus wouldn't be able to participate.
Well, if the audience is education, the audience is teachers
and learners, then we ought to have some language that is to
communicate with people, not intimidating. If we have something to say, we should be able to find the words that say it
to the people who want to hear it and must hear it, and would
hear it if it were in the right words and had the right metaphors attached to it.

There is another critical aspect of language development -- once you build the concept, it can be escalated back
into the labelling of the concept. There are certain terms in
language without the label that are difficult to talk about.
Phonics is one. We are at a point where we want to build
concepts and label them so that people have the experiential
base to understand. Basically, I learned what I now know by
messing around with the program. Understanding the results of
the program helped explain the labels.

Most teachers feel rotten about themselves. A lot of
people in society feel rotten and we are coping with a lot of
alienation. The reason is that people feel out of control,
and we know from cognitive psychology that locus of control is
critical. We have to give control back to the people. We
have to start the needs assessment, where we're at. If we
start looking at a lot of the implementation models we will
see that they are grassroots efforts where teachers teach each
other and where principals teach each other. The expert is
looked upon as the foreigner and doesn't give the control to
the user. We are all pioneers and because we are pioneers we
write the rules.

●   It is surprising that there has been almost no discussion
about the use of computers in managing the classroom. Until
the teachers perceive day-to-day use of micro computers in
managing their classes, computers will remain a gimmick to be
used on occasion for window dressing. That includes data
accumulation, such as attendance, test scoring, grade processing, intra-school communications such as ordering supplies
from ordering film to the daily attendance reporting to the
principal, and word processing such as tests and letters and
the curriculum materials. An agency, perhaps one of the
classroom teacher organizations, or the Business Teachers
Association, should ask for funds to explore the development
of programs for classroom management -- unique problems of
classroom management as opposed to an office atmosphere.

The egalitarian approach to computer literacy is favorable because "the truth shall keep us free." Who will benefit most from computer literacy? Will it be used to fragment our society or unify it? Is the cost of employing computers always worth it or are some of our more time tested ideas as good? Should education anticipate the computers demand or should it use and teach it in a judicious manner?

The local use of computers is preferable to the establishment of a new computer establishment with our new bishops of "computerdom" ensconced in the new temple of computer centers. Universities, community colleges, county systems, educational TV stations, could all be involved in this program. Establishing large centers with satellite centers and so-called fast communication, removes the people from direct use and it puts another layer between them and understanding. New structures tend to become self perpetuating. Grassroots support for computers use and development is a far better to keep local control and initiative.

● Consider the case that the career, environmental education, and MIS groups made a few years ago. They made the case that career education was going to pervade all the existing disciplines. Particularly in the elementary and secondary levels, we should continue to build on the existing subject matter areas and not propose a new discipline. We are not at the point where we can justify a new discipline.

Finally, there is a need for possible Federal legislation. Several weeks ago a new act, the Information Science and Technology Act of 1980, was introduced in the House of Representatives by Representative Brown from California. That Act speaks to a lot of the things that we have talked about here and particularly in our round table discussions on national strategy. They recognize the need for cooperation between the private and public sector. They recognize the relationship between Information and Science productivity. They recognize that microcomputers are around. The Act proposes a National Institute made up of the private sector, education in the public sector, the federal government, and people appointed by the President. In effect, the Act amends the National Science and Technology Policy and Organizations Act of 1976. It requests an authorization of $20 million for fiscal year 1982 and Representative Brown (CA) in the Congressional Record speaks to the fact that this is a draft. For those of you who are interested, the file number on that is H.R. 8395. It was introduced on December 1, and it is in the Congressional Record of that date. It would be in our best interest to react to the Act rather than try to introduce new legislation.

●   A number of people have raised issues here that deal with
something often not discussed but needs to be discussed. The
reason it may not be discussed is because computer people or
people closely associated with this area attempt to accept the
labors of others and take them for granted. When you sign on
a system, you don't question the way people have developed
software necessarily, unless you have a problem with it. But
we tend to do the same thing nationally and that is not necessarily the right idea. We have to take seriously the possibility that many people in the government do not know what
they are doing. They know even less what they are doing than
we do. The best example is the amount of money we are now
spending on weapons systems that we do not ever dare use and
if we do use, all efforts for education will be for zero anyhow. The amount of money that we are wasting represents an
amount that would more than cover the costs of anything that
any of us could dream up. Some of the comments about war-like
games and so on are at one end of the spectrum. Some of the
long discussions we had last night about basic issues of
national priorities and shortages of massive amounts of money
are all related to this same question. It is important for
those of us who have some insight into the problems and the
shortages of money, the problems of national economic paraly-
sis and decline when billions and billions of dollars each
year are put into the systems that are non-productive -- you
can not expect the economy to grow. It is going to be a problem. As far as computer literacy goes, if we continue to put
our best products in terms of human minds that come out of all
these institutions into industries who are spending most of
their time and money creating weapon systems that are of no
value to any human being on the face of the earth, we can not
expect to survive or to prosper. It is important to contact
our political representatives and say, look this is enough, we
can kill all the people on the face of the earth 40 or 50
times over. It is wrong to go on spending more money for this
kind of thing when we badly need the money for more creative
human activity. This should be said among the groups that you
all belong to and it should be said to your political representatives because if we are looking for money, that is where
the money is. If you want to know how much money was spent on
weapon systems, since World War II, it would stagger the
imagination compared to any educational activity.

●   Two years ago, a group of us met with representatives
from NSF. One of the important things that came out of that
meeting was a concept of making sure that some way or other
there was no barriers to people getting the kind of computing
access needed. There are a lot of people beginning to worry
very much about the rich getting richer and the poor getting

poorer. One element of the national commitment has got to be making sure that the South Bronx's in this country aren't cut out of this revolution, and that they are provided in some way with the kinds of facilities as those in Dix Hills. There are computers all over Dix Hills, but there aren't computers all over the South Bronx. This causes a very serious disjointedness in our society.

There is an important point which to be made about initiative and activism at the local level. The idea of network, of national centers, regional centers, and networks reaching into the local level, is intended to identify, define it and support it. So the most important point, perhaps, in all of this, might be to find at least one activist at the local level.

● One other issue alluded to is the whole issue of language. There are virtually no programs for second language students. It's something that both the public and private sectors have to deal with. If people want to use those machines, they're going to have to be in a language that they can read and understand. That's something we have to think about when talking about the kinds of programs that have been alluded to at this conference.

● If the home market does become as important as many of us think, and as a new educational centers through computers in our society, then it's quite likely to be the more affluent homes, who will be most likely to get the new machines. It's hard to think that many new computers are going to come into the home with very low income. So that seems to be more an area where the government needs to give some special thought and special concern. Likewise, the same issue but applied to a different consideration -- the teacher education program -- the kinds that are started as possible models to follow in computer literacy or computers in education, more generally -- have to be very careful to look at the problem and how it can be used all around the country. Too often programs of this kind have been done in areas with very affluent school districts -- people who are already oriented in that direction, and so they become a way of further enhancing that particular district. The critical thing in many of these areas is how to avoid the previous problems that led to educational inequalities.

● If education is to be merely driven by the commercial market, many areas may be left out because science has force of its own. And if it's not being supported, then that is the role for the federal government. Likewise, there are many

communities that aren't being attended to because they are
either too small or not financially significant, and that is
another role of the federal government -- to ensure that no
sector of society goes below accessibility level and access to
education. Those are the things that are carried on to us
from the 50's and 60's as a federal responsibility. Of
course, our programs are responsive to those things. We are
essentially an agency that responds to initiatives as the
community sees them.

WORKING GROUP VI*

*NATIONAL STRATEGIES FOR IMPLEMENTING
COMPUTER LITERACY*

QUESTIONS

1. *Some computer literacy objectives can be integrated into
    math, social studies, science curricula. Others don't
    "fit" (for example, fundamentals of computers, program-
    ming). How should computer literacy objectives that do
    not conveniently fit into existing disciplines be imple-
    mented in K-8 curriculum?*

2. *From a national standpoint, what are some possible strate-
    gies for implementing computer literacy, e.g., state
    initiatives, federal initiatives, professional society
    initiatives?*

3. *With respect to the school district level, how can imple-
    mentation be successful if responsibility for teaching
    computer literacy to students rest with the teachers, but
    authority for what to teach rests with the administrative
    staff?*

4. *What national recommendation can be made for school
    districts to get started in computer literacy? What
    should be done first, etc.? What kinds and how much
    computer equipment are necessary for initiating a mean-
    ingful program?*

**Participants: Karl Zinn, J.C.R. Licklider, Steven Gilbert,
    Ludwig Braun, Robert Taylor, Art Luehrmann, Nellouise
    Watkins, Sylvia Charp, Portia Isaacson, and Andrew Molnar.*

Copyright © 1982 by Academic Press, Inc.
All rights of reproduction in any form reserved.
ISBN 0-12-634960-6

5.   What local models for implementation could be suggested?
     Roles for the community -- PTA, city councils, school
     boards, etc.?

6.   Should any standards or guidelines be proposed for mini-
     mal computer literacy for high school graduates? Who
     should propose such standards?

7.   Is it necessary, important and realistic to attempt to
     provide universal educational opportunity for computer
     literacy on a national scale? How might this be achieved?
     What timetable is realistic?

8.   What are realistic national goals and timetables for
     achieving minimal computer literacy on the part of school
     administrators? Elementary school teachers? Junior high
     and high school teachers? How might such goals be
     achieved?

9.   Who should establish the national goals and timetables?

10. How might various agents assist this effort? Profes-
     sional societies? Federal government? State and local
     governments? Educational agencies?

11. Should state-wide computer and communications networks be
     established for use by students and teachers?

HIGHLIGHTS

- A national needs assessment focusing on
  individual and national benefits should be
  established.

- Regional centers should be established.

- Public and private sectors should cooperate
  to make educational products and services
  profitable.

- White papers on the requirements and opportunities for improved computer literacy
  should be prepared and disseminated.

- *Government agencies as well as NSF should increase their support; government regulations affecting information technology and education should be revamped to support new opportunities in this area.*

WORKING GROUP VI

NATIONAL STRATEGIES FOR IMPLEMENTING
COMPUTER LITERACY

        This report reflects the ideas and issues that were dis-
cusses by Working Group VI in the format of recommendations.
No votes were taken and no consensus was attempted. These
recommendations are taken from Thursday and Friday afternoon
working sessions of Group VI as well as expended on group
discussion on Friday evening.

        1. A national assessment of needs related to computer
literacy should be conducted to focus attention on benefits to
individuals and the nation.

        2. White papers discussing the requirements and oppor-
tunities for improved literacy regarding computers should be
prepared and distributed by professional organizations, industry associations, federal agencies, and perhaps others.

        3. The private and public sectors should be encouraged
and assisted in cooperative work, in general to make educational products and services profitable. The more beneficial
the educational products, the more profitable they should be.

        4. Regional centers should be established (perhaps work-
ing collectively as a "national center") to assist with local
training and consultation, and to support local efforts
through development and dissemination.

        5. Government regulations affecting information tech-
nology and education should be revised to accommodate and
encourage the new opportunities provided to educational institutions and networks by the new technologies.

        6. The National Science Foundation and other government
agencies should increase their attention to computing and in-

formation processing as a field of science as well as a tool
in other sciences, and as a language for communication as well
as a technology for instruction.

The next four items concern the report of this conference.

   7. Present the case for supporting each of up to a dozen
approaches to providing literacy in computing: single course,
diffused throughout the curriculum, emphasis on social issues,
development skills, exploiting mass media for delivery ("Open
University"), using community centers or science museums, focusing on materials authored or adapted locally, etc.

   8. Present the case for supporting half-a-dozen approaches to training teachers for courses related to computing, reflecting the diverse approaches to providing literacy:
schools of education, discipline-based programs, (e.g., MAT),
self-instruction, Open University (or regional centers), vendors, etc.

   9. Present the case for supporting a few approaches to
providing support services (consultation, assistance, perhaps
development): regional centers (collectively a "national center"), local experts, national communication network, etc.

   10. Recommend follow-up activities which involve concerned and contributing parties in the planning and decision
making: school people (teachers, administrators, resource
people, board members, etc.), minorities, handicapped, elderly, professional associations (representing teachers, administrators, disciplines, etc.), vendors, publishers, employers,
etc.

The last recommendation is intended for attendees at this
conference and other interested persons.

   11. Provide support of concerted action to remedy the
problems caused by illiteracy regarding computers and to extend the benefits of improved knowledge and skill regarding
computing and information systems: endorse general recommendations, consider a variety of approaches, encourage all
those activities which appear to help, contribute to all those
activities for which you have skills and time.

SECTION VI

SUMMARY OF THE CONFERENCE

     This section is a summary of the presentations, comments,
and discussion of the conference proceedings by the sponsor,
Andrew Molnar, National Science Foundation.

SUMMARY OF THE CONFERENCE[1]

Andrew Molnar

National Science Foundation

There is not a lack of input; there is the lack of an ability to hear it all and synthesis it. Clearly, what we have heard is that there is a problem. That is the lowest common denominator. It reminds me of a cartoon with the student standing at the board and it says 2+2 with a line drawn and the student turns to the teacher and says, "Is this the trick problem?"

In fact, there are several problems. Throughout the meeting, we heard what computer literacy is, not what it should not be and what it can't be. Tom Dwyer set the conference right when he asked, "What is it, what should it be and what could it be?" Those are all three different questions and all valid questions.

Another point that we heard was there is a log jam, there is a bottleneck. The closest metaphor is the centipede. That is, business, industry, military, schools, all have similar problems and none can seem to move that first leg of the 100 legs that we all have to move together if we are going to make the thing move.

Apparently, we have had a lot of miscommunications with regard to the target groups. It does appear that there is a strong feeling that we must make a national commitment. Nothing can happen without some sort of national commitment. The French government, the President of France, made a national commitment to have a computer literate society. The British Prime Minister equally did the same thing. The Japanese have

[1]*The opinions and views expressed herein are those of the author and do not necessarily reflect the views of the National Science Foundation.*

301

said that an information society is better than an industrial
society and set down a plan. The national commitment also
heard went beyond just the federal government. It included
state and local commitments, that is with the national commitment, all of the pioneers will have some sort of license or
legitimacy to do the things that they feel are important.

   Not all national commitments need money. When the federal government decided to declare a national commitment on
reading literacy the argument went something like this: What
can we do, we're at a time when we have no money at the federal level and we don't want to put a lot of money into something. How can we do something in the meantime? The argument
was to point to a national problem -- reading -- and the problem is not dissimilar from computer literacy. First of all,
we don't know too much about reading. We certainly can't set
standards, it is far more complex than we ever realized.
There are all types of reading capabilities in literacy. It
is another problem that has to be attacked at the local level.

   The other group that we are talking to really are professionals or colleagues. That is, on the one hand, while we
believe people should be doing something, we ought to also
have a plan. There is a saying that if you don't know where
you're going, any road will get you there. I think we must,
as individuals, act as representatives. That is why you were
invited here: you are leaders. You can talk to your colleagues. If this is important, leadership should be grassroots leadership. I talk about what the federal government
doesn't do, but in fact, I am the federal government in the
sense that I do make decisions. Policy is usually written by
historians anyhow.

   Another issue: everybody agrees that there is strength
in diversity and that there should be no one position. On the
other hand, that creates some problems. An issue that Dr.
Licklider pointed out and that others emphasized: the public
schools really are the crossroads and we have not engaged in
discussion of what would happen without a public school system. Referring back to that is the problem of opportunity of
access. Under "opportunity" is the need for equipment at the
K-8 level, computers in the classroom. It's clear that without opportunity of access, very little can take place. And at
the 8-12 level, computers can fit conveniently into laboratory
type courses.

   Second, high quality courseware and software. That is,
if we do have access, if we do have opportunity, it would be
for naught unless it was high quality material. Thirdly, is

the awareness that computing is important, but the student should be able to program as a basic skill and should have hands-on experience. It seems that those type of access problems we can pay attention to in supporting research and development activities.

Another issue that came out strongly during the conference was the importance of people. That is, the model of massive programs, massive instruction, is not quite as important as talent development -- identifying talent and developing it, the teacher training on a broader basis through talent development. In fact, the people are the most important investment in this activity. Along those lines, such approaches as master teachers, national centers for the collection of expertise, workshops to get people who are willing to go in this area, and suggestions for looking at the models have been discussed -- how can we have the greatest impact? That is, what is the quickest and most efficient route to impact on the most people? It may be through teachers colleges; on the other hand, it may be through engineering schools, or computer science departments. It may be easier to teach computer scientists and engineers, education than it will be to teach computing to educators. But certainly, we've got to start looking at models -- models for impact.

Another area is the uncertainty. It's true, we're moving into a different realm where a lot of past experiences may be good suggestions, but we need really to gather more empirical information, to perform national needs studies as Karl Zinn has suggested, and probably another suggestion that we should take a look at the "way out" ideas -- the think tank. As a model, Xerox Parc was cited as a case where we should not be afraid to think of what could be. That is, the fact this area may produce many discontinuities from which we can't build upon past experiences, we would have to look for new experiences to build.

Another area is the encouragement of literacy, not only in the school, but in the home and in the work environments. In fact, this is a national problem of public understanding. Public understanding deserves the general good of the society and to make decisions that impact on the information communications areas. And that television and the medium should be used as one means of impacting upon large groups of people.

Then we heard from the various disciplines, and it's clear that the mathematics groups have come to some resolution of at least a minimal direction that mathematics ought to be going. It's clear that we can entertain proposals from the

math community on problem solving in computer literacy. The
idea of holding workshops which set up materials, directions,
curricula, and pilot projects can easily be supported within
the domain of our programs.

The science groups are more diffuse. Some are ready and
some are not. And it's clear that related to this is the
problem of survival. But, science is in a sharp decline in
the school systems and it is going to be very difficult to do
both types of things. On the other hand, it may be argued
that survival of science may depend upon technology. Now
students are not interested in science as taught in the
schools. They are very much interested in computers. This
may be a way to accomplish both goals.

In the social sciences, it is clear that this is the
group to which the problem of values and ethics is going to
fall, as well as the uses of computers in instruction. It's
not clear how this very complicated and difficult issue can be
solved. But it is clear that need additional thinking about
the problem and additional research.

PARTICIPANTS

Ronald E. Anderson, *Minnesota Educational Computing Consortium, St. Paul, Minnesota 55133*

Robert M. Aiken, *Department of Computer Science, University of Tennessee, Knoxville, Tennessee 37916*

Richard W. Arnold, *American Telephone & Telegraph Co., New York, New York 10007*

Karen Billings, *Microcomputer Resource Center, Teachers College, Columbia University, New York, New York 10027*

Alfred Bork, *Department of Physics, University of California, Irvine, California 92717*

Gerald Bracey, *Evaluation and Testing, Virginia Department of Education, Richmond, Virginia 23216*

Ludwig Braun, *Department of Technology and Society, College of Engineering & Applied Sciences, State University of New York, Stony Brook, New York 11794*

John Seely Brown, *Cognitive & Instructional Sciences, Xerox Palo Alto Research Center, Palo Alto, California 94304*

Kenneth E. Brumbaugh, *Minnesota Educational Computing Consortium, St. Paul, Minnesota 55133*

Joseph Caravella, *Professional Services, National Council of Teachers of Mathematics, Inc., Reston, Virginia 22091*

Sylvia Charp, *Instructional Systems, Instructional Computer Center, School District of Philadelphia, Philadelphia, Pennsylvania 19140*

Dorothy K. Deringer, *Science Education Directorate, National Science Foundation, Washington, D. C. 20550*

Richard A. Diem, *Division of Education, University of Texas, San Antonio, Texas 78285*

Thomas Dwyer, *Department of Computer Science, University of Pittsburgh, Pittsburgh, Pennsylvania 15260*

Wes Fasnacht, *Computer Services, West Chester State College, West Chester, Pennsylvania 19380*

James R. Fridie, *Franklin Research Center, Silver Spring, Maryland 20910*

Jane D. Gawronski, *Planning, Research and Evaluation, Department of Education, San Diego County, San Diego, California 92111*

Steven W. Gilbert, *Consultant, Princeton, New Jersey 08540*

Shiela Grinell, *Association of Science Technology Centers, Washington, D. C. 20036*

Joyce Hakansson, *Childrens' Television Workshop, New York, New York 10023*

Henry Hamburger, *Division of Information Sciences and Technology, National Science Foundation, Washington, D. C. 20550*

Tom Hansen, *Educational Computing Consultant, Barrington, New Hampshire 03825*

Carol Hargan, *Educational and Training Systems Division, Human Resources Research Organization, Alexandria, Virginia 22314*

John Haugo, *Minnesota Educational Computing Consortium, St. Paul, Minnesota 55133*

Rachelle S. Heller, *Department of Computer Science, University of Maryland, College Park, Maryland 20742*

Michael J. Hillelsohn, *Educational and Training Systems Division, Human Resources Research Organization, Alexandria, Virginia 22314*

Irwin Hoffman, *Department of Mathematics, George Washington High School, Denver, Colorado 80224*

Beverly Hunter, *Educational and Training Systems Division, Human Resources Research Organization, Alexandria, Virginia 22314*

Portia Issacson, *Future Computing, Inc., Richardson, Texas 75080*

Charles J. Jackson, *Shooshan and Jackson, Inc., Washington, D. C. 20036*

David C. Johnson, *University of London (CSME), Chelsea College, Center for Science Education, Bridges Place, London, England SW6 4HR*

Greg Kearsley, *Educational and Training Systems Division, Human Resources Research Organization, Alexandria, Virginia 22314*

Kent Kehrberg, *Minnesota Educational Computing Consortium, St. Paul, Minnesota 55133*

Daniel Klassen, *Office of Educational Research, St. Olaf's College, Northfield, Minnesota 55057*

William H. Kraus, *Educational Department, Wittenberg University, Springfield, Ohio 45501*

Barbara Kurshan, *Academic Computing, Hollins College, Hollins, Virginia 24020*

Richard Lavine, *Principal, Wolftrap School, Reston, Virginia 22090*

Saul Lavisky, *Human Resources Research Organization, Alexandria, Virginia 22314*

Kenneth C. Laudon, *Croton Research Group, Inc., Croton-On-Houdson, New York 10520*

Stephen Lewis, *SRA, Inc., Chicago, Illinois 60606*

Thomas Liao, *Department of Technology and Society, College of Engineering and Applied Sciences, State University of New York, Stony Brook, New York 11794*

J. C. R. Licklider, *Laboratory of Computer Science, Massachusetts Institute of Technology, Cambridge, Massachusetts 02139*

Doris Lidtke, *Department of Mathematics, Towson State University, Baltimore, Maryland 21204*

Joseph Lipson, *Division of Science Education, Development and Research, National Science Foundation, Washington, D. C. 20550*

Laurette F. Lipson, *National Medical Audiovisual Center, National Libarary of Medicine, Chevy Chase, Maryland 20015*

Arthur Luehrmann, *Computer Literacy, Berkeley, California 94708*

Phyllis R. Marcuccio, *Directory of Elementary Education, National Science Teachers Association, Washington, D. C. 20009*

Richard E. Mayer, *Department of Psychology, University of California, Santa Barbara, California 93106*

Sue Moats, *Computer-Related Instruction, Montgomery County Public Schools, Rockville, Maryland 20851*

Andrew R. Molnar, *Science Education Directorate, National Science Foundation, Washington, D. C. 20050*

Catherine Morgan, *Computer Education Consultant, Kensington, Maryland 20795*

David Moursund, *Computer and Information Science Department, University of Oregon, Eugene, Oregon 97403*

Wayne A. Moyer, *National Association of Biology Teachers, Inc., Reston, Virginia 22090*

Carol Muscara, *Franklin Research Center, Silver Spring, Maryland 20910*

Gary Olson, *Department of Psychology, University of Michigan, Ann Arbor, Michigan 48109*

Joseph Psotka, *Learning and Development, National Institute of Education, Washington, D. C. 20208*

Charles C. Philipp, *Division of Career Programs, Montgomery County Public Schools, Rockville, Maryland 20850*

James Poirot, *Computer Sciences Department, North Texas State University, Denton, Texas 76201*

Richard Pollack, *Minnesota Educational Computing Consortium, St. Paul, Minnesota 55133*

Donald G. Rawitsch, *Minnesota Educational Computing Consortium, St. Paul, Minnesota 55133*

Jean Rice, *5132 Tifton Drive, Minneapolis, Minnesota 55435*

Richard Ricketts, *Multnomah County Education Service District, Portland, Oregon 97216*

Linda G. Roberts, *Division of Educational Technology, Department of Education, Washington, D. C. 20202*

James B. Sanders, *CSR, Inc., Columbia, Maryland 21045*

Beverly Sangston, *Instructional Planning and Development Department, Montgomery County Public Schools, Rockville, Maryland 20851*

Martin Schneiderman, *Educational Testing Service, Princeton, New Jersey 08541*

Robert J. Seidel, *Educational and Training Systems Division, Human Resources Research Organization, Alexandria, Virginia 22314*

Gary B. Shelly, *Anaheim Publishing Company, Fullerton, California 92631*

Elliot Soloway, *Department of Computer and Information Science, University of Massachusetts, Amherst, Massachusetts 01003*

John Sonquist, *Department of Sociology, University of California, Santa Barbara, California 93106*

Doris Stein, *Educational and Training Systems Division, Human Resources Research Organization, Alexandria, Virginia 22314*

Bruce Taylor, *Educational Testing Service, Princeton, New Jersey 08541*

Robert Taylor, *Center for Computer Information Management Service, Teachers College, Columbia University, New York, New York 10027*

Martha Torn, *William H. Sadlier, Inc., New York, New York 10007*

William Underhill, *Educational and Training Systems Division, Human Resources Research Organization, Alexandria, Virginia 22314*

Harold Wagner, *Educational and Training Systems Division, Human Resources Research Organization, Alexandria, Virginia 22314*

Nellouise Watkins, *Computer Center, Bennett College, North Carolina 27420*

Daniel H. Watt, *LOGO Project, Massachusetts Institute of Technology, Cambridge, Massachusetts 02139*

Cheryl Weiner, *EDL/McGraw-Hill, New York, New York 10020*

Fred Weingarten, *Office of Technology Assessment, U. S. Congress, Washington, D. C. 20510*

Wayne Welch, *Department of Social and Psychological Foundation of Education, University of Minnesota, Minneapolis, Minnesota 55455*

Ingrid Zadrozony, *Computer-Based Education Center, The University of Akron, Akron, Ohio 44325*

Karl L. Zinn, *Center for Research on Learning and Teaching, University of Michigan, Ann Arbor, Michigan 48104*